The Perception of Christianity as
a Rational Religion in Singapore

American Society of Missiology Monograph Series

Series Editor, James R. Krabill

The ASM Monograph Series provides a forum for publishing quality dissertations and studies in the field of missiology. Collaborating with Pickwick Publications—a division of Wipf and Stock Publishers of Eugene, Oregon—the American Society of Missiology selects high quality dissertations and other monographic studies that offer research materials in mission studies for scholars, mission and church leaders, and the academic community at large. The ASM seeks scholarly work for publication in the series that throws light on issues confronting Christian world mission in its cultural, social, historical, biblical, and theological dimensions.

Missiology is an academic field that brings together scholars whose professional training ranges from doctoral-level preparation in areas such as Scripture, history and sociology of religions, anthropology, theology, international relations, interreligious interchange, mission history, inculturation, and church law. The American Society of Missiology, which sponsors this series, is an ecumenical body drawing members from Independent and Ecumenical Protestant, Catholic, Orthodox, and other traditions. Members of the ASM are united by their commitment to reflect on and do scholarly work relating to both mission history and the present-day mission of the church. The ASM Monograph Series aims to publish works of exceptional merit on specialized topics, with particular attention given to work by younger scholars, the dissemination and publication of which is difficult under the economic pressures of standard publishing models.

Persons seeking information about the ASM or the guidelines for having their dissertations considered for publication in the ASM Monograph Series should consult the Society's website—www.asmweb.org.

Members of the ASM Monograph Committe who approved this book are:

Robert Gallagher, Associate Professor of Intercultural Studies
 and Director of M.A. (Intercultural Studies),
 Wheaton College

Margaret Guider, O.S.F., Associate Professor of Missiology, Boston College

RECENTLY PUBLISHED IN THE ASM MONOGRAPH SERIES

Jenny McGill, *Religious Identity and Cultural Negotiation: Toward a Theology of Christian Identity in Migration*

John Hubers, *I Am a Pilgrim, a Traveler, a Stranger: Exploring the Life and Mind of the First American Missionary to the Middle East, the Rev. Pliny Fisk (1792–1825)*

The Perception of Christianity as a Rational Religion in Singapore

A Missiological Analysis of Christian Conversion

Clive S. Chin

PICKWICK Publications · Eugene, Oregon

THE PERCEPTION OF CHRISTIANITY AS A RATIONAL RELIGION
IN SINGAPORE
A Missiological Analysis of Christian Conversion

American Society of Missiology Monograph Series 31

Copyright © 2017 Clive S. Chin. All rights reserved. Except for brief quotations in critical publications or reviews, no part of this book may be reproduced in any manner without prior written permission from the publisher. Write: Permissions, Wipf and Stock Publishers, 199 W. 8th Ave., Suite 3, Eugene, OR 97401.

Pickwick Publications
An Imprint of Wipf and Stock Publishers
199 W. 8th Ave., Suite 3
Eugene, OR 97401

www.wipfandstock.com

PAPERBACK ISBN: 978-1-4982-9808-7
HARDCOVER ISBN: 978-1-4982-9810-0
EBOOK ISBN: 978-1-4982-9809-4

Cataloguing-in-Publication data:

Names: Chin, Clive S.

Title: The perception of christianity as a rational religion in Singapore : a missiological analysis of Christian conversion / Clive S. Chin.

Description: Eugene, OR: Pickwick Publications, 2017 | Includes bibliographical references.

Identifiers: ISBN 978-1-4982-9808-7 (paperback) | ISBN 978-1-4982-9810-0 (hardcover) | ISBN 978-1-4982-9809-4 (ebook)

Subjects: LCSH: Christianity—Singapore. | Conversion—Social aspects—Singapore.

Classification: BR1200.5.S55 C46 2017 (print) | BR1200.5.S55 (ebook)

Manufactured in the U.S.A.   03/21/17

Contents

Acknowledgments | vii
Abstract | ix

1. Research Problem | 1
  Missiological Context · 1
  Research Question · 6
  Research Methodology · 7
  Biblical and Theological Assumptions · 12

2. Evangelical Contextualization in Asia | 17
  Review of Literature · 20
  Doing Theology in the Era of Globalization · 38
  Summary · 41

3. Modernization, Globalization, and Religious Change | 43
  Modernization Theory · 44
  The Phenomenon of Globalization · 56
  Religious Change · 68

4. Christian Conversion and Identity in Singapore | 81
  The Singapore Context · 82
  Review of Conversion Theories · 89
  Rationalization of Religion in Singapore · 108

5. Research Methodology | 125
General Procedure · 125
Interview Process and Data Analysis · 127
Criteria for the Selection of Informants · 130

6. Research Findings | 133
Views and Attitudes toward Chinese Religions and Rituals · 133
Christian Conversion Experience · 145
Christianity as the True Religion · 159
Christianity as a Logical or Rational Religion · 164
Formation of Christian Identity · 174

7. Analysis of Research Findings | 183
Summary of Research Findings · 184
Christian Conversion in Singapore · 186
Active Engagement Over Passive Acceptance of Religion · 189
Perception of Christianity as a Rational Religion · 194
Perception of Christianity as a Western Religion · 198
Christian Identity in Singapore · 200
Rationality, Rationalization, and Rationalism · 202
Explaining Conflicting Viewpoints · 204

8. Conclusions and Missiological Implications | 207

Appendices
1. Informant Profiles | 215
2. Interview Protocol | 217

Bibliography | 219

Acknowledgments

THIS BOOK IS A revision of a dissertation submitted to the faculty of Trinity Evangelical Divinity School for the PhD degree. The completion of this book would not have been possible were it not for the many people who helped me along the way. No words can adequately express my deep sense of gratitude and indebtedness to them. Firstly, I wish to give thanks to members of the Intercultural Studies faculty—Drs. Harold Netland, Craig Ott, James Plueddemann, Robert Priest, and Tite Tiénou—for their inspiring scholarship, teaching, and guidance throughout the course of my studies. Dr. Netland, my dissertation director, and Dr. Ott, my second reader, deserve a special word of thanks for guiding me through the research and writing process, and for prodding me to the finish line. Their academic expertise, wise counsel, and passion for Christian mission made the learning process both an enriching and enjoyable experience. Although their individual contributions will never be publicly acknowledged, I am particularly indebted to the thirty-five men and women who shared their conversion experiences with me. Their willingness to be interviewed and their personal stories truly constitute the heart of the book. Last but not least, I would like to thank my dear wife, Rhonda, and our children, Elisabeth and Stephen, for journeying with me and supporting me with their unending patience and love.

Soli Deo gloria

Abstract

THIS STUDY DRAWS UPON Chee Kiong Tong's thesis of the perception of Christianity as a rational religion in Singapore and explores the extent and ways to which this is a factor for Christian conversion among younger Chinese Singaporeans. Taking the mode of qualitative research, the study involves interviews of thirty-five Chinese Singaporeans who converted from Buddhism and/or Taoism to Christianity. The findings are then analyzed in view of three domains of literature, including (1) contextualization of Christianity in Asia, (2) modernization, globalization, and religious change, and (3) Christian conversion theories in Singapore, in order to better understand the phenomena in Singapore.

In particular, the study addresses the common criticism that Christianity in Asia is Westernized due to the intrusion of rationalistic Western theology in that part of the world and is therefore contextually inappropriate. Recent sociological research suggests that younger Chinese Singaporeans are converting to Christianity in part because they perceive it as a rational religion in contrast to their perception of Chinese religions as illogical or irrational. The research findings indicate that the perception of Christianity in Singapore as a more rational religion is, to a large extent, an important factor for conversion. Not only did many informants favor Christianity as a rational religion, but they did not regard Christianity in Singapore as a Western religion at the point of their conversion. Moreover, all informants insisted that becoming Christians did not eclipse their Singaporean or Chinese identities.

These changes reflect not only the personal or micro-level and societal or meso-level factors, but the structural and macro-level factors of modernization and globalization impacting conversion patterns. Religions in Singapore are not declining but are transformed as a result of the processes of modernization and globalization. The changes are evident in terms of both the inner coherence and the social significance of religions in Singapore. The science-oriented educational system and the emphasis on intellectual pursuits in Singapore have facilitated a growing number of conversions to Christianity. The preference for the more rational Bible teachings of Christianity reflects a shift from passive acceptance of religion to one that is perceived as intellectual, logical, and relevant. There is a strong correlation between education and religion inherent within the overall structure of Singapore society, which plays a significant role in influencing one's religious choice. The observation that informants perceive Christianity as a global religion as opposed to a strictly Western religion indicates the social significance of religion in Singapore to facilitate the formation of a more cosmopolitan social identity.

1

Research Problem

Missiological Context

SINCE THE EARLY 1980S, a number of Asian evangelical theologians, missiologists, and church leaders have lamented about the Western and, hence, alien nature of Christianity in Asia. At the root of their complaint is the intrusion of Western theology into Asian contexts. They characterize Western theology as rationalistic in nature, dualistic in approach, individualistic in emphasis, and argue that it is shaped by Enlightenment thought, presupposes a naturalistic worldview, and disconnected from pastoral, social, and religious concerns. Since theology and mission are inseparable, Western theology is inappropriate for effective mission in Asia. In order to facilitate effective mission and to cultivate indigenous communities of faith, researchers seek to "de-Westernize" Asian theological education and the church in Asia by calling for appropriate contextualization of Christianity in that part of the world.[1]

Perhaps the greatest antipathy toward rationalistic, Western theology is that it leads to skepticism and the erosion of one's confidence in the gospel of Jesus Christ.[2] Due, in part, to its association with Western colonialism and the observation that much of theological education in Asia is rooted in Enlightenment rationalism, Christianity is largely perceived by people in Asia as a Western and foreign religion.[3] The acrimonious statement—

---

1. Ro, "Contextualization: Asian Theology," 63–77; Conn, *Eternal Word and Changing Worlds*; Yeung, *Theology of Reconciliation*; Yu, *Being and Relation*; Dyrness, *Learning About Theology*; Siew, "Theological Education in Asia," 58–68; Hwa, *Mangoes or Bananas?*; Wan, "Sailing in the Western Wind"; Caldwell, "How Asian," 23–45.

2. Newbigin, *The Gospel*.

3. Hwa, "The Gospel," 92.

1

"Theological ideas are created on the European continent, corrected in England, corrupted in America, and crammed into Asia"—is often quoted as a source of ridicule. One Asian theologian insists that "shoving the 'Westerner's Christianity' upon other nationals is no longer acceptable."[4] Those words are indeed less than charitable, and evoke the controversial rhetoric of "Orientalism" versus "Occidentalism"[5] or the "Clash of Civilizations."[6] One surmises that such negative assessments of Western mission have contributed to the so-called "Western guilt complex," and partially account for the recent decline of missionary output from the West in general and America in particular.[7]

There is no doubt that Asian missiologists offer important insights to the subject of contextualization in Asia. However, one wonders if their assessments accurately reflect the variegated lived experiences of all Asians, and if their recommendations are applicable to all cultures in Asia. One notable exception seems to stand out. In *Rationalizing Religion: Religious Conversion, Revivalism and Competition in Singapore Society*, Chee Kiong Tong, a sociology professor at the National University of Singapore, argues that religiosity in Singapore has increased despite the nation undergoing modernization and secularization.[8] According to the 2010 Census of Population, 44.2 percent adhere to Buddhism/Taoism, 14.7 percent profess Islam, 5.1 percent follow Hinduism, 0.7 percent declare "other religions," and 17 percent profess "no religion." Adherents to Christianity, which constituted 5 percent of the total population in 1920 when the data were first collected, has increased to 14.6 percent in 2000 due to a favorable perception of Christianity as a "rational" religion.[9] That percentage has since risen to 18.3 percent, according to the 2010 census of population.[10] Tong concludes that there has been a dramatic shift in the religious landscape in Singapore, with a "substantial growth in the number of Christians, and a rapid decline in adherence to traditional Chinese religion."[11]

The growth of Christianity in Singapore is a unique cultural phenomenon in that it is instigated by several key factors including (1) a growing trend on the part of many Chinese Singaporeans to renounce traditional

---

4. Ro, "Contextualization: Asian Theology," 63; Ro, "Asian Theology," 106.
5. Said, *Orientalism*.
6. Huntington, *Clash of Civilizations*.
7. Hwa, "A Fresh Call," 42–46.
8. Tong, *Rationalizing Religion*, 12; Tong, "Rationalization of Religion," 189–212.
9. Tong, *Rationalizing Religion*, 4.
10. Wong, "Census of Population 2010," 13.
11. Tong, "Religious Trends and Issues in Singapore," 49.

Chinese religions, (2) the modernization of Singapore society, and (3) the nature of Christianity as an ethnically neutral, global, and all-encompassing religion.[12] Though religion and ethnicity are closely correlated, as with Hinduism and Islam being restricted to Indian and Malay communities respectively, the case with traditional Chinese religions and Chinese Singaporeans is not so straightforward, and the correlation is not as strong. People of Chinese descent, who constitute about 75 percent of the total population, are the most heterogeneous of the three major ethnic groups. Some convert from Buddhism and Taoism to Christianity because they perceive it as a modern, rational religion in contrast to traditional Chinese religions. A second group opts to declare no religious affiliation at all, though it is possible a small percentage of people actually follow some variation of Buddhism. The third alternative, which came about as a result of the growth of Christianity between 1950 and 1980, involves the rationalization of traditional Chinese religions to compete with Christianity and other so-called rational religions.[13]

The rationalization of religion occurs as Singaporeans, who are educated in English-stream, Western educational systems, respond to the effects of modernization and globalization. In the process of transformation, religion is intellectualized, where one's acceptance of religious faith is based upon active reflection and thinking as opposed to passive acceptance based upon oral tradition.[14] Christianity, as a religion of the book, is a prime example of a religion that has become socially appealing to a particular sector of the population. The growth of Christianity can be attributed to several socio-demographic variables, including age, language, education, occupation, socioeconomic status, and ethnicity.[15] This socio-demographic profile characterizes Christian converts as mostly (1) ethnically Chinese from Taoist and Buddhist backgrounds, (2) well-educated, (3) belonging in higher income brackets, and (4) switching their religion between ten and twenty-nine years of age (approximately 72.2 percent of converts).[16] The well-educated background of Protestant Christians in Singapore is widely observed and documented, and researchers claim that "over 40 percent of a total of 350,000 Protestant Christians hold a university degree."[17]

---

12. Tong, *Rationalizing Religion*, 191.
13. Ibid., 4–9, 265–72.
14. Ibid., 267.
15. Ibid., 10, 82.
16. Ibid., 81–101.
17. Chong and Hui, *Different under God*, 2.

It would appear that religious affiliation in Singapore is culturally or ethnically structured.[18] Tong argues that, in comparison to Chinese religions (i.e., Taoism and Buddhism), which are characterized as "illogical," "irrational," and largely "superstitious," many Singaporeans convert to Christianity because they perceive Christianity as a "rational, modern, ethnically neutral religion that partly explains its attractiveness to younger Singaporeans, who are themselves socialized into an English-stream, Western oriented educational system."[19] The appeal of Christianity to younger Singaporeans is related to the perceived connections between the English language, Western educational systems, and the transplantation of Christianity into Singapore from the West.[20]

Tong concedes, however, that the perception of Christianity as an "English-based western religion," which reflects a specific socio-demographic sector, is problematic and "might have prevented many Chinese-educated Chinese from converting to Christianity, as they see it as counter to Chinese culture."[21] Thus, there are strong correlations between Chinese religion with working class status and Chinese dialects on the one hand and the association of Christianity with middle class status and with English or Mandarin on the other hand.[22] In other words, religious conversion to Christianity is a marker for social, educational, and occupational mobility.[23]

One sociologist raises the contextualization issue with a direct question: "Is Christianity in Singapore actually very Western in form, and does this, or the perception that this is so, hinder evangelism?"[24] He goes so far as to state that "it is actually quite fashionable to be a Christian today in Singapore and unfashionable or *suaku* (as it is called in popular Hokkien) to be a Chinese religionist (better to be a Theravada or Soka Gakkai Buddhist than that!). However by the same token, it makes many working class people regard Christianity as 'rich-man's religion,' too foreign (literally), too wordy and altogether too alien and ethically demanding for their sort-of-people."[25] As disturbing as these comments may appear, perceptions do not necessarily reflect reality and can change over time. What seems striking

18. Tong, *Rationalizing Religion*, 49; Clammer, "Singapore," 16–19; Yeow, *Doing Christian Theology*, 154.
19. Tong, *Rationalizing Religion*, 32–33, 82.
20. Ibid., 89.
21. Ibid., 90.
22. Ibid., 93; MacDougall and Chew, "English Language Competence," 294–312.
23. Tong, *Rationalizing Religion*, 82.
24. Clammer, "Singapore," 19; Clammer, *Sociology of Singapore Religion*, 25.
25. Clammer, "Religious Pluralism," 206.

is Tong's thesis that a particular socio-demographic segment of the Singapore population is attracted to Christianity as a rational religion. This is an observation which deserves further examination. Tong acknowledges the general nature of his findings and the need for further research. He writes,

> These observations must be further developed for it has important theoretical implications and should be sensitive to the fact that theorising on the relationship between modernity, social change and religion is based on western society. There is a necessity to develop an Asian perspective, as the process of modernization and the nature of Asian religions, such as Chinese religion and Hinduism, are quite different from the West.[26]

From the foregoing discussion, several disconnects can be identified. Firstly, there are conflicting perspectives on the value of the rationalistic or rational element in Christianity. On the one hand, Asian evangelical missiologists criticize Christianity in Asia as a Western religion due to the intrusion of rationalistic theology and is therefore inappropriate for effective mission. This is evident in Ro's statement that Western theological ideas are "crammed into Asia" and that "shoving 'the white man's Christianity' upon other nationals is no longer acceptable."[27] On the other hand, Tong's research indicates that the perception of Christianity as a rational religion is precisely one of the main factors for conversion among younger Chinese Singaporeans, who are "socialized into an English stream, scientifically oriented educational system."[28]

Secondly, there are conflicting opinions on the relationship between the categories of "rational" and "Western." Asian thinkers see a strong correlation between the two in their criticism of rationalistic, Western theology in Asia. In other words, rational is necessarily equivalent to Western. But what exactly is Western? What is Asian? Tong seems to differentiate the two in suggesting "the perception of Christianity as an English-based western religion" may have prevented the Chinese-educated Chinese Singaporeans from conversion but unlikely in the case of younger Chinese Singaporeans who converted because they perceive Christianity as a rational religion.[29] What Tong's study does not explicitly demonstrate is whether people who converted to Christianity due to their positive perception of it as a rational religion also regarded it as a Western religion. The current study will need

---

26. Tong, "Religion," 401.
27. Ro, "Contextualization: Asian Theology," 63; Ro, "Asian Theology," 106.
28. Tong, *Rationalizing Religion*, 4.
29. Ibid., 90.

to assess the relationship between what is meant by the terms rational and Western.

A third apparent disconnect is between the missiologists' critique of Western theology as too rationalistic and Tong's thesis that Christianity in Singapore is appealing because it is, in part, regarded as a rational religion. There are some obvious overlaps in these issues, but there is a difference between Christianity in general and theology in particular. The former represents a much broader category than theology. It seems that Asian missiologists not only fail to make this important distinction, but their critiques of rationalistic theology as being too Western often lapse into general critiques of Christianity as being too Western. The above conflicting perspectives are indeed problematic and various issues need clarification.

Research Question

The central research question is as follows: To what extent and in what ways is the perception of Christianity as a rational and/or Western religion a factor in Christian conversion among younger Chinese people in Singapore?

In examining the missiological context, it appears that Tong's thesis—younger Chinese Singaporeans are predisposed to Christianity because they perceive it positively as a rational religion—challenges the prevailing criticisms of rationalistic theology and Westernized Christianity in Asia. The study draws upon Tong's thesis and examines whether his claims are reflected in the conversion narratives of some Chinese converts to Christianity. The implications of Tong's thesis and the findings from Chinese converts are then evaluated with respect to Asian missiologists' critique of rationalistic theology and Western expressions of Christianity in Asia. The study examines Tong's claim of the perception of Christianity as rational religion in Singapore in relation to the nation's Western educational system and vision for a modern society.

In addressing this important question, the study reviews three domains of literature, namely, (1) evangelical contextualization in Asia, (2) the impact of modernization and globalization processes on religious patterns in Singapore, and (3) how younger Chinese Singaporeans understand their conversion experience to Christianity and form their newfound Christian identity.

The investigation of the research question uses the mode of the sociological analysis of religion and is framed by broader questions that emerge in the review of three distinct yet interrelated domains of literature. The review of literature on evangelical contextualization in Asia examines, in particular, the nature of the criticisms advanced by missiologists concerning rationalistic theology and Westernized Christianity in Asia. A second review explores the issue of religious change through the processes of modernization and globalization with special focus on Singapore. The third review—Christian conversion and identity in Singapore—analyzes conversion theories and Tong's argument that Christianity is perceived as a "rational" religion in contrast to the perception of "irrational" Chinese religions.

In particular, the discussion clarifies the distinction between the perception of Christianity as a rational religion in Singapore and criticisms of Western, rationalistic theology in Asia. Literature reviews serve to underpin and provide a theoretical framework for interpreting qualitative interviews of Chinese Christians in Singapore regarding the extent of the perception of Christianity as a rational religion as a factor for their conversion experience. Finally, the study draws missiological implications on Christian contextualization in Asia from the findings.

Research Methodology

General Procedure

This study used the mode of qualitative research to investigate why younger Chinese Singaporeans have been converting to Christianity in recent decades. In doing so, it draws upon Chee Kiong Tong's thesis that the perception of Christianity as a rational religion in Singapore is a key factor for conversion. This recent sociological study on religious conversion in Singapore appears to challenge the common assumption in missiological literature that rationalistic theology is responsible for the Western and alien expressions of Christianity in Asia, rendering it inappropriate for effective Christian mission.

Specifically, the study addressed the central research question: to what extent and in what way is the perception of Christianity as a rational and/or Western religion a factor in the conversion of younger Chinese in Singapore to Christianity?

In conducting interviews, a narrative inquiry method of research was used, whereby the subtleties and complexities of lived human experience were probed. The findings were then analyzed in the light of three domains of literature, including (1) contextualization of Christianity in Asia, (2) modernization, globalization, and religious change, and (3) Christian conversion and identity in Singapore. The purpose of literature review served to determine what writers are saying about the nature of the missiological problem in Asia, the issue of religious change in the midst of modernization and globalization, and how those processes impact Christian conversion and identity in Singapore.

As a point of reference consistent with the claims of social scientists, this study defines Christianity as a rational religion as involving an active thinking process in search of a codified religion that is systematic, logical, and relevant. Religious conversion, in this sense, is primarily understood as an intellectual process. Consistent with the claims of missiologists, the markers of "Western" Christianity include focus on religious truth as abstract, universal, or rationally coherent, and framed by the concerns, questions, topics, and categories of Western systematic theology. Ability to speak Mandarin or dialects, adherence to Chinese ritualistic practices, and ascriptive features are typically used as markers for Chinese identity. The study also examines Christian converts' attempt to preserve Chinese identity by reinterpreting traditional Chinese birth, marriage, and death rituals in accordance with biblical teaching. One common example is the Christian substitution of holding a rose instead of joss sticks at Chinese funerals.

The research involved private interviews with interview protocols as the basis for information gathering.[30] Specifically, thirty-five interviews were conducted with Chinese Singaporeans who were selected based on a particular set of criteria. The bases for selection include individuals who: (1) were roughly between fifteen and thirty-five years old, (2) converted to Christianity from non-Christian homes and traditional Chinese religions within the last ten years or so, and (3) were educated in English schooling systems from either local or foreign institutions representing various levels of academic achievement. Individuals who were trained in technical or scientific fields were especially appropriate. Of the thirty-five informants interviewed, twenty were males and the remaining fifteen were females. Informants were selected from churches across denominational lines, independent churches, and those from Charismatic and Pentecostal backgrounds.

In selecting informants, the researcher cast a wide net and used a variety of approaches. He contacted church leaders or pastors via email correspondence, as well as personally approached friends and acquaintances to identity suitable candidates. Once contact was made with potential informants, the researcher then contacted those individuals to gain their consent to be interviewed. Letters were sent, followed by telephone calls, to explain in detail what the research project entailed. Informants under the age of eighteen were not interviewed unless permission was granted by a parent or

---

30. Rubin and Rubin, *Qualitative Interviewing*.

guardian. The interviews were conducted in a variety of venues, including private offices and open public places.

With permission from informants, all interviews were recorded, transcribed, and the results were coded. A written introduction was read to each informant before the start of the interview on the nature and purpose of the study. No time limit was placed on interviews, although interviews typically ranged between forty-five to seventy-five minutes in duration. Interviews were conducted with utmost discretion, and careful attention was given to protect the identity of informants and the reputation of churches represented. The book culminates by stating conclusions and missiological implications.

Limitations

While the study seeks to address the central research question, it must be noted that the intention is not to either prove or refute Tong's thesis. Rather, it attempts to see the extent to which Tong's claims can be found in informants' responses. The study is also limited to examining the perception of a narrow socio-demographic sector of Singapore society, and, therefore, cannot explain why people from other segments would or would not respond to Christianity. After the empirical data was collected and transcribed, the researcher used a word processor to manually code the findings for the purpose of analysis. Additional potential for bias in undertaking such a study on Christianity in Asia, religion, and evangelical missiology, includes the researcher's personal background. The researcher is a Chinese-American born and raised in Hong Kong. Brought up in a family that practiced Chinese religions, he converted to evangelical Christianity in America. He is an ordained minister and pastored Chinese churches in the United States for significant periods of time before embarking on teaching and administrative roles in theological education in Asia.

Chapter Outline

The first chapter introduces the research problem in terms of the missiological context in which Christianity in Asia is widely criticized as Westernized. It points out that recent sociological research on Christian conversion in Singapore seems to challenge Asian missiological assumptions. The chapter also introduces apparent disconnects between the criticism of Western theology and the perception of Western Christianity in Asia. Research limitations, approach, and the overall structure of the book are also discussed.

Chapter two—evangelical contextualization in Asia—reviews studies in which researchers discuss why they regard certain elements of "Western" theology as inappropriate for Asia. For many Asian missiologists, Western theology is often described in association with Enlightenment rationalism, dualism, individualism, a naturalistic worldview, and as disconnected from pastoral, social, and religious concerns in Asia. The categories of "Western" and "Asian" theology are far from monolithic entities, and are typically conceived from philosophical and theological reflections. The study of indigenous Christianity must triangulate various disciplines, including theological and socio-cultural dimensions in order to effectively contextualize Christianity. Discussion of "Western" theology must also take into consideration major shifts in Western thought from colonialism to anti-colonialism and to globalism.

Chapter three—modernization, globalization, and religious change—seeks to clarify the interrelationship of those concepts within social science literature. Much of the discussion centers on the phenomenon of globalization as arising from modernization. Religion, in the era of globalization, undergoes much transformation. In that sense, religion is both a vehicle and a product of globalization. The impact of economic, political, and cultural factors is examined in relation to Singapore's emphasis on Western education and capitalism as primary carriers of globalization. The chapter clarifies that globalization does not necessarily lead to Westernization, and underscores the processes of religious change in modern society.

The fourth chapter on Christian conversion and identity in Singapore surveys major theories advanced by social scientists. In particular, Chee Kiong Tong's argument that younger Chinese Singaporeans are converting to Christianity due to their perception of Christianity as a rational and/or Western religion is examined. What does Tong mean by "rational" in contrast to the "irrationality" of Chinese rituals? Since Tong derives much of his research from Max Weber's concept of the rationalization of religion, the chapter focuses on the nature of religious change in Singapore, especially in terms of Christian conversion and the role Christianity plays in shaping identity formation.

The fifth chapter offers a brief introduction to the empirical methodology of qualitative research used in the book, including gathering, handling, and analyzing qualitative data.[31] The aim of qualitative research is to explore human behavior and the reasons underlying such behavior. As such, qualitative methodology investigates not only the "what" but especially the "why" and "how" of human phenomena.

---

31. Richards, *Handling Qualitative Data*, x–xi.

Chapter six presents significant research findings from the thirty-five interviews on Christian conversion experience in Singapore. The nature of the chapter is primarily descriptive, summarizing key themes, patterns, and concepts from discussions with the informants. The exploration of major topics include informants' views and attitudes toward Chinese religions and rituals, Christian conversion experience, their understanding of Christianity as the true religion, perception of Christianity as a rational religion, and the formation of Christian identity.

Chapter seven underpins and analyzes new empirical findings derived from the thirty-five qualitative interviews with Chinese Singaporean converts to Christianity. Interviews were conducted using interview protocols and informants were probed for their perceptions of traditional Chinese religions and their conversion experiences. The chapter summarizes the major findings and explains the meaning and the importance of the data in the light of the three literature reviews. Key issues analyzed include explanations for informants' negative perception of Chinese religions and practices and positive perception of Christianity as a rational religion, the extent to which Christianity is perceived as a rational and/or Western religion, the social significance of Christianity as a source for identity formation, and the various nuances of the terms rational, rationalization, and rationalism.

The eighth and concluding chapter of the book summarizes major points in addressing the central research question and offers qualified conclusions on the challenge of evangelical contextualization in Asia. Several missiological implications are drawn from the study to point toward the development of effective mission in Singapore and beyond.

Glossary

The subject matter of the study involved research in various domains of literature. The following is a list of related terms used in different subject fields or areas of studies with their accompanying definitions. This glossary attempts to define and explain difficult or unusual words and expressions used in the text. It must be noted that not all of the definitions provided are technical in nature. Rather, they reflect this present writer's own understanding as he consulted and interacted with different and often conflicting viewpoints in various domains of literature.

Rationalistic. This term, used mostly by Asian missiologists (chapter 2) to describe the inappropriateness of Western theology in Asia, refers to a kind of theology, which is shaped by Western philosophy, primarily concerned with intellectual matters, and aligned with a modern, scientific and naturalistic worldview characteristic of the Enlightenment. Asian missiologists often correlate the term "rationalistic" with the term *Western* in their critique of Western theology in Asia. In that sense "rationalistic" and "Western" theology refers to not only theology shaped by Enlightenment philosophy but one that is overtly abstract and unconcerned with human lived realities. Asian missiologists typically juxtapose Western with *Asian* theology to indicate the latter as a way doing theology that is holistic and engages with human lived realities.

Rationalism. Used mostly by Asian missiologists, this term indicates an overall philosophical commitment that regards reason as the chief source and test of knowledge. In Western philosophy, it refers to one's use of reason as the sole arbiter of truth.

Rational. This term is used mostly by sociologist Tong in chapter 4 with reference to his thesis that Chinese Singaporeans perceive Christianity in Singapore as a rational religion. In that context, it denotes the intellectual aspect of Christianity, which is regarded as systematic, logical, and relevant. Moreover, converts are attracted to rational Christianity because they favor a codified religion or a religion of the "book." When informants used the term "rational" in qualitative interviews with reference to Christianity (chapter 6), various shades of meaning emerged, including Christian faith "is logical," "makes sense," "corroborates with reality or learning," "is objective or intellectual because it can be examined," and "answers the questions of the origin of the world and life."

Rationalization. According to Weberian sociology of religion, traditional religions and customs are guided by habits and emotions. Rationalization of religion refers to a shift from the unthinking or passive acceptance of traditional religions and rituals to the active engagement of religion whereby conscious ideas emerge in guiding belief and action. Consistent with Weber, Tong adds that "Rationalization involves the clarification, specification, and systematization of the ideas which men have concerning their reason for being."[32]

Biblical and Theological Assumptions

Religious conversion experience is a complex phenomenon, which can be examined through various perspectives.[33] In the field of Christian conversion, this topic has evolved into an interdisciplinary endeavor pursued by

32. Tong, *Rationalizing Religion*, 5.
33. Rambo, "Theories of Conversion," 259–60; Rambo, "Anthropology and Study of Conversion," 216–17.

various experts including social scientists as well as biblical scholars and theologians. While social scientists often focus on the socio-cultural dimension and seek to examine the "what," "why," and "how" of conversion, biblical scholars and theologians tend to assess if one's experience is a "good," "right," or genuine conversion process.[34]

Four biblical terms are commonly used to denote the conversion process. The Hebrew term נָחַם (*nacham*) refers to "lament or grieve" or more generally "repent," while the more common term שׁוּב (*shub*) indicates "repent."[35] The Greek term μεταμέλομαι (*metamelomai*) refers to "to have a feeling of regret," while μετανοέω (*metanoeo*) means "to think differently or to have a mind."[36] Taken together, these terms describe a turning of faith and repentance that reflect a radical change of loyalty and allegiance in the life of a Christian. These terms, along with others like them, denote a progressive redirection of the entire person, in which thought, affection, and will are transformed. Thus, the notion of conversion refers to a person's "fundamental change and transformation" and describes the process of change in one's overall outlook on everything in life.[37]

Recent literature is not in complete agreement on the nature of Christian conversion. Examining conversion primarily from a biblical-theological perspective, David Wells argues that "Conversion can be spoken of as a single act of turning," but "is better understood if we view it as a complex process."[38] For Wells, the biblical definition of conversion as a process "involves forsaking sin, with its self-deifying attitudes and self-serving conduct, and turning to Christ, whose death on the cross is the basis for God's offer of mercy and forgiveness."[39]

Given that conversion involves both point and process, the question is raised as to how these concepts are personified in the Bible. In *Conversion in the New Testament: Paul and the Twelve*, Richard Peace observes that conversion is both point and process. Citing Acts 26:18, Peace argues that conversion is a dramatic experience with the apostle Paul as the paradigmatic figure.[40] The conversion experiences of the twelve, however, indicate a gradual process whereby they clarified Jesus' unfolding identity as teacher,

---

34. Rambo, "Theories of Conversion," 264.
35. Erickson, *Christian Theology*, 866.
36. Ibid., 867.
37. Dearman, "Observations on 'Conversion,'" 22.
38. Wells, *Turning to God*, 63.
39. Ibid., 27.
40. Peace, *Conversion in the New Testament*, 27.

prophet, Messiah, Son of Man, Son of David, and Son of God, which is the organizing principle of Mark's gospel.[41]

Scot McKnight, in *Turning to Jesus: The Sociology of Conversion*, takes issue with Peace and insists that Paul's conversion experience is the exception and not the norm.[42] Peter's turbulent relationship with Jesus probably best represents the kind of conversion as a process in which no singular pattern predominates.[43] For McKnight, conversion is a process, where "many have no comprehension of a time and date on which they became a Christian."[44] Christian conversion is not so much about "making a decision" than it is about "following Jesus as the shaping core of one's identity."[45]

Theologically, the biblical data on Christian "conversion" point to a three dimensional perspective, including the concepts of salvation, sanctification, and glorification. In Eph 2:8, Paul writes, "For it is by grace you have been saved, through faith—and this not from yourselves, it is the gift of God." In this passage, salvation is understood as a past event, indicating perhaps a completed action. It involves one having been saved from the penalty of sin. In Cor 1:18, however, Paul says, "For the message of the cross is foolishness to those who are perishing, but to us who are being saved it is the power of God." The emphasis in this verse is the dimension of salvation known as "sanctification," in which believers are "being saved," a present ongoing process that will not be completed until the end. Salvation in the present tense involves being saved from the power of sin. The idea of final salvation or "glorification" is suggested in Rom 5:9, where Paul states, "Since we have now been justified by his blood, how much more shall we be saved from God's wrath through him!" Paul is clear about the future dimension of salvation when believers will be delivered from God's wrath. That is, the believer will be saved from the presence of sin. The Christian life is about conversion, the process of becoming a Christ-follower or a disciple of Jesus Christ.

From the foregoing discussion, conversion can be properly understood as a binary reality. Firstly, conversion refers to a spiritual reality where one is born again or is alive to Jesus Christ (John 3:7). In that sense, conversion is a positional, completed, and past event. It is positional in that the believer is considered holy, blameless, and a saint. Secondly, conversion is progressive, whereby the positional status must steadily be reflected in the actual

---

41. Ibid., 109.
42. McKnight, *Turning to Jesus*, 23.
43. Ibid., 176.
44. Ibid., 5.
45. Ibid., 181.

life experience of a Christian as he or she continues to be conformed to the image of Jesus Christ.

Beyond paradigmatic issues, the important question of whether religious conversion is best understood as a point/event or process must be carefully examined. In addressing the categories "Christian" and "Christian identity," Paul Hiebert uses set theory as the theoretical framework for his missiological analysis.[46] There are various categories or typologies to account for Christian identity and conversion.[47] These include bounded set, centered set, and fuzzy sets.

The bounded set category is defined by a clear intrinsic boundary. A fruit, such as an apple, is either an apple or it is not. An apple cannot be partly apple or partly a pear. That is, an apple is a static category.[48] Applied to the identity of a Christian, the bounded set prescribes the terms by which one is identified a believer. Bounded set seeks to determine the theological edges that define Christian orthodoxy.[49]

The centered set category is defined by a center and the relationship of things to it is determined by their movements away or toward that center.[50] Applied to the category of a Christian, one is identified in terms of his or her relationship to Christ. The process of conversion is indicated by one's relationship to Christ as he or she either walks away or toward Christ in Christian discipleship. It is a highly dynamic process.[51]

Unlike the bounded or centered sets, where well-formed edges are defined, fuzzy sets have no defined boundaries. There are, according to Hiebert, "degrees of inclusion within them."[52] In fuzzy categories, no strict boundary is used to determine whether one is a Christian or not. It is conceivable that one can be straddling or negotiating two or more religions at the same time without strict adherence to a particular one. In that case conversion to Christianity does not involve a decisive point but rather a series of small movements.[53]

---

46. Hiebert "Conversion, Culture," 24–28; Hiebert, "Sets and Structures," 217–27; Hiebert, "The Category 'Christian,'" 421–27; Hiebert, *Anthropological Reflections*; Yoder et al., "Understanding Christian Identity," 177–88.

47. Hiebert, *Anthropological Reflections*, 110–11.

48. Hiebert, "The Category 'Christian,'" 422; Hiebert, *Anthropological Reflections*, 111–13.

49. Ibid., 115–16.

50. Hiebert, "The Category 'Christian,'" 423.

51. Ibid., 424; Hiebert, *Anthropological Reflections*, 124–27.

52. Hiebert, "The Category 'Christian,'" 424.

53. Ibid., 425–26; Hiebert, *Anthropological Reflections*, 131–33.

There are obviously valid points advanced by each of the aforementioned models. The bounded set rightly defines salvation in terms of orthodox belief and practices. The center set, with its focus on relationship with Christ and obedience to him, underscores the dynamic process of Christian discipleship. The fuzzy set rightly acknowledges that people are often eclectic in their faith journey and practices, and only God knows the nature and extent of their faith.

Therefore, it is crucial to conceive Christian conversion as a binary reality, including both point and process. Salvation is a boundary set. One is either born again or not in Christ. Christian discipleship or conversion encompasses more than making a decision for Christ or getting people saved. Rather, it is a journey whereby one follows Jesus in the process of transformation. Hiebert rightly argues that the category "Christian" is best conceptualized in terms of the centered set theory.[54] In this life, we do commit sin, and we struggle to overcome it with God's help. But what is the difference between a believer and an unbeliever? Is the difference between the two merely a difference in degree? The differences are very substantial. The change is not a change from sin to sinlessness, but a radical change in direction or outlook in life.

Given the evangelical orientation of this work, the foregoing discussion establishes the theological basis upon which missiological analysis is built. However, as a missiological analysis of conversion, it takes a primarily sociological approach to the study of the subject. As such, the study considers both the biblical-theological and socio-cultural approaches as complementary endeavors and seeks to provide a balanced understanding to what is otherwise an extremely complicated phenomenon.

---

54. Ibid., 134.

2

Evangelical Contextualization in Asia

ASIA, COMPRISING OVER FORTY countries, is the most diverse continent in the world in terms of its ethnic, socio-cultural, political, and religious make-up. Situated within the so-called "10/40 window," it is also one of the least evangelized areas of the world.[1] Yet despite its relatively strong resistance to Christianity, Asia has long been considered a strategic outpost for missionaries. According to the *Acts of Thomas*, an early third-century apocryphal text, the initial entry of Christianity into Asia came by way of the apostle Thomas, who presumably landed at the Malabar coast of Kerala, South India to proclaim the gospel. He was allegedly martyred in AD 72.[2] Alopen, a Nestorian missionary from the Syrian Church, reached China in AD 635, according to a stone tablet discovered in Xian, China in 1625.[3] Protestant missions began earnestly in the eighteenth century, most notably with the entry of William Carey into Calcutta, India in 1793. The pioneer work in Asia was followed by Robert Morrison, who landed in Macau in 1807 and subsequently translated the Bible into Chinese.[4] Other notable missionaries, serving for long periods, include Adoniram Judson who arrived in Rangoon, Burma in 1813.[5]

The aforementioned discussion reveals the first wave of Protestant missionaries was sent from the West, including Britain and the United

---

1. Ro, "Asia," 82.
2. Ibid.
3. Ibid.
4. Ibid., 83.
5. Ibid.

States. As the seeds of the gospel were planted and the church in Asia began to grow, Christianity, particularly in the last century, became a global phenomenon. Particularly noteworthy is the decline of Christianity in Europe and its expansion outside of the non-Western world.[6] Reports of church growth after WWII indicate tremendous expansions in such areas as South Korea, China, India, the Philippines, and, to a lesser degree, in such countries as Nepal, Malaysia, and Singapore.[7] As Christianity spread from the West to other parts of the world, new churches, along with the unique questions and concerns that they bring to theological discourse, began to arise. Researchers have noted the tremendous growth of Christianity in the last century, particularly as it has spread from the Northern to the Southern hemispheres.[8] The significant development of world Christianity—sometimes called "polycentric Christianity" or "Christian faith with many cultural homes"—has occasioned the need to (re)examine of the issues of Christian identity and theology.[9]

The subject of Christian identity in an era of world Christianity involves, particularly from a sociological perspective, the study of religion as a facilitator of one's identity formation. That is, religious conversion indicates not only a change in personal belief but the formation of a new identity as one responds to surrounding socio-cultural changes. The perception of Christianity in Singapore as a rational and/or Western religion requires sociological analysis within the larger contexts of modernization and globalization. The use of social sciences for contextualization has tremendous implications on the nature, task, and method of theology. In fact, the neglect to use the social sciences for appropriate contextualization is a significant methodological issue for doing theology or missiology.[10] Christian identity and Christian theology are related subjects and both must be considered in order to produce insightful missiological understanding. On the one hand, theological formulation needs to incorporate sociological analysis. On the other hand, sociological insight needs to be scrutinized by sound Christian doctrine.

Despite the growth of the Majority World Church outside of the West in recent decades, the perception of Christianity as a Western religion persists. This misunderstanding not only perpetuates the view of Christianity as provincial but overlooks the reality that Christianity has become a worldwide

---

6. Netland, "Introduction: Globalization," 14–15.
7. Ro, "Asia," 83.
8. Jenkins, *The Next Christendom*.
9. Tiénou, "Christian Theology," 38.
10. Stults, *Grasping Truth and Reality*, 240.

phenomenon. It has been pointed out that "As long as people continue to perceive Christianity as Western, the changes in world Christianity will not have the impact they deserve."[11] One way forward in correcting the perception of Christianity as a Western religion is for Western biblical scholars and theologians to admit that many operate with a "hegemony postulate," the assumption that Western scholarship represents normative Christianity, and acknowledge the need to listen to the voices from the outside.[12]

For example, the 1991 publication of *Doing Theology in Today's World* represents such a need for Western theological scholarship to be exposed of its provincial blind-spot. Although the book claims to be global in scope, it is written primarily by Western thinkers addressing Western theological issues without much regard for voices outside the West.[13] In an effort to rectify this lacuna, one needs to acknowledge the contextual nature of all theologies and the significant theological contributions of those from developing world countries.[14] And in order to entertain multiple voices, theology, Western or otherwise, has to make methodological adjustments to ensure the task of theology attends to both local and universal dimensions.[15] That is, traditional Western systematic theology needs to engage contextualization as a discipline in doing theology and to recognize the necessity of producing appropriate missional theology.[16]

As one peruses the studies on contextualization in Asia, one of the key questions is whether Western theology adequately addresses the lived experiences or "living situations" in Asia. Researchers consistently highlight issues in Asia, including but not limited to oppressive regimes, poverty, suffering, war, the demonic realm, and social injustice.[17] One can argue that theological methodology remains a contentious issue in Asia. Evangelical biblical scholars and theologians need to seriously consider contextualization as a vital discipline in doing theology in the light of new realities around the world today.

---

11. Tiénou, "Christian Theology," 43.
12. Ibid., 46; Tennent, *Context of World Christianity*, 11.
13. Ibid., 17.
14. Dyrness, *Learning about Theology*.
15. Tiénou, "Christian Theology," 50.
16. Ibid.
17. Ro, "Asian Theology," 106.

Review of Literature

The first set of literature review analyzes the criticism of Christianity in Asia that is shaped by rationalistic theology and is thus Westernized. The following survey reveals that criticisms focus on the assumptions, nature, and task of Western theology. In response to the negative perception of Christianity in Asia as Westernized, Asian thinkers sought to fashion the gospel more relevantly to their cultural contexts.

The initial formulation of Asian contextual theology can be traced to the historical development of indigenous Christian movements. In the early 1970s, the concept of indigenization was then applied in the area of mission when the Theological Education Fund introduced the concept of "contextualization" to promote local theologies.[18] Appearing in a 1972 Theological Education Fund (TEF) publication entitled, *Ministry in Context*, the term "contextualization" was defined as "the capacity to respond meaningfully to the gospel within the framework of one's own situation." While the main purpose of the publication was to set out principles on the distribution of funds for the Third Mandate of the TEF, the publication also lamented about the failure of the gospel to address particular contexts due to its captivity to Western theological frameworks and presuppositions.[19]

Local Asian theologies began to emerge in the aftermath of WWII as theologians attempt to de-Westernize Christianity in Asia. Prominent indigenous expressions, such Kazoh Kitamori's *Theology of the Pain of God*, Kosuke Koyama's *Water Buffalo Theology*, South Korea's *Minjung* theology, and Song Choan-Seng's *Third-Eye Theology*, were produced. The studies by Kitamori and Koyama, in particular, focus on Christ's suffering as the central motif for theology, as the former relates it to the Japanese experience of suffering in the aftermath of WWII and the latter to the deprivation of life experiences in Thailand with significant interaction with Buddhism.

Kitamori, for example, seeks to move beyond traditional Western theories on Christ's atonement by arguing that the pain of God serves as the basis for divine grace. The *Theology of the Pain of God* has significant implications not only for one's understanding of the character of God but the relevance of the gospel message in Japanese culture.[20] In *Water Buffalo Theology*, Koyama is less concerned with theoretical discussion on methodology typical of Western theology. Rather, he is primarily concerned with theology's engagement with culture and the promotion of interreligious dia-

---

18. Ibid.
19. Ibid.; Gilliland, "Contextualization," 225.
20. Kitamori, *Pain of God*, 8.

logue.²¹ According to Koyama, "Third World Theology" begins by raising issues and addressing "raw situations."²²

What is the nature of Asian theology? As one gives a cursory reading of the literature of this topic, several key characteristics emerge. In contrast to Western theology, Douglas Elwood maintains that Asian theology does not necessarily take the form of systematic theology as in the "construction of comprehensive, logical systems whose parts stand or fall together," which typifies Western theology. In this sense, the latter tends to be too narrow and disengaged from culture and society. Asian theology is described as "living theology," which seeks to address the questions, dilemmas, sufferings, and aspirations of Asian people.²³ As if speaking for all Asians, one writer states the difference between Western and Asian theology as follows: "Asian theology cannot afford to be purely academic and philosophical, but rather it is valid only if it is produced not primarily in between piles of books, but in the 'field' where it is put to the test each day."²⁴

Moreover, Asian theology must not over-emphasize the eschatological or futuristic dimension of Christian faith to the neglect of Asian realities of everyday life.²⁵ Noting the complexity of Asia and the diversity of Asian theologies, Gnanakan observes that "All Asian theologians have one thing in common. There is a strong desire to address the context within which their people live. There is a missiological focus in their theologies, but this focus varies with one's definition of mission. Evangelicals will stress the need to directly make known the redemptive message of Jesus Christ in the diverse context of Asia."²⁶

It must be acknowledged that Asian theology has been articulated primarily from Roman Catholic and Protestant "mainline" denominations. Three distinct "strands" characterize Asian contextual theology. Particular theological initiatives can be identified as the *sine qua non* of Asian theology. One, Asian theology seeks to negotiate with social, political, and economic realities in Asia. This strand is represented by the M. M. Thomas of India and *Minjung* theology, a version of liberation theology in Korea.²⁷ Two, Asian theology seeks to engage cultural realities in Asia. This involves the subject of gospel and culture and the latter's role as a hermeneutical filter in

21. Koyama, *Water Buffalo Theology*, x–xi.
22. Ibid., 3.
23. Elwood, "Asian Christian Theology, 30.
24. Athyal, "Asian Christian Theology," 75.
25. Gispert-Sauch, "Asian Theology," 472–73.
26. Gnanakan, "Asian Theologies," 90.
27. Lee, "Asian Theology," 75.

indigenizing Christianity. Raimon Panikkar of India, C. S. Song in Taiwan, and Kosuke Koyama are clear representatives.[28] Three, Asian theology seeks to advocate for interreligious dialogue. Here, the significant concern is with Christian engagement with world religions. C. S. Song of Taiwan, C. C. Lee of Hong Kong, and Yeow Choo Lak from Singapore are good examples of this strand.[29]

More recently, however, Asian evangelical theologians have emerged to challenge mainline perspectives. Theologians, such as Rodrigo Tano in the Philippines, Hwa Yung in Malaysia, Carver Yu of Hong Kong, and Vinoth Ramachandra in Sri Lanka, are among those who rigorously engage religious and cultural Asian realities with the Christian gospel. The main concerns of evangelicals seem to surround de-Westernizing Asian Christianity and the creation of re-contextualized Asian theologies.[30] Bong Rin Ro, former executive secretary of the Asian Theological Association (ATA), cautions: "national Christians must seriously evaluate their own contextual situation in order to find the most effective indigenous ways to communicate the gospel of Jesus Christ."[31] Given the plurality and complexity of the Asian context, it is imperative that Christianity be contextualized without compromising the integrity of the gospel.

To be sure, Asian theology is quite diverse and has been variously classified as syncretistic, accommodation, situational, and biblical theology.[32] While these categories are simplistic and can be misleading, this study focuses primarily on "biblically oriented Asian theology." One of the earliest efforts to contextualize Asian theology from an evangelical perspective came as a result of the 1982 Third World Theologians Consultation in Seoul. This consultation produced "The Seoul Declaration" and a collection of essays on the contours of an Asian evangelical theology under the title, *The Bible and Theology in Asian Contexts*. The Seoul Declaration, in particular, describes the nature and problems of Western theology as follows:

> Western theology is by and large rationalistic, moulded by Western philosophies, preoccupied with intellectual concerns, especially those having to do with the relationship between faith and reason. All too often, it has reduced the Christian faith to abstract concepts which may have answered the questions of the past, but which fail to grapple with the issues of today. It

28. Ibid., 74–75.
29. Ibid., 76.
30. Ibid., 75–76.
31. Ro, "Asia," 83.
32. Ro, "Asian Theology," 106–8.

has consciously been conformed to the secularistic worldview associated with the Enlightenment. Sometimes it has been utilised as a means to justified colonialism, exploitation, and oppression, or it has done little or nothing to change these situations. Furthermore, having been wrought within Christendom, it hardly addresses the questions of people living in situations characterised by religious pluralism, secularism, resurgent Islam, or Marxist totalitarianism.[33]

Within this collection of essays, one in particular focuses on the critique of Western theology and its misplaced philosophical assumptions. In "A Critical Evaluation of Western Theology: Towards a Reappraisal of the Biblical Faith," Han Chul Ha blames Western theological liberalism for espousing rationalistic scientism with its basis in a naturalistic worldview. That is, a modern scientific rationalism presupposes "that nothing exists beyond the sensible world of time and space."[34] Methodologically, Western liberal theology reinterprets the miraculous and supernatural elements of the Bible in accordance with the Cartesian dictum of the human cogito, "I think, therefore I am." Thus, all spiritual power has been divested from Christianity as a result. According to Han, the destructive influence of Enlightenment thinking is evident in the theology of Helmut Thielicke. On the one hand, one can travel the route of Cartesian or liberal theology by positing human judgment over divine revelation. On the other hand, one can take the route of non-Cartesian theology or Neo-orthodoxy, where he or she separates the Word of God from Scripture, thus undermining the literal truth of biblical authority. While one can distinguish the methodological approaches of these theologies, they share the same presupposition—"the emancipating world of Enlightenment thought."[35]

Han concludes that the rationalistic character of the modern scientific worldview and the negative effects of natural theology have no place in biblical Christianity. The former denies supernaturalism and seeks to demythologize the biblical account. The latter presupposes atheism and that the world is uncreated.[36] For Han, once people posit the modern scientific worldview (as opposed to the biblical worldview) as the Archimedean point from which reality is evaluated, one has no recourse but to accept atheism.[37]

---

33. Ro, "Contextualization: Asian Theology," 23.
34. Han, "Western Theology," 3–47; Han, "Towards a Reappraisal," 32.
35. Ibid., 39.
36. Ibid., 42.
37. Ibid., 43.

The chapter by Han presents a sustained critique of Western theological liberalism and its concomitant bastard child, Western theology. Han's critique of Western rationalism proceeds by way of a Reformed, if not an overtly Barthian, theological framework in which he separates the theology of the Word from Cartesian epistemology. Han is correct to point out that much of the dispute over theology surrounds the question of methodology.[38]

There are a few noticeable limitations in this chapter. The first one is Han's simplistic definitions of Asian and Western theology, failing to show nuance, depth, and variety in both camps. For example, Han generalizes that Asian theology expressed in an Asian context is similar to the context of the Bible, while the Western mind works primarily in abstract terms. Secondly, in his criticisms of modernism, rationalism, and theological liberalism, he tends to define these complex subjects in a catch-all fashion. Moreover, what is modernism and is one's commitment to rationalism as a philosophical tenet equivalent to the rational or intellectual dimension of life? All these terms and concepts need to be nuanced or used in a qualified manner.

However, the most glaring weakness, evident throughout the volume, is that Asian authors limit their contextualization efforts to theological analysis. One wonders about the value of this approach when Asian thinkers do not agree on the nature, sources, and tasks of theology. Viewed from the broader context of the volume, Han's chapter is not only limited because of its singular (Reformed) theological assumptions, but it fails to explain how theology triangulates Scripture, culture, and tradition in its attempt to formulate a contextualized Asian theology. Is it possible or permissible, within Han's Reformed theological framework, for theology to interact with social sciences in contextualizing the gospel?

In *Eternal Word and Changing Worlds*, Harvie Conn critiques Western paternalism in mission by triangulating theology, anthropology, and missiology. He writes, "These pages are the closest I feel a white Westerner can come to theologizing for another culture's set of problems while avoiding the ethnocentric paternalism I see at the root of so many missionary mistakes in the past."[39] With the so-called Western and white evangelical community in view, Conn traces the problem of Western theology to Enlightenment rationalism. In his critique of "the ferment of the eighteenth century," Conn holds the Enlightenment period and the rationalistic thinkers responsible for developing a view of "religion" that privileges reason, the empirical

---

38. Ibid., 39.
39. Conn, *Eternal Word*, 14–15.

scientific methods, the undermining of ancient cultures as "primitive," and the assumption that progress is facilitated by "enlightened education."[40]

The negative outcomes, articulated in "consciousness one," represent phase one of the trialogue between theology, anthropology, and mission when theology and mission took an antithetical view of anthropology. The results include depersonalizing humans as "primitive man," dichotomizing people as religious beings from the whole person, creating a static view of culture, and passivity where people within various cultures are viewed as recipients of blessings from Western missionaries.[41] These results produce not only inaccurate depictions of culture and religion but the bifurcation of static truth and Christian living.[42]

In the second phase of the trialogue, articulated as "consciousness two," Conn observes that mission began to use the results of anthropology, though with increasing isolation from theology. This tendency is evident in the way the natures of religion, man, culture, and language are understood via functionalism and particularization.[43] The result is a shift from "a static view of culture to a static of cultures."[44] He argues that the rationalistic presuppositions of "functionalism," particularly characteristic of early cultural anthropologists such as Malinowski, were responsible for marginalizing mission to strategic rather than theological concerns. He states, "Consciousness two moves in a similar dehumanizing direction. But the reason now becomes its reduction of culture and religion to the level of the usable."[45]

Instead, Conn advocates for a triangulation of theology, anthropology, and missiology to overcome traditional Western theology. Conn concludes his study with a brief section on "consciousness three" in which the trajectory for future discussion are focused on issues related to paradigm, worldview, symbolism, and relativism.[46] He contends that "Theologizing becomes more of a dynamic process rather than one virtually completed in the West."[47] Such a process of theologizing involves "the normative perspective of the Bible, social time and place, and the existential perspective of our humanity as images of God," yet "embraces relativism in a creative

---

40. Ibid., 41.
41. Ibid., 47–88.
42. Ibid., 333.
43. Ibid., 116–22.
44. Ibid., 121.
45. Ibid., 116.
46. Ibid., 315–38.
47. Ibid., 338.

sense."⁴⁸ What seems clear is that Conn understands traditional Western theology as a form of "naïve realism" and intricately connected to Enlightenment rationalism.

Conn should be commended for his significant contributions to triangulating theology, anthropology, and mission. In particular, his observation of Western theology as a form of naïve realism is a valid criticism. His depiction of the three phases of conversation between theology, anthropology, and mission is also helpful. The limitations of Conn's study include his failure to acknowledge that Western theology has gone through various phases of development, and that, for many, naïve realism is a thing of the past. Thus, his treatment of Western theology as a monolithic vestige of Enlightenment rationalism does not do justice to the variegated and globalized forms, which exist in the contemporary era.

The critique of Western thought, with its dependence on Enlightenment rationalism, is further explored in a significant study by a Chinese theologian. In *Being and Relation: A Theological Critique of Western Dualism and Individualism*, Carver Yu offers a trenchant theological analysis of the cultural condition in the West and argues that Western thought can be traced to its roots in Greek dualism. Citing a number of Chinese writers,⁴⁹ he draws on their perceptions of Western culture as representing a "scientistic-mechanistic model of reality,"⁵⁰ which produces a dichotomy between matter and spirit, subject and object, and facts and values. According to Yu, "the problem of Western culture is due to the fact that the Greek and Christian humanistic spirit has given way to realism and naturalism."⁵¹ This dualism finds its roots in pre-Socratic Greek philosophy, particularly in the concepts of nature (*physis*) and substance (*ousia*).⁵²

The pre-Socratic Greeks understood the universe as a rational order, which is complete-in-itself, self-subsistent, and self-motivating. The concept of nature, which came out of this background, was used to express "the notion that thing or the totality of things all have the fundamental principles of determining what they are immanent in themselves, that things exist in and through themselves. That means, things are to be explained in virtue of themselves without recourse to anything other than themselves."⁵³ This

---

48. Ibid.
49. Yu, *Being and Relation*, xii–xxii.
50. Ibid., xii.
51. Ibid., xx.
52. Ibid., 49–63.
53. Ibid., 67.

perception of reality as *physis* or nature was responsible for the development of a naturalistic-mechanistic worldview.[54]

Although Plato rejected this worldview, he nevertheless later built his theory of "ideas" upon this theory of reality as "reality-in-and-through-itself," which has no place for any dynamic interaction or interpenetration. This laid the seed of individualism in Western thought.[55] Similarly, Aristotle developed his notion of substance on the concept of being as "being-in-itself." Each substance has a particularity of its own, having its identity in and through itself, and identified as a substance precisely because it is self-subsistent. The world is composed of discrete substances and any relation among individual entities composed of discrete substances is merely accidental.[56]

Yu goes on to suggest that Descartes built his understanding of self upon these Greek philosophical ideas, rooted in the concept of reality as "being-in-itself." For Descartes, the self-conscious "I" in *cogito ergo sum* (I think therefore I am) is implicitly understood as a substance, which is self-subsistent and needs no other for its existence.[57] The self or "ego-subject" subsists in its own self-consciousness, without intrinsic relation to the world or to other selves. This is the foundation which views humans as "being-in-itself," or the autonomous self. Western individualism is, thus, conceived. Moreover, the spiritual malaise in the West is antithetical to a "more holistic system of meaning and value" relevant to China.[58]

For Yu, the cultural dilemma in the West is "the common experience of the erosion of the personal."[59] At the heart of this challenge is a metaphysical problem found in one's tendency to view reality as the "thing-in-itself." Citing Martin Heidegger's phenomenological givenness of *Dasein* (being-in-the-world), this disastrous outlook conditions us to not only approach the world in an "objectivistic" way, but to view reality in terms of "things" as opposed to "events of encounter."[60] An integrated view of culture or reality, based on biblical meanings of being and relation, facilitates "intimate communion and a lively interpenetration" between God, humans, and the cosmos.[61] A person, in this sense, is considered primarily as "an acting agent

54. Ibid., 78.
55. Ibid., 78–86.
56. Ibid., 88–98.
57. Ibid., 98–105.
58. Ibid., xiii.
59. Ibid., 50.
60. Ibid., 55–59.
61. Ibid., 232.

in communion rather than a thinking substance." The interpenetration of being is reflected in the fact that one's identity is shaped, to a large extent, by culture and society.[62]

Yu points out that rampant Western individualism is antithetical to biblical teaching. Although influenced by Greek philosophy, Christianity took a somewhat different path rooted in biblical teachings. The Bible seeks to combine a strong emphasis on commitment to community, with an intense concern for the dignity and value of the individual.[63] In contrast to Western individualism, the Chinese approach to reality begins with "reverence" or the "intuitive confidence of the existence and infinite value of man and the cosmos."[64] Such biblical themes as humans being created in the image of God (Gen 1:26), the love commandment (Matt 22:37–39), and the equality of all in Christ (Gal 3:28) support this balance. From a biblical perspective, individualism is only one aspect of what it means to be human and how reality is perceived. For Yu, Western individualism needs to be balanced with an understanding of self in relation with others. He writes, "The individual who is truly an individual before God is also truly communal at the same time."[65]

From the above discussion, one surmises that Yu would have a natural affinity for the social sciences in understanding Christian identity. However, his philosophical examination of the Enlightenment reflects a truncated understanding. Moreover, his view of Western culture as a static entity lacks engagement with a sociological approach to understanding modernity's impact on culture and religion. Rather than being informed by social sciences to understand Christian identity, his notion of being is largely informed by Heideggerian existentialism, and his epistemology is derived from the Barthian notion of knowing God in personal encounter.

In *Theology of Reconciliation and Church Renewal*, Arnold Yeung, a theologian from Hong Kong, develops a contextual theology specifically for China. In doing so, he not only criticizes Western theology for adopting an "either-or" methodological approach to theology, which is unhealthy for the holistic cultural orientation of China, but he also follows in the footsteps of Yu's characterization of Western theology as dualistic. Given the return of Hong Kong to China, Yeung argues for the motif of "reconciliation" as a way forward. The process of "doing theology" is a matter of conceptualization closely related to cultural conditioning. The perception of reality

---

62. Ibid., 226.
63. Ibid., 219–22.
64. Ibid., xxi.
65. Ibid., 232.

and the conception of spirituality cannot be separated from the enculturation process of members of a cultural group. For example, such a theology emphasizes the unity of heaven and mankind, the equilibrium of yin and yang, harmony in relationships, unity of knowledge and action, and the solidarity of family and nation. Thus, the focus on a "both-and" approach is clearly characteristic of Chinese culture in thought, action, relationship, sentiment, and institution, which should also serve as the foundation for a "Sino-theology."

According to Yeung's observation of recent history, two groups of Chinese departed from the traditional "both-and" approach with devastating consequences. One, the scholars during the May Fourth Movement chose to embrace the "either-or" approach of Western thought, and gathered the tares with the wheat.[66] The other group is conservative Christian leaders in China during the period of the 1920s to the 1940s, such as Chia Yu-ming, Wang Mingdao, and Watchman Nee. This group's "either-or" approach was influenced by fundamentalist missionaries, who resisted humanism and the social gospel.[67]

What Yu does in his philosophical treatment of Western thought as rooted in Greek dualism, Yeung does in his historical treatment of significant events related to China's encounter with Western Christianity. The results are similar. Yeung's conclusions are predictable, reflecting sweeping, and sometimes anachronistic depictions of significant events in the history of China in general categories. Yeung is not a historian by training and his theological biases show forth all too readily. A more careful examination of modern historiography would demonstrate that this is not a reliable historical treatment of the May Fourth Movement, nor is it a nuanced depiction of early Chinese leaders influenced by fundamentalist missionaries.

The nature of contextualization as a hermeneutical process or method in theology is addressed in William Dyrness' *Learning About Theology from the Third World*.[68] Endemic to much of Western theology is what Dyrness describes as a triumphalistic paternalism that privileges itself as the final standard by which all other theologies are judged. Here, the author reflects on the complexity of theological contextualization, and argues that the "Third World" has much to offer to the limitations of "Western" theology. He rightly admits that all theological formulations are historically and culturally conditioned, and acknowledges the contributions of African, Latin American, and Asian theologians. He writes, "While neat boundaries are

---

66. Yeung, *Theology of Reconciliation*, 24.
67. Ibid., 30.
68. Dyrness, *Learning about Theology*.

not possible, I will argue that there are distinctive styles that Latin American, Asian, and African people reflect in thinking about Christianity (just as there is a distinctive style we Americans bring to our faith)."[69]

Concerning those in Asia, he continues, "Asian theologians have sought to relate their faith to religious values, especially as these are found in the ancient and ever-present traditions of the major religions (Buddhism and Hinduism). As a result, they have reflected more on the religious and philosophical nature of reality than others have.[70] In the process of interacting with one another, Dyrness insists that one must resist the temptation to judge theologies by positing Western theology as the benchmark. He states, "we must at all costs avoid giving the sense that these theologies must all be judged and corrected from any one particular point of view, which for us usually turns out to be Western."[71]

There are many important and helpful points in the book. Particularly important is Dyrness' claim that all theology is historically conditioned and contextualization is a hermeneutical process. One must ask, however, what Dyrness means by "Western" and how it is distinct from "Asian?" In an earlier study, for example, Dyrness characterizes American culture as pragmatic, optimistic, and individualistic.[72] These traits reflect Enlightenment ideals, such as freedom, progress and autonomy. Are these generalizations valid? Are the terms "Western" and "Asian" static entities? Without careful examination, descriptions may seem like overstatements in need of nuance or qualification.

In "Theological Education in Asia: An Indigenous Agenda for Renewal," Yau Man Siew, a Singaporean educator, laments the "uncritical importation" of Western models of education into Asia in an age of globalization, where geographical boundaries are blurred by enhanced accessibility in world travel. As a result of this cross-fertilization, there has been "a blind copying of the Western models of training, including wholesale adoption of curricula and philosophies without thoughtful critique or recognition of contextual differences."[73] The consequences are great, according to Siew. The Western models are characterized by the fragmentation of disciplines (and, hence, specialization), a dichotomy between seminary and church, an

---

69. Ibid., 16.
70. Ibid., 17.
71. Ibid., 19.
72. Dyrness, *Hear the Gospel?*
73. Siew, "Theological Education in Asia," 58.

emphasis on intellectual pursuits and formal schooling, and a disconnect between theory and practice.[74]

For Siew, these characteristics are not relevant for Asia. Instead, he articulates an "indigenous philosophy of theological education" for Asia that effectively triangulates the gospel, world, and the church.[75] He states, "The purpose of theological education is not to train in theological abstractions for respectable scholarship but to 'form' people in the church to participate effectively in God's local and global mission."[76] For Siew, the church must hold in tension both the global and the local when it comes to theological education. One must be sensitive to the richness and diversity of the global church while respecting the uniqueness and relevance of local contexts.[77]

Siew's article offers helpful insights on the limitations of the Western model imported to foreign soil in Asia. In particular, his discussion on the disastrous outcome of theological fragmentation is valid. A potential problem is detected in the study. One wonders if Western models are directly reproduced and transferred to Asia without modification, as Siew claims? Consideration of scholarly literature on globalization would indicate a certain degree of hybridity occurs. Here, the relationship between globalization and Westernization deserves careful examination.

Perhaps the most comprehensive study on evangelical contextualization from an Asian perspective is Hwa Yung's *Mangoes or Bananas? The Quest for an Authentic Asian Christian Theology*.[78] Hwa, former Bishop of the Methodist Church in Malaysia and Director of the Centre for the Study of Christianity in Asia at Trinity Theological College, Singapore, laments about the Western nature of the church in Asia. In his effort to de-Westernize theology in Asia, he argues for contextualization as an integral element of theological methodology and proposes a missional theology for Asia.

Several prominent themes run throughout the text, including a Wesleyan emphasis on the experiential dimension of Christianity, pastoral concerns, and a deep dissatisfaction with the Enlightenment or rationalistic nature of Western theology. The culprit for the lack of an authentic Asian Christianity is the presence of Western theology in Asian contexts, which gives rise to a secular understanding of reality. Such a worldview is devoid of spiritual quality. Since theology and mission are methodologically inseparable, he argues for a truly contextual theology to empower the church

74. Ibid., 60–62.
75. Ibid., 63–64.
76. Ibid., 64.
77. Ibid., 66–67.
78. Hwa, *Mangoes or Bananas?*

in Asia. He discusses four reasons for the Asian church's disenchantment with Western theology. One, since theologies are products of particular cultures and histories, the limits of Western theology is inadequate to address the existential realities of the rest of the world.[79] Two, Western theology presupposes a naturalistic worldview and does not sufficiently address the spirit world of Asian folk religions.[80]

Hwa's most trenchant critique of Western theology is directed at Enlightenment rationalism and empiricism. For Hwa, the detriment of rationalism is best characterized as Cartesian individual self-consciousness as the final arbiter of truth, as personified in the writings of Lessing, Schleiermacher, Bultmann, and Tillich.[81] Empiricism is "the view that the sole source of knowledge comes from sense perception." This understanding contributed to Hume's skepticism of miracles and religious belief.[82] Lastly, Hwa criticizes Western theology as an "unengaged theology" in the way it dichotomizes static truth and praxis. As such, Western theology lacks the power for human and social transformation.[83] An authentic Asian Christian theology must be guided by four criteria: relevance to socio-political context, connection to church evangelistic and pastoral ministries, inculturation, and faithfulness to Christian tradition.

Hwa uses these criteria to assess various missional theologies in Asia, including theologians from the pre-WWII era, ecumenical theologians from the postwar era, and conservative Asian theologians associated with the Asian Theological Association. He concludes that none of those theologians fully meet all the criteria, though his favor for the conservative theologians is quite evident. In his critique of those theologians, the most glaring weakness, according to Hwa, is that they lack adequate engagement with the spirit world, or what Hiebert calls the "flaw of the excluded middle." This major lacuna is responsible for the Asian church's ineffectiveness in evangelism and providing proper pastoral care for its members. In his concluding comments, he compares the present state of Christianity in Asian to a banana, which is yellow on the outside but white in the inside. An authentic Asian contextualized theology should be more like a mango, yellow on the outside and yellow on the inside.

While Hwa should be commended for his important study, several limitations can be enumerated. The typical treatment of Western theology

79. Ibid., 2.
80. Ibid., 3–4.
81. Ibid., 5.
82. Ibid., 6.
83. Ibid., 8.

as a static or monolithic entity is again evident. Like many before him, Hwa does not seem to appreciate both the depth and variety of Western theology in existence today, which makes his criticisms appear like "straw-man" arguments. In his essay, "The Gospel in Twenty-First-Century Asia," Hwa argues that an authentic Asian gospel must contain at least four key elements. (1) The gospel is holistic and does not dichotomize the spiritual and physical, or the socio-political and economic elements. (2) The gospel is supernatural in that it engages the Asian religious worldview of gods, spirits, demons, magic, and healing through prayer. (3) The gospel should be inculturated so that faith and practice are expressed in more indigenous Asian forms. (4) The gospel must be incarnated for authentic gospel proclamation to be carried out.[84] One surmises that a vast majority of Western theologians today would agree with those elements, at least in theory if not in practice.

Secondly, Hwa's treatment of Enlightenment rationalism, as with most missiological critiques, is approached primarily from a philosophical perspective. In particular, the terms "modernity' and "modernism" are certainly debatable in scholarly circles today and should be understood beyond philosophical boundaries. Again, is one's commitment to philosophical rationalism tantamount to the rational or intellectual dimensions of life? Are they mutually exclusive ideas? Terms such as "rationalism" and "rationalistic," used in philosophical contexts, need to be nuanced and properly distinguished from human rational or intellectual capacities in general. Thirdly, Hwa's study is largely a deconstructive work and lacks a genuine constructive trajectory that points theology forward to overcoming the so-called Asian-Western impasse. Lastly, Hwa points out that Christianity in Asia is still perceived as a Western and foreign religion, due, in part, to its association with Western colonialism and the observation that seminaries in Asia still use texts and methodologies rooted in Enlightenment rationalism. However, he concedes that the problem "is not very apparent in highly Westernized societies like Singapore," and that "some people are attracted to Christianity precisely because of its Western features."[85] Unfortunately, he does not explain why Singapore is an exceptional case or the reasoning for this important observation.

Missiologist Enoch Wan's collection of seven articles in *Chinese Around the World* revisits previous criticisms of Western theology as rooted in Greek dualism. In arguing for appropriate contextualization for Chinese contexts, he insists that the gospel in the Chinese mind embraces a "both-and" approach to theology. Wan's approach to theology is both critical and

---

84. Hwa, "The Gospel," 87–102.
85. Ibid., 93.

constructive. One, he critiques what he calls the "either-or" thought pattern of traditional Western theology, which is derived from Greek philosophy.[86] For Wan, this "either-or" approach has several variations: the dualistic cosmology of ancient Greek philosophy, the dialectic idealism of Hegel, the dialectic materialism of Marx, and Augustine's dialectic sociology of the kingdom of God and the kingdom of man.[87]

In contrast, Chinese thought pattern is characterized by a "both-and" orientation, which is completely free from Aristotelian logic. The pictographic symbol of "*tai-qi*" or the yin and yang depicts this concept, and is expressed in the Chinese cultural themes of unity, harmony, integration, equilibrium, wholeness, or balance.[88] The constructive aspect of Wan's thought is the development of a Sino-theology, which involves a synthetic, integrative cognitive process, as opposed to the either-or approach of the West. For example, the Chinese's way of social interaction favors a relational or complementary paradigm rather than a dichotomistic or confrontational approach of the West.[89] Wan's Sino-theology is uniquely contextual in terms of conceptualization, expression, and application.

Wan's missiological critique of Western theology is built upon prior scholarship done by Chinese theologians, particularly Carver Yu, in that he presents a static view of Western theology as reflecting Greek dualism, resulting in either-or conclusions.

The critique of Western theology and its alliance with Enlightenment rationalism is evident in several essays published in 1999 in the *International Journal of Frontier Missions*. These authors argue not only for the de-westernization of the gospel but do so with an overtly Reformed insistence on the recovery of a biblical worldview.[90] Dutch missiologist Hans Weerstra points out, however, that de-westernizing the gospel does not necessarily involve making it more Eastern. For him, the primary problem with the Western version of Christianity is that it is a form of syncretism. He writes, "There is no doubt that the 20th century birthed a non-Christian worldview that has spawned a tornadic like whirlwind of non-Christian beliefs and paradigms in the form of scientific rationalism, secular humanism, materialism and consumerism, plus pluralism and its kissing cousin relativism

---

86. Wan, "Calling for Sino-Theology," 12–17.

87. Ibid., 13.

88. Ibid., 15.

89. Wan, "Theological Contributions of Sino-Theology to the Global Christian Community," 19.

90. Weerstra, "De-Westernizing the Gospel," 129–34; Weerstra, "Rediscovering the Sacred Myth," 135–40; Campbell, "Releasing the Gospel," 167–71.

where everything is true and nothing is true."[91] For Weerstra, the root problem of Western civilization is the Enlightenment and Greek philosophy, which supported the emergence of empiricism in that reality is determined by the observable and measurable.[92] The only way out of this morass is the recovery of a biblical worldview, one that embraces creationism, the reality of the spirit world, a biblical view of humanity, and an authentic Christian lifestyle.[93]

Judy Weerstra echoes the sentiment that de-westernizing the gospel does not necessarily make it Eastern. For her, the effort means divesting Christianity of its modernism and Greek philosophical trappings and restoring the holistic nature of faith exemplified in the Old Testament Scripture.[94] Only in this way can the gospel become Eastern and more appropriate for those in our postmodern societies.[95] In "Releasing the Gospel from Western Bondage," Jonathan Campbell also identifies "modernity" as the debilitating element of Western Christianity. The "hollowness" of the Western gospel is especially evident in the light of its inability to answer to the charges and meet the needs of those living in postmodern times. He compares modernity with secularization, individualism, relativism, and syncretism.[96]

In "Reconfiguring Western Theology in Asia," Korean theologian Lee Moon Jang acknowledges that while Asian theologians have sought to de-westernize theology in Asia in the last three decades or so, they have not reached a consensus on the goals, tasks, and methods of formulating an authentic Asian theology.[97] Citing Scott Sunquist, Lee identifies the quest to "Asianize" the gospel in Asia revolves around the perennial issues of the nature of theology and the contextualization of theological education in Asia.[98] Although Lee credits the contributions of Western theology in Asia, he takes pain to "revisit" some of its problems. Three in particular are highlighted.

One, Lee complains about "the influx of Western theologies *en masse* suppresses the creativity of Asian Christians."[99] Taking a more irenic tone,

---

91. Weerstra, "De-Westernizing the Gospel," 131.
92. Ibid., 132.
93. Ibid., 132–34.
94. Weerstra, "Rediscovering the Sacred Myth," 136–37.
95. Ibid., 138–40.
96. Campbell, "Releasing the Gospel," 168.
97. Lee, "Reconfiguring Western Theology," 31.
98. Ibid., 32.
99. Ibid., 33.

Lee argues that the existence of Western theology is not a problem in itself, but it is the "massive presence," which has suppressed or hindered indigenous theologians to create local expressions of the Christian faith.[100] A second problem is that "Western methods for theological studies are imposed."[101] Lee contends Asian theologians have perpetuated Western methods of doing theology to the impoverishment and neglect of Asian Christianity. This is so because imported theologies bring with them answers to unique Western questions, which are not relevant to Asia. The tragic result "is the monopoly of theological discourse by those theologians trained in the Western methods."[102] As a result of the first and second problems, the final problem of Western theology in Asia is that "the goal of theological studies is not effectively achieved."[103] Rather than serving Asian religious seekers or Christian practitioners, Western theology in Asia serves "scientific, historical, and positivistic researches," with their goal of amassing objective knowledge as opposed to practical ends.[104]

Lee notes it is not realistic for Asians to remove or undo Western theology in Asia. However, he is hopeful that Asian thinkers can "reconfigure" it so it becomes more relevant to Asian realities.[105] Lee proposes three ways forward. One, Western theology should be revised as spiritual theology. Seeking truth is not merely an intellectual endeavor, but one that is 'holistic" and "spiritual" in orientation. Here, the deficiencies of the scientific or positivistic approaches become glaringly apparent, because they fail to provide hermeneutical engagement with the spiritual world inherent of the Asian worldview.[106]

Secondly, Western theology in Asian needs to be reconfigured as missiological theology. Lee cites approvingly of Paul Hiebert, who "is interested in a rendezvous between gospel and our concrete life situations."[107] For Lee, "missiological theology seeks to bridge the gospel and Asian cultures" by holding in tension the transcendent and immanent elements in Asian theology.[108] That is, theology must relate to the concrete realities of everyday

---

100. Ibid.
101. Ibid., 34.
102. Ibid.
103. Ibid., 35.
104. Ibid., 35–36.
105. Ibid., 36.
106. Ibid., 36–37.
107. Ibid., 37–38.
108. Ibid., 38.

Asian life, because the validity of Asian theology is "a living orthodoxy and orthopraxis."[109]

Lastly, Lee identifies the problem of Western theology for its dualistic orientation, the strict dichotomy between subject and object of inquiry. In contrast to this objectivistic approach, "the goal of Asian learning is to embody and personify the object of learning through a non-dualistic engagement."[110] For Lee, theological studies are not merely intellectual pursuits but ways to help Asians "embody" the Christian message so that their lives can be transformed. Western theology harms the church by relegating theology to the realm of speculation, removing it from the historical and cultural context of Asia, and formulating theory to the neglect of the identity and integrity of Christianity in Asia.[111]

Lastly, the ATA, on the occasion of the 40th anniversary of its founding, published a collection of essays under the title, *Tending the Seedbeds: Educational Perspectives on Theological Education in Asia*. Noting the concerns about the effectiveness of theological education in the last few decades, the editor states the aim of the book: "This volume does not explicitly address the question, 'How effective are our seminaries?' Rather, the articles in this collection relate to a more formative question: How could the tending of our seminaries be enhanced to ensure appropriate growth towards maturity and fruitfulness of those who participate in our ventures in theological education?"[112]

In "How Asian is Asian Theological Education," Larry Caldwell links much of theological education in Asia to Western colonialism. He argues that the influence of colonization in Asia is evident in what and how subjects are taught. As a result of colonization, many Asians have uncritically accepted Western curricula and pedagogical methods to the detriment of appropriate content and local ways of teaching and learning.[113] The uncritical acceptance of Western theology is evident by the prevailing use of Millard Erickson's *Christian Theology* in which discussion on the "spirit world" is largely ignored.[114] Caldwell observes that many theological educators in Asia are not adequately trained for the realities of Asia, nor are courses and curricula appropriately contextualized for Asian contexts.[115]

109. Ibid.
110. Ibid., 39.
111. Ibid.
112. Ibid., 10.
113. Caldwell, "Asian Theological Education," 25–29.
114. Ibid., 29.
115. Ibid., 32–40.

There is much to be commended for in Caldwell's essay, including the lingering negative effects of Western colonialism on theological education in Asia and the sobering reality that many Western educators are not well-suited for the complex and variegated Asian contexts. However, a case can be made against interpreting the history of world missions solely through the lens of colonialism. Some things have changed. As Tennent observes, "Many people believed that the presence of these new Christians was only an unfortunate by-product of Western, imperialistic colonialism and that in the wake of colonialism it would wither and die."[116] However, Christianity has globalized in the last century as the center of gravity of Christianity has shifted from the North to the South. The history of world missions, properly understood, needs to be reinterpreted through the lens of globalization.

Doing Theology in the Era of Globalization

It is clear from the foregoing review that criticisms of Western theology in missiological literature focus primarily on theological methodology. The issue is how theology is formulated or done that contributes to the negative perception of Christianity as a Western or alien religion in Asian contexts. This is particularly prominent in the 1982 Seoul Declaration in which Western theology is criticized for its captivity to Western individualism and rationalism. Hwa Yung, for example, identifies Western theology as allied with Enlightenment thought, which is the root cause for its disengagement from Asian lived experiences. These are detriments to effective mission in Asia. In critiques of Western theology, what seems clear is that missiological literature uses terms like "modernism" or "rationalism" as catch-all words to depict all-encompassing ideas or concepts that lack nuance or qualification.

The notion of "rationalism" in the history of Western philosophy refers to the view that reason alone is the source and final arbiter of knowledge.[117] In other words, a rationalist attempts to arrive at incontestable truths or principles. Such an epistemological assertion rests on specific methodological assumptions. What are some alternative ways to construct theology that avoids the pitfalls of rationalistic, Western theology? Evangelical thinkers have long recognized the problems of overt rationalism and Western theology and sought to overcome them by addressing three key issues. These include the postmodern critique of modernistic theological methodology,[118]

---

116. Tennent, *Theology in the Context*, 7.

117. Geisler and Feinberg, *Introduction to Philosophy*, 110.

118. Vanhoozer, "But That's Your Interpretation," 21–28; Vanhoozer, *Drama of Doctrine*; Vanhoozer, "One Rule to Rule," 85–126.

the need to formulate global theology,[119] and the limitations of Western dualism.[120]

Although it is beyond the scope of this study to examine these issues, it is sufficient for now to point out that doing theology in the global era needs to attend to the universals and the particulars. The former refers to universal theological principles that transcend culture. The latter refers to the need to indigenize and ground the gospel in particular cultures.[121] In this sense, the complementarity between biblical, systematic, and mission theology keeps theologians asking relevant questions and missiologists grounded in biblical truths. Dialogue within a hermeneutical community of missiologists and theologians from around the world exposes biases, holds in tension "universals and particulars," and keeps "past revelation and the gospel to the present" connected.[122] The aim of missional theology is realized when it "makes theology live for us, because theology is no longer an abstract understanding of truth, but a map for living our lives."[123]

Authentic theology in the era of globalization, whether Asian or Western in orientation, must manifest the qualities of "universality" and "particularity."[124] In order to rectify Western theology's tendency to break down disciplines into separate domains, such as biblical, systematic, historical, and practical theologies, one must reintegrate the theological disciplines so that theology can more accurately reflect biblical revelation and local historical and cultural settings.[125]

This two dimensional nature of theology—universality and particularity—is evident in Simon Chan's treatment of evangelical theology from a Singaporean's perspective. In his essay "Evangelical Theology in Asian Contexts," Chan demonstrates how an Asian theologian can hold in tension both global and local perspectives, only he does not use such terminologies. Although written to address the broader umbrella of evangelical theology in Asia, he has the Singaporean context in view. He argues that "Asian evangelicalism has much in common with evangelicalism in the West" in terms of "explicit" theology.[126] Here, the term "theology" is understood as "criti-

---

119. Hiebert, *Anthropological Insights for Missionaries*, 53–73; Tiénou and Hiebert, "From Systematic to Biblical," 117–33.

120. Hiebert, *Anthropological Reflections*, 189–209; Anane-Asane et al., "Paul G. Hiebert's," 189–97.

121. Tennent, *Theology in Context*, 12.

122. Tiénou and Hiebert, "From Systematic to Biblical," 131.

123. Ibid., 133.

124. Tennent, *Theology in the Context*, 264; Walls, *Missionary Movement*, 227.

125. Tennent, *Theology in the Context*, 251.

126. Chan, "Evangelical Theology," 233.

cal reflections" in terms of church doctrine, confessions, or statements by institutionally accredited theologians.[127] Citing David Bebbington's "working definition" of evangelicalism, the common features include conversionism, activism, biblicism, and crucicentrism.[128] What Asian evangelicals take issue with their Western counterparts is theological methodology. Asians typically prefer non-dualistic and concrete ways of doing theology in contrast to the Cartesian, abstract, Greek-dualistic way of Western rationalism. While issues have been identified, Asian theologians have yet to actually apply the "Asian way of thinking" to the formulation of theological treatises.[129]

In dealing with evangelical theology in Asia, Chan insists that one's assessment must go beyond explicit theology to implicit theology done at the grassroots in terms of stories, testimonies, and sermons. This type of implicit Asian "evangelicalism" is unique and must not be defined by institutional terms as in the West. Moreover, the evangelical character of Asian Christianity "has much in common with the spiritual instinct of Asians," especially evident in those who convert from Buddhism and Taoism.[130] This is so because the worldview in Asia is "primal" in that people view "reality in its totality and affirm a spiritual world behind the world of observable reality." Accordingly, such a worldview is similar to evangelicalism with its emphasis on spiritual conversion.[131] In particular, an implicit theology in Asia, especially expressed in Charismatic and Pentecostal sign gifts, shares a "sacramental" worldview with Asian religions in that the "physical acts as a vehicle for spiritual power."[132]

Chan concludes, "Although Asian evangelicals often contrast the 'Asian way of thinking' with the rationalism of the West, it should be noted that this way of thinking is not exclusively Asian as it has much in common with the spiritual exegesis of the church fathers and certain strands of postmodern thought."[133] For Chan, the defining characteristics of evangelical theology in Asian contexts include those that grapple seriously with the "spiritual" realm and one that addresses social realities by formulating "political theology" as a primary way of engagement.[134]

---

127. Ibid., 226.
128. Ibid., 225, 227–30.
129. Ibid., 228–29.
130. Ibid., 226–27.
131. Ibid.
132. Ibid., 232.
133. Ibid., 233.
134. Ibid., 234.

Summary

This chapter has reviewed various Asian missiological studies that point to the problems of rationalistic and Western theology in Asia. Yet the spread of Christianity across the globe is quite evident, particularly in the last century. What are some implications of the global spread of Christianity and the development of local indigenous theologies over the past century? One, as long as people continue to perceive Christianity in Asia as a Western religion, the globalization of Christian faith will not be recognized. Two, the negative perception of Western Christianity in Asia is rooted in how Western theology is formulated, which often opts for grand schemes to the neglect of local lived realities. Three, the categories "Asian" and "Western" theology are not monolithic and variations exist in both camps. One must avoid using such misleading categories, as if all Westerners follow Western theology and all Asians adhere to Asian theology. In fact, many Western evangelicals have moved beyond Western to global theology, the latter of which takes into account local realities in formulating theology. That is, evangelicals must seriously consider contextualization as a discipline in formulating theology in a world where thinkers engage in dialogue and learn from one another. Only by listening to one another can we expose our own theological blindspots and overcome the perception of Western Christianity in various parts of the globe where Christianity has taken root.

Craig Ott notes that, while the days of Western theological hegemony are likely behind us, there is still much that the Western church can offer to the global church. The Western church can serve the global community by globalizing theology "in the sense that it surrenders its position of privilege and enters genuine dialogue with theologians from non-Western traditions."[135] Globalizing theology is a way of doing theology that recognizes local expressions of faith, yet seeks to incorporate those perspectives to inform the global church on topics of relevance to global Christianity. Such an approach overcomes the limitations of the individualistic and rationalistic tendencies of Western theology. Ott rightly summarizes, "The point is to move beyond an East versus West critique, which often employs gross generalizations while failing to point the way forward."[136]

The study by Singaporean sociologist, Chee Kiong Tong, indicates that Christianity in Singapore is, in fact, growing due to the perception of Christianity as a rational religion. More importantly, Tong's study sheds light on the "East versus West" impasse in his observation that the "Chinese-educated"

---

135. Ott, "Conclusion: Globalizing Theology," 311.
136. Ibid., 314.

non-believers tend to reject Christianity because they perceive it as a Western religion and the fact that a growing number of English-educated young people convert to Christianity because they perceive it as a rational religion. These claims, if substantiated, could potentially counter the prevalent Asian missiological criticism that the intrusion of rationalistic theology into Asia is responsible for the Western and alien expressions of Christianity in that part of the world. This study seeks to examine the topic of Christian conversion in Singapore and attempts to explain the conflicting views between Asian missiologists and sociologist Tong. The next chapter then explains not only why religions change over time in the contexts of modernization and globalization but also the ways in which people perceive them differently in various cultural settings across the globe.

3

Modernization, Globalization, and Religious Change

THE PREVIOUS CHAPTER REVIEWED literature that critiques theology in Asia as rationalistic, Western, and a vestige of Enlightenment thinking and the modern age. The validity of that judgment depends, of course, upon how one defines the term "rationalistic" and the phenomenon of "modernity." If, on the one hand, modernity is defined narrowly on philosophical grounds, as a period starting roughly in the seventeenth century associated with the rationalism of Descartes, the criticism may be valid.[1] If, on the other hand, modernity is examined broadly in a socio-cultural perspective, a case can be made that modernity should be understood "in terms of the ongoing processes of modernization and globalization." These two approaches are "not mutually exclusive," and together provide a fuller understanding of the subject.[2]

According to Wilson, "modernity refers to the cultural conditions that set the terms for all thought and action in a particular culture."[3] The concept indicates "an openness and a commitment to the new as opposed to the old," and refers to "the consciousness of cultural change."[4] Moreover, "modernity" is associated with a number of interrelated concepts, including "modern," "modernism," and "modernization." First, the term "modern" is a comparative concept, indicating the changing perception of "what is new as opposed to what is ancient." Since one's perception is a subjective judgment of what is modern, the phenomenon of modern can vary greatly from

1. Netland, *Encountering Religious Pluralism*, 65–77.
2. Ibid., 89.
3. Wilson, "Modernity," 6108.
4. Ibid., 6109.

culture to culture.⁵ Concomitantly, the terms "modernism" and "modernization" refer, respectively, to "cultural and social attitudes or programs dedicated to supporting what is perceived as modern."⁶ The former denotes a "commitment to the modern in intellectual and cultural spheres," while the latter indicates "a programmatic remaking of the political and economic aspects of society in support of the 'new.'"⁷ This second set of literature review examines three distinct, yet interrelated subjects, namely, modernization, globalization, and religious change. The chapter examines the processes of modernization and globalization and their impact upon religion, particularly in terms of the rationalization and hybridization of religion within the local culture in Singapore.

Modernization Theory

A classic treatise on modernization is *The Homeless Mind: Modernization and Consciousness* by Berger, Berger, and Kellner. The authors argue that modernization processes—technology, bureaucracy, and pluralization—are contributing to a growing feeling of anxiety and confusion when competing viewpoints are introduced. The authors define modernity as "the institutional concomitants of technologically induced growth." In other words, economic growth brought about by technological advances brings with it certain institutions, which are incorporated into everyday life. Thus, modernization "consists in the growth and diffusion of a set of institutions rooted in the transformation of the economy by means of technology."⁸ The crux of the argument is that the processes of modernization are facilitated by two carriers, namely, technology and bureaucracy. The impact of emerging technological and bureaucratic realities shapes our consciousness and worldview. Technology offers new ways of doing and thinking about things. Bureaucracy creates "red tape" in daily life as one loses control to external restrictions. The individual in modern society responds by compartmentalizing life and identifies himself or herself in accordance with roles and responsibilities.

As a result, modernization contributes to the pluralization of social life-worlds. In comparison to traditional society, where viewpoints are shaped and shared by a group as a whole, modernization introduces the individual to multiple viewpoints. These varying viewpoints often conflict

---

5. Ibid., 6108.
6. Ibid.
7. Ibid.
8. Berger et al., *Homeless Mind*, 9.

and introduce tension. In an effort to reduce cognitive dissonance, modern people adopt separate thought processes for public and private life. One of the results of this erroneous dichotomy is the privatization of religious faith.

As a sociological discipline, modernization theory seeks to analyze social, ideological, and cultural change from a premodern to a modern society.[9] It does so primarily as a historical investigation, dating back to premodern times.[10] Modernization can be defined as "the process of change from small, traditional societies to the contemporary world. It is assumed that when the most technologically advanced societies existing at various points in time are compared, they will reveal directions of social change. That is, it is assumed that increasing technological sophistication produces social changes in a predictable manner."[11] Inglehart argues, in particular, that economic development, cultural change, and political change go together in coherent and even, to some extent, predictable patterns. He writes,

> The central claim of modernization theory is that industrialization is linked with specific processes of socio-political change that apply widely . . . Economic development is linked with a syndrome of changes that includes not only industrialization, but also urbanization, mass education, occupational specialization, bureaucratization, and communications development, which in turn are linked with still broader cultural, social, and political changes.[12]

Netland attributes the beginning of this historical transformation process to the industrial revolution in late seventeenth-century Europe, spreading later to America and the entire world. The advancement of technology intensified in the twentieth century. This growth created not only massive population shifts in terms of urbanization throughout the globe, but impacted social interactions in terms of how people viewed themselves and the rational ways in which people functioned within complex societies.[13]

To be sure, modernization theory is notoriously difficult to define and various positions exist. Despite such difficulties, social scientists agree that indicators can be identified which suggest modernization. These include (1) self-sustaining economic growth, (2) political participation, (3) the diffusion of secular norms, (4) a high degree of geographical and social mobility,

---

9. Tamney and Chiang, *Modernization, Globalization and Confucianism*, 1.
10. Ibid., 7.
11. Ibid.
12. Inglehart, *Modernization and Postmodernization*, 8.
13. Netland, *Encountering Religious Pluralism*, 77–80.

and (5) personality transformation.[14] From such indicators, modernization can be viewed "as part of the increasing control of his environment by man" along three dimensions: technological, organizational, and attitudinal.[15] Technology involves industrialization, which contrasts pre-industrial and industrial societies. The organizational aspect reflects degrees of differentiation and specialization and contrasts between simple and complex societies. The attitudinal dimension refers to that of rationality and secularization and contrasts the scientific versus the religious-magical perspective.[16]

In the long-term process of modernization, five components can be identified, including "technological development, societal expansion, structural differentiation, fragmentation of a society's culture, and the growing importance of the individual at the expense of groups."[17] A defining characteristic of modernization is technological innovations, which, in turn, contribute to the expansion of societies. As societies expand, differentiated social structures also emerge. In contrast to traditional societies, modern societies no longer differentiate responsibilities based upon family and kinship units. All these factors contribute to cultural fragmentation. As societies expand, along with the mechanisms of urbanization, nation building, and globalization, cultures become more diffused and pluralistic. Lastly, as structural differentiation and cultural fragmentation take place, the result is individuation. People are no longer identified by group values and expectations. Rather, they are defined by individual roles and personal choices in modern society.[18]

Modernization and Rationalization of Religion

What are some implications of modernization theory for religion? Such a view of modernization assumes that the viability and durability of religion depends, to a large extent, on how it fits or adjusts to its historical context. Modernization theory implies that socio-cultural changes at the societal level precede and change religions. Impacted by the processes of modernization, religions are transformed both in terms of their internal constitution and social significance within culture. However, these changes do not necessarily indicate a linear movement. Although social scientists do assume that most social changes can find their roots in secular forces,

---

14. Von der Mehden, *Religion and Modernization*, 5.
15. Ibid.
16. Ibid.
17. Tamney and Chiang, *Modernization, Globalization and Confucianism*, 7.
18. Ibid., 7–8.

they do recognize that the consequences of such changes are affected by the religious responses to them. As a result, social change is facilitated by a group's successful ability to accommodate the patterns of change. In other words, religions are more likely to be successful in modernizing societies to the extent that people are able to adjust to increasing technological development, societal expansion, structural differentiation, cultural fragmentation, and individuation.[19]

To be sure, cultural change does take place in all societies and at all times. No society is exempt from it, but how does cultural change relate to modernity? According to John Wilson, modernity is a "special case" of cultural change. Several key characteristics of modernity toward religion can be enumerated. (1) "Modernity includes a systematic commitment to rationality, that is, a conviction that logically consistent and universalizable principles ought to be the basis for change." (2) "Modernity tends to undervalue the role of symbols and the subconscious." (3) "Human life is highly malleable." Modernity is a "special case" of cultural change in the contemporary world, because it is a "self-conscious" response.[20] This descriptive approach to modernity, as stated above, can also apply to modernity's impact on religion, whereby patterns of religious change are identified under the conditions of modernity.[21]

Modernity's overall impact on religion is considered ubiquitous regardless of the tradition. Key examples include the concepts of "bureaucratization" and "rationalization."[22] Bureaucratization refers to religious change in the modern world as religious institutions are permeated by the techniques and procedures derived from other sectors of society. Some of these management techniques are neutral in effect but most transform religion into a bureaucratic institution.[23]

In sociology, rationalization refers to the replacement of traditions, values, and emotions as motivators for behavior in society with rational and calculated ones. Specifically, rationalization indicates the necessity of making reasonable decisions relevant to the demands and constraints of the modern world. In *The Homeless Mind*, sociologists consider the effects of modernization on religion. They argue that the processes of modernization—technology, bureaucracy, and pluralization—give rise to a feeling of

19. Ibid.
20. Wilson, "Modernity," 6109.
21. Ibid., 6109–10.
22. Ibid., 6110.
23. Ibid.

anxiety or confusion in the modern world.[24] As a result of these processes, religion has been rationalized, particularly in terms of the privatization of religious faith. For Berger, Berger, and Kellner, rationalization "does not mean the reflective rationality engaged in by a scientist or philosopher, but rather immediately available functional rationality, as it is thematizable in the everyday life of the individual."[25] Functional rationality refers, above all, to "the imposition of rational controls over the material universe, over social relations and finally over the self."[26]

For example, since modernity involves the ordering of time, traditional religions can no longer structure festivals and feasts to involve the public domain, because they have to compete with wider social obligations that constrain or impinge on traditional religions. As a result, religions are often transformed or relegated to the private realm. Religion—in its public expression—no longer carries as much weight as before, while religion—in its private expression—is given greater emphasis. The dichotomization of religion between the public and private realms is characteristic of modernity and its impact on religious behavior.[27]

Beyond the general impact of modernity on religion, there are explicit identifiable religious responses to modernity. The degree of response falls roughly into five categories. One, religious response to modernity can yield new religious ideas. In particular, religious cults have mushroomed in the last few decades throughout the world as a result of new insights and resources gained from modernity. Two, religious response to modernity can result in the accommodation of religion to the surrounding cultural milieu. Protestant liberalism is a prime example of this category, whereby divine revelation as codified in the Bible is reinterpreted according to modern science and a naturalistic worldview. A third pattern of response is for religious traditions to preserve their uniqueness, albeit within the parameters of their new environment. The Roman Catholic Church's reluctance to update its traditions in the light of the Vatican II Council is a prime example. Four, religious responses to modernity can also take the form of strident resistance, opting for the purity of some original or primitive form. Religious fundamentalism is a manifestation of resistance and a form of purified reductionism. Lastly, religious response to modernity can spawn new religions. The creation of new religions can be eclectic in nature, combining idiosyncratic modern forms and ancient elements. It should be noted that these are rather

---

24. Berger et al., *The Homeless Mind*, 23–82.
25. Ibid., 111–12; Wilson, "Modernity," 6110.
26. Berger et al., *The Homeless Mind*, 202.
27. Wilson, "Modernity," 6110.

artificial and arbitrary categories, where the lines separating them often shift. Far from the assumption that religions rival or disappear in the midst of modernity, religious traditions react differently and are transformed in varying degrees and manners.[28]

Max Weber and Rationalization of Religion

The literature on modernization theory has a long history in sociology from Karl Marx to Max Weber. In general agreement with Marx and Weber, Inglehart maintains that modernization occurs when "Economic, cultural, and political change go together in coherent patterns that are changing the world in predictable ways."[29]

The sociological analysis of modernity, as it is associated with the processes of rationalization and the disenchantment of the world, is rooted in the seminal work of Max Weber (1864–1920). Tong writes, "The crux of the Weberian thesis is that the world we live in is undergoing a continuous process of rationalization." Society as a whole tends toward *zweckrational* organization. In traditional society, "action is largely determined by habit and emotions." However, modern society tends toward rational action, "as conscious ideas emerge in the orientation of action."[30] In the rationalization of religious ideas, the process is at least a historical process resulting from disenchantment. For Weber, disenchantment refers to one's observation of the natural realm as being stripped of its religious meaning in favor of scientific or naturalistic explanations.[31] Modern life, as impacted by the processes of rationalization and the disenchantment of the world, is viewed with a set of assumptions. Weber observes, "There are no mysterious incalculable forces that come into play, but rather that one can, in principle, master all things by calculation. One need no longer have recourse to magical means in order to master or implore the spirits, as did the savage for whom such mysterious powers exist."[32]

The process of religious rationalization involves the clarification, specification, and systematization of the ideas that inform people of their reason for being. Such ideas imply metaphysical and theological conceptions of the cosmic and world orders, as well as humans' position in relation to such

---

28. Wilson, "Modernity," 6110–11.
29. Inglehart, *Modernization and Postmodernization*, 7.
30. Tong, *Rationalizing Religion*, 5.
31. Wilson, "Secularization," 8216.
32. Tong, *Rationalizing Religion*, 114.

wider orders.[33] In *The Protestant Ethic and the Spirit of Capitalism*, Weber considers the impact of modernization on society and argues that ascetic Protestantism fosters rational social action. Protestantism is the most rational of all world religions, because it is characterized by a methodical control of every activity of daily life and imbues all human action with an integrated set of conscious meaning.[34]

Specifically, Weber identifies certain aspects of Calvinism that shift human efforts toward rationalizing tendencies. These spur the creation of the Western capitalistic system, and spread throughout the world. For Weber, the phenomenon of religion is an important historical factor that serves as a source of social and economic change.[35] Religion, in this sense, is viewed primarily as a set of historical ideas, beliefs, and regulations, which, in turn, impact group interests (material and ideal), shape activities, and spur economic change.[36] For example, Weber cites two kinds of prophets, the exemplary prophet and the emissary prophet. The exemplary prophet challenges the status quo by living an exemplary life, with the Buddha as a prime example. The typical emissary prophet is the kind found in the Hebrew Bible, one sent by God to bring a message that people need to live differently. For Weber, it is the emissary prophet who calls for change—active ascetic change—that ultimately leads to modern capitalism.

On the question of how a religion shapes society and culture, Weber notes a causal connection between ascetic Protestantism and economic success.[37] In other words, there seems to be a linear relationship between religion and social institutions. The underlying force of the spirit of capitalism is a work ethic that finds its roots in Protestantism. At the core of this impetus is the Calvinistic doctrine of predestination.[38] This doctrine contains several key elements, including God's decree to elect the church and damn the reprobate, divine election without the benefit of divine foresight, and salvation as a free gift.[39] In contrast to Roman Catholicism, which provides an assurance of salvation for those who partake of the sacramental system and submit themselves to the clerical order,[40] Weber claims that Calvinists experience a deep sense of terror, helplessness and loneliness because they

33. Ibid., 5.
34. Weber, *Protestant Ethic*.
35. Ibid., 44.
36. Ibid., 40, 47, 155.
37. Ibid., 155.
38. Ibid., 109.
39. Ibid., 98–128.
40. Ibid., 105.

MODERNIZATION, GLOBALIZATION, AND RELIGIOUS CHANGE 51

cannot know for certain about their eternal destiny until they persevere to the end.[41] Aside from the internal witness of the Holy Spirit, Calvinists look for some external evidence of salvation. Such an outward sign might include worldly success, which would involve ascetic, rational regulation of one's life conduct as a genuine sign of eternal security. One could thus prove oneself before God, not to earn salvation (which was impossible) but to assure oneself that one already possessed it.[42]

According to the new Protestant traditions, an individual is religiously encouraged to follow a secular vocation with as much zeal as possible. It is particularly advantageous in technical occupations for workers to be extremely devoted to their craft. Religion would serve to facilitate the view that one's craft as an end in itself or as a "calling."[43] This attitude is notable in certain classes, which have endured religious education, especially of a pietistic background. However, Calvinism discourages wasteful spending of hard-earned money and identifies the purchase of luxuries as sinful.[44] A paradox is thus created. The manner in which this paradox is resolved, according to Weber, is the investment of money, which gives an extreme boost to nascent capitalism.[45] The Protestant work ethic, therefore, reinforces or legitimizes the spirit of capitalism within a larger cultural context.

What social factors and processes, in turn, influence the strength and character of religious communities and traditions? Through his analysis of the spirit of capitalism, and Calvinism's tendency toward asceticism, Weber notes the process of rationalization actually confirms or assures one's standing with God.[46] Weber argues that Protestant Christians look for other "signs" that serve as confirmation of their salvation. The Protestant work ethic or self-confidence provides assurance of God's blessings.[47] Worldly success becomes one measure of that self-confidence. The most vital feature of the spirit of capitalism is that it attributes "economizing" with high moral significance. The individual who engages in capitalistic ventures would test his or her inner resources and thus affirm one's moral worth. A major effect of this spirit is that the entrepreneur performs his tasks with an earnestness of purpose that places those tasks at the center of his life, and endows him with intrinsic dignity. Ultimately, the point of the spirit of capitalism is to

41. Ibid., 121.
42. Ibid., 170.
43. Ibid., 154.
44. Ibid., 171.
45. Ibid., 48–50.
46. Ibid., 172.
47. Ibid.

attribute moral significance to entrepreneurial activity and lend meaning to the existence of those committed to it.

Weber's goal is to explain how the process of rationalization, as a way of thinking and acting, becomes increasingly dominated by "the purposive orientation of one's actions with respect to the actions of others and with respect to the means employed in achieving freely chosen ends."[48] That is, modernity is the result of cultural, social, and political rationalization or transformation by which the world is controlled and regulated by an ethic of world mastery. Modernization is the imposition of rationality—by way of an ends-means scheme—applied to the control of the total human environment.[49]

Weber's notion of rationality, variously defined, is associated with the phenomenon of modernity. Simply stated, rationalization, whether manifested in religion or other domains of society, refers to the historical drive to fashion a world in which "one can, in principle, master all things by calculation."[50] Eisen enumerates six components: purpose, calculability, control, logical, universality, and systematic.[51] These can be organized under two broad headings—formal and substantive rationality. When applied to religion, a particular religious tradition found inconsistent with those principles would be considered irrational or unsystematic.[52]

Social scientists observe that rationalization is epitomized by bureaucratization or "McDonaldization," where efficiency, calculability, predictability, increased control and use of non-human technology are manifested.[53] Weber's notion of rationalization can be distinguished in four sub-categories. By "practical" rationality, Weber refers to the methodical approach to ensure a practical and most expedient way of dealing with everyday matters. Pragmatic action in dealing with daily matters is privileged, while one gives attention to precise calculation of the most adequate means in achieving end results. The uniqueness of "This type of rationality exists as a manifestation of man's capacity for means-end rational action."[54]

---

48. Gay, "An Ironic Cage," 253.

49. Netland, *Encountering Religious Pluralism*, 80.

50. Weber, *Protestant Ethic*, 139.

51. Eisen, "Meanings and Confusions," 58–61.

52. Ibid., 60, 65.

53. Ritzer, "Professionalization, Bureaucratization and Rationalization," 627–34; Ritzer, *The McDonaldization of Society*.

54. Kalberg, "Max Weber's Types," 1152.

"Theoretical" rationality involves "an increasingly theoretical mastery of reality by means of increasingly precise and abstract concepts."[55] Characteristic of this type of rationality include such principles as logical deduction, causality, and arranging of symbolic meaning, whereby "systematic thinkers practice this type of rationality to offer "comprehensive explanations" of the world. Scientists, for example, rationalize in offering a scientific worldview.[56] In other words, worldviews are developed as a result of prolonged theoretical rationality.[57] Likewise, the Calvinist doctrine of predestination and the Indian concept of Kharma are examples of theoretical rationality offered to provide comprehensive understanding of the world from a religious point of view.[58]

For Weber, "substantive rationality directly orders action into patterns" by postulating values in terms of past, present, and future possibilities.[59] As such, "this type of rationality exists as a manifestation of man's inherent capacity for value-rational action."[60] Examples of substantive rationality, such as communism, Calvinism, hedonism, egalitarianism, socialism, Buddhism, and Hinduism, refer only to limited areas of life situated in particular historical contexts.[61] Substantive rationality—ordering action into patterns—serves as a "canon" or "standard" by which "reality's flow of unending empirical events may be selected, measured, and judged." The crux of Weber's substantive rationality is its "radical perspectivism." Since there are endless perspectives in which to form and examine patterns, the value judgment of those patterns ultimately rest upon the "points of view" or "directions" of observers.[62] The manifestation of substantive rationality in the public or secular sphere include, for example, the "Enlightenment's faith in reason and classical liberalism's credo of the rights of man and freedom of conscience."[63]

Lastly, Weber understands "formal" rationality with reference to "spheres of life and structures of domination" that relate to the economic, legal, and the bureaucratic form of domination.[64] As such, formal rationality

55. Ibid.
56. Ibid., 1153.
57. Ibid., 1154.
58. Ibid.
59. Ibid., 1155.
60. Ibid.
61. Ibid.
62. Ibid.
63. Ibid., 1168.
64. Ibid., 1158.

is typically institutionalized in such large-scale structures as the bureaucracy, modern law, scientific sphere, and the capitalist economy. The choice of means to ends is determined, to a greater extent, by those large structures along with their rules and regulations. In this sense, bureaucratization is the ultimate expression of formal rationalization because it emphasizes efficiency, calculability, predictability, and exchanges human social interaction with non-human technology as means to justify ends.[65]

For Weber, the crux of these fine delineations of rationality is that they represent "heuristic tools he employed to scrutinize the historical fates of rationalization as sociocultural processes." In that sense, the construction of rationalism as a worldview to deflect what is considered irrational, reflects vested "interests, power, historical chance, and other random factors." For Weber the sociologist, "rationalism is a historical concept that contains a world of contradictions within itself."[66] Researchers note that the practical, theoretical, and formal rationalities dominate substantive rationality in the West, where a scientific worldview has overwhelmed the theistic worldview.[67] The irony is that the scientific worldview—seen as distinct from religious values—is itself a substantive rationality.[68]

The polymorphous nature of Weber's concept of rationality reflects not only its inherent complexity but also Weber's unsystematic usage of the term. For Weber, rationalization refers to the process as a whole, that is, societal change, as well as its parts, such as religious action. In the rationalization of religious ideas, the process of rationalization is at least a historical process resulting from the disenchantment of the world. The religious process of rationalization involves the clarification, specification, and systematization of the ideas, which inform people of their reason for being. Such ideas imply metaphysical and theological conceptions of the cosmic and world orders, as well as human's position in relation to such wider orders. At least three different concepts of rationalization are identified in Weber's work, namely, (1) rationalization of society as a whole, (2) rationalization of religion as an historical process, and (3) rationalization of religion itself.

What are some implications of the Weberian rationalization of religion? For some scholars, Weberian rationality is more of a psychological premise upon which action is generated than a method to differentiate worldviews.[69] Is it appropriate to characterize Weber's rationality

---

65. Ritzer, "Professionalization, Bureaucratization and Rationalization," 42–43.
66. Kalberg, "Max Weber's Types," 1172.
67. Ibid., 1173.
68. Ibid., 1174.
69. Kalberg, "Rationalization of Action," 58–84.

as an expression of modernism? His writings reflect the tension of modern Enlightenment epistemology. His views on reason and objectivity place him squarely within modernism. However, his views on science and knowledge led him to a very pessimistic outlook on society, which certainly did not accord with the optimism of the Enlightenment.[70] As a result of the rationalization of religion, the process of secularization, which Weber calls "the disenchantment of the world," can be recognized throughout history. That is, one's observation of the natural realm is stripped of its religious meaning in favor of scientific or naturalistic explanations.[71]

For other scholars, Weber's rationalization of religion serves as a crucial explanation for religious change. Since modern religions have become rationalized, many adherents favor a more rational religion in comparison to those perceived as irrational. Thus, religious conversion is viewed as one's active engagement of religion in contrast to one's uncritical acceptance of ritual practices.[72] Three key premises underscore religious conversion as a result of modernization. (1) Social change comes about as people constantly orientate themselves in accordance with increasing rational thought and action. (2) World religions, such as Judaism, Buddhism, Islam, and Christianity, represent superior forms of religious rationalization when compared with traditional counterparts, such as animism and ancestor worship. (3) Religious rationalization occurs not only within world religions but also instigates conversion between religions.[73] Through the processes of modernization, traditional religions, regarded as superstitious and irrelevant, are slowly replaced by rationalized world religions that effectively address the emotional, ethical, and intellectual issues of modern life.[74]

Interpreters of Weber's sociology of religion explain the fading away of traditional religions is due, in part, to the way in which religions conceive the notions of the "self" and the "world" as inseparable symbols. The detrimental correlation of the two becomes evident, if religion cannot be differentiated from society. The tragic result is that traditional religions "provide little intellectual leverage with which to evaluate or criticize received arrangements."[75] In other words, traditional religions—by virtue of their "this-worldly" orientation—are obsolete because of their inability to

70. Koch, "Rationality, Romanticism and the Individual," 123–44; Wallace, "In Weber's Theory," 199–223.
71. Wilson, "Modernity," 8216.
72. Dawson, "Self Affirmation, Freedom, and Rationality," 141–63.
73. Woods, "Geographies of Religious Conversion," 442.
74. Hefner, "World Building," 8.
75. Ibid.

challenge the status quo.[76] Conversely, world religions—with their dualistic cosmology of "world-rejection"—offer a transcendent explanation of reality in which "the received world is evaluated in light of higher ideals."[77]

For Weber, traditionalism refers to the "unthinking acquiescence in customary ways."[78] According to Geertz, the so-called "disenchantment" of traditional religions is driven by an intellectual element inherent in charismatic prophets of world religions in their rejection of passive acceptance of the divine.[79] The process of religious rationalization refers then to "the formal systematization and codification of rite, doctrine, and authority."[80] World religions succeed because they demonstrate a strong preoccupation to standardize religious ideas and actions through the use of technology, uniformed rites, sacred Scriptures, and a formalized clergy.[81]

It must be noted that not all social scientists agree with Weber's view on rationalization. Contemporary anthropologists challenge the notion of whether the systematization of ideas at the level of world religions necessarily translates to the transformation of the worldview or rationality at the individual level. Here, one must distinguish between rationalization and rationality. The former refers to the systematization of ideas and truths within a cultural system, and the latter refers to the efficacy of those ideas, impacting the individual in ways that make sense.[82] The distinction is crucial because the rationalization or systematization of religious ideas and its impact on individual rationality are embedded in socio-cultural systems, which vary from culture to culture across the globe. In fact, religious doctrines formalized in canons and creeds are not in themselves the true driving factors for why believers embrace them.[83]

The Phenomenon of Globalization

Views on Globalization

If one were to examine important studies on world trends in recent years, two in particular would come to mind, namely, Samuel Huntington's *The*

76. Ibid.
77. Ibid., 9.
78. Weber, *Economy and* Society, 30.
79. Geertz, *Interpretation of Cultures*, 174.
80. Hefner, "World Building," 14–15.
81. Ibid., 15.
82. Ibid.
83. Ibid., 16.

Clash of Civilizations and Thomas Friedman's *The Lexus and the Olive Tree*. In what he regards as the final phase of conflict in the post-Cold War modern era, Huntington argues that cultural and religious, not ideological, conflicts around the world expand into a sharp clash of civilizations. He posits, in particular, the concept of "civilization" as the touchstone of cultural identity. Conflict occurs primarily between nation states, representing different civilizations. Moreover, the clash is between the "West and the rest."[84] Contrastingly, Friedman argues that if one seeks to understand the post-Cold War world, he or she must start by understanding the phenomenon of globalization, a new international system that has succeeded it. Under the global system, one will find a unique blend of both the clash and the homogenization of civilizations.[85]

These two views generally represent the contrasting discourses on global trends, ranging from the "clash" to the "homogenization" of cultures. The former school of thought argues that cultures across the globe are becoming more rigid, unyielding, and even militant, as they seek to protect themselves from intrusive outside forces. In particular, the emergence of the Islamic world challenges Western dominance and universal Western ideals. The latter school of thought maintains that, under the guise of Westernization, world forces are leading to homogenization of culture worldwide, albeit in a blended fashion.

The "clash of civilization" can be characterized as a reaction to the "McDonaldization" thesis, which considers the homogenization of worldwide cultures "through the impact of multinational corporations."[86] George Ritzer is one of the contemporary proponents of this school of thought. According to Ritzer, McDonaldization is "the process whereby the principles of the fast-food restaurant are coming to dominate more and more sectors of American society as well as the rest of the world."[87] This process of converging world cultures is often attributed to the Weberian understanding of rationality in which bureaucratization and other rational social technologies laid down the rules and regulations contributing to greater efficiency, calculability, predictability, and control.[88] From Ritzer's statement, one can detect the association of the convergence or McDonaldization thesis with modernization or Americanization. In other words, there seems to be a strong connection between modernization and globalization.

84. Huntington, *Clash of Civilizations*, 3.
85. Friedman, *Lexus and Olive Tree*, xx–xxi.
86. Pieterse, *Globalization and Culture*, 51.
87. Ritzer, *McDonaldization of Society*, 19.
88. Pieterse, *Globalization and Culture*, 51.

Indeed, modernization and globalization are distinct, yet interrelated phenomena or processes. Of course, not all scholars agree on the nature of modernity. Unlike Ritzer, who views modernity as epitomized by formal rationality applied to means-end efficiency, Anthony Giddens, in *The Consequences of Modernity*, views modernity as a "juggernaut" or "a runaway engine of enormous power."[89] These destructive powers include, among other things, capitalism and industrialization. Although disagreeing with Ritzer, Giddens rightly notes that "Modernity is inherently globalizing."[90] The veracity of this claim is based upon two defining characteristics of modernity, including "disembeddedness" and "reflexivity."[91] Modernity is characterized by (1) the separation between time and space, (2) the processes of disembedding and embedding social activities across time and space, and (3) the systematic appropriation of history to shape the future.[92]

By the separation between time and space, Giddens describes time in pre-modern cultures as intricately connected with social activities. In the modern period, time is separated from space when it becomes standardized and uniformed in precise measurement by the mechanical clock.[93] This provides the means for temporal and spatial zoning.

By disembeddedness, Giddens refers to "the lifting out of social relations from local contexts of interaction and their restructuring across indefinite spans of time-space."[94] In pre-modern societies, for example, space is the area in which one moves, and time is the experience one had while moving. In modern societies, however, the social space is no longer confined by the boundaries that set the space in which one moves. One can now imagine what other spaces look like, even if he or she has never been there. This is virtual space and time. Similarly, modernity is characterized by specialized knowledge. In pre-modern societies, elders are considered as those who possess knowledge. They are defined in time and space. In modern societies, one must rely on expert systems. Those are not restricted to time and space. The technology we use also hold much risks and we must trust them.

Another characteristic of modernity is reflexivity, both at the individual and institutional levels. Regarding the latter, in particular, there is always a component in modern institutions which studies the institutions

---

89. Giddens, *Consequences of Modernity*, 139.
90. Ibid., 63; Tiryakian, "From Modernization to Globalization," 296–323.
91. Giddens, *Consequences of Modernity*, 63.
92. Ibid., 20.
93. Ibid., 17–18.
94. Ibid., 21.

themselves for the purpose of enhancing its effectiveness. This enhanced reflexivity was enabled as language, became increasingly abstract with the transition from pre-modern to modern societies, and institutionalized into universities. Giddens explains, "The reflexivity of modern social life consists in the fact that social practices are constantly examined and reformed in the light of incoming information about those very practices, thus constitutively altering their character."[95] In other words, the development of social life and thought was no longer contingent upon tradition. Thus, Giddens concludes that "modernity is inherently globalizing" because its institutions are characterized by disembeddedness and reflectivity.

But what is the nature of globalization? Giddens writes, "Globalisation can thus be defined as the intensification of worldwide social relations which link distant localities in such a way that local happenings are shaped by events occurring many miles away and vice versa. This is a dialectical process because such local happenings may move in an obverse direction from the very distanciated relations that shape them."[96]

Scholars, who distance themselves from the view of globalization as stemming from the modern period, argue that globalization implies a long-term human evolutionary perspective. Over against the "clash" and "convergence" theses, Jan Nederveen Pieterse, in *Globalization and Culture: Global Mélange*, introduces a third alternative and argues that globalization leads to cultural hybridity. Pieterse takes issue with Giddens and the notion of globalization as a corollary of modernity, because it narrowly presupposes Western capitalism as the structure, with its roots in the modern period of the 1800s. He prefers Roland Robertson's understanding of globalization as "multidimensional" with "sociocultural processes," and finds its roots in the 1500s.[97]

For Pieterse, "hybridity" refers to a mixing of cultures, "one that is historically deep and geographically wide."[98] As such, "Hybridization goes under various aliases such as syncretism, creolization, métissage, mestizaje, crossover."[99] In particular, two forms of hybridization are at work: structural, which leads to new, mixed forms of social cooperation, and cultural, which is the development of mélange cultures that span multiple locations and identities.[100]

- 95. Ibid., 38.
- 96. Ibid., 64.
- 97. Pieterse, *Globalization and Culture*, 67–68.
- 98. Ibid., 2.
- 99. Ibid., 55.
- 100. Ibid., 70–77.

That social scientists observe the fact of the increasing interconnectedness of the world is a given. While social scientists may not agree on the derivation of globalization and its starting point, what is clear is that globalization is not a recent development that began in the 1980s.[101] There is another significant element of globalization, which one must consider. That is, why has this topic only emerged as a subject of recent scholarly inquiry? Unlike any period of time before us, what is new about globalization in contemporary life is one's conscious awareness of it.[102] For example, Lechner and Boli write,

> We are witnessing the consolidation of a new global society. After World War II, the infrastructure for communication and transportation improved dramatically, connecting groups, institutions, and countries in new ways. More people can travel, or migrate, more easily to distant parts of the globe; satellite broadcasts bring world events to an increasingly global audience; the Internet begins to knit together world-spanning interest groups of educated users. Such links are the raw material of globalization. The world is becoming a single space, in which different institutions function as parts of one system and distant peoples share a common understanding of living together on one planet. This world society has a culture; it instills in many people a budding consciousness of living in a world society. To links and institutions we therefore add culture and consciousness. Globalization is the process that fitfully brings these elements of world society together.[103]

In other words, globalization includes more than the fact of interrelatedness worldwide but also the awareness of such interconnectedness. The latter point is described by Malcolm Waters as "a social process in which the constraints of geography on economic, political, social and cultural arrangements recede, in which people become increasingly aware that they are receding, and in which people act accordingly."[104] Noting that globalization grew out of the economic and political influences of the Western modern world, Netland defines "globalization" as both the "fact of worldwide interrelatedness" and "our heightened awareness of this interconnectivity and the effects of this consciousness on local patterns and identities."[105]

---

101. Eriksen, *Globalization*, 5.
102. Ibid.
103. Lechner and Boli, "General Introduction," xvii.
104. Waters, *Globalization*, 5.
105. Netland, "Introduction," 19.

Key Concepts of Globalization

In examining the phenomenon of globalization, one must recognize that global and local elements often become hybridized. This has strong implications on religions as both a vehicle and a product of globalization. What are the key processes of globalization that result in hybridity? In *Globalization: The Key Concepts*, Thomas H. Eriksen enumerates eight concepts to explain the nature and complexity of globalization.[106] Through the concepts of disembedding, acceleration, standardization, interconnectedness, movement, mixing, vulnerability, and re-embedding, Eriksen argues that globalization refers "both to the compression of the world and the intensification of consciousness about the world as a whole." Globalization indicates for both "increased interconnectedness and increased awareness of it."[107] Although discussed for centuries, the recent emergence of this term is spurred by three factors: (1) the end of the Cold War, (2) the internet, and (3) identity politics.[108] However, globalization should not be considered as a recent phenomenon, equated with Westernization, construed as homogenization of cultures, or viewed as the erosion of local identities. In fact, the term "glocalization" is probably more accurate to describe global trends.[109] What are the key concepts of globalization?

Disembedding. Due to recent developments in technology, economic growth, and politics, global boundaries have been blurred. Disembedding refers to "deterritorialization." Distance is no longer a barrier for communication, spread of trade, and the dissemination of information. It is a "lifting out" of their local contexts and a "restructuring across indefinite spans of time-space." It is a shift away from the concrete and tangible to the abstract and virtual worlds. The disembedding process is facilitated mainly by the exchanges of printed information and money. Even music—as a form of entertainment—is dislodged from its local context and shared. Local time and contracts become standardized measurements. There are cultural and political implications to disembedding, including nationalism, where it is regarded as an ideology rather than a personal loyalty. Nationalism—as a form of integration—must be viewed as a lived experience as well as an ideology. Eriksen cautions that alienation and fragmentation as possible outcomes of disembedding.[110]

---

106. Eriksen, *Globalization*.
107. Ibid., 4.
108. Ibid., 3–4.
109. Ibid., 5–6.
110. Ibid., 15–31.

Acceleration. Speed is a key characteristic of globalization made possible by electronic communication and efficient transportation. Eriksen states, "Everything, it seems, happens faster and faster, bringing disparate parts of the world closer to each other." Time-space compression refers to "the squeezing together of time and space," which is facilitated chiefly by technological advances, such as email, the jet plane, and the satellite dish. Consequently, change is accelerated around the world. Thomas Friedman writes about the "ten flatteners" of the twenty-first century. An important mark of accelerated change is not "a totalizing phenomenon." Rather, globalization is partial. There are many developing world countries, which may not have readily access to technology, are removed from globalization. Simultaneity refers to how people from even remote places are becoming "contemporaries" with the rest of the world for the first time in history. Another significant implication is that acceleration seems to support global capitalism, where speed facilitates production, distribution, and consumption.[111]

Standardization. Eriksen observes that globalization actually perpetuates the work of nation building by creating shared standards or "bridging principles of translation" between what used to be very discrete worlds. Everything from consumer tastes to measurements and values are standardized at an alarming global level. Standardization implies comparability and shared measurements. The various forms of standardization include a monetary economy, formal education, political parties, and nationalism along with rights and privileges, such as citizenship. One of the consequences of standardization is the erosion of local traditional craft skills, beliefs, and practices. English—as a medium of communication—has become a dominate language worldwide. There are two tendencies—standardized goods cater to globalization and products that can only be produced in a specific location cater to glocalization. As a result, the world seems to be a bipolar place, where capitalism and local resistance compete against each other. Microsoft Word has dominated written communication, suppressing competitors along the way. Shared standard eases communication across boundaries. However, it can also undermine local uniqueness. Muslim countries and China have protested against the Christian calendar. The effects of standardization can affect the spread of human rights ideas and a global ethics. The discussion of human rights, in particular, has to be interpreted in its local cultural context in order to be useful. Human rights are universal, Eriksen insists, but contain a local element.[112]

111. Ibid., 33–48.
112. Ibid., 51–68.

Interconnectedness. Many infra-structures and networks now exist to facilitate global interconnectedness at a denser, wider, and faster rate each year. As a result, a "transnational" phenomenon is created, where corporations, transnational rights, religion, and the world market ultimately eclipse local interests. The transnational phenomenon includes communication networks and an increasingly globalized economic network. Interconnectedness has possible political, economic, and cultural implications. Some international agencies, including NGOs, have raised important questions, such as human rights and environmental issues. The notion of "global governance" can be seen in international treaties concerning workers' rights, greenhouse gases, and peace-keeping. Others (e.g., Samuel Huntington) view international cooperation perhaps as a source of conflict due to competition for resources and deep cultural and religious differences. The English language, migration, and even sporting events facilitate interconnectedness.[113]

Movement. Eriksen says that "the world is on the move." Where rigid geographical boundaries existed in the mid-twentieth century, now migration, tourism, business travel, and refugees have dissolved them. Thus, the concept of culture is made more complex due to frequent and rapid movements characteristic of globalization. Transnational migration is evident by the moving about of several streams of people, including North Atlantic expatriates living in the south, people from southern countries moving to other southern countries, and those from south to north. National boundaries are stretched by way of outsourcing goods and services. However, a second kind of outsourcing involves finding others—albeit poorer people—to do typically undesirable work. There are obvious economic advantages to the latter approach. Tourism has evolved from local to regional to global. For the most part, this pattern is typical of most wealthy countries. In contrast to tourists, refugees are marginalized people, who are economically dependent. The movement of people often results in "hyphenated identities." However, people who hold to "long-distance nationalism" have strong influence on the politics of countries where they now reside. With the vast movements of people around the globe, there exist those who stay put and preserve traditionalism for nostalgia sake. Globalization involves the forming and reforming of social identities.[114]

Mixing. People of diverse ethnic and cultural origins are interacting and mixing in large proportions. There is, on the one hand, a trend toward cosmopolitanism and hybridity. Yet, on the other hand, there is a trend toward withdrawal and boundary-marking. The notion of a "pure culture" is

113. Ibid., 69–89.
114. Ibid., 91–105.

a myth. And not all cultural dynamics can be viewed as "Westernization." Many forms of mixing exist today. These include such models as the mixing of diverse influences, colonization, diffusionism or borrowing, juxtaposition (where opposites are accepted without an attempt at integration), assimilation or imitation, and innovation and creativity. All these imply mixing at the levels of identity, symbolic meaning, or both. Hybridity or creolization refers to the "intermingling" of two or more discrete cultures to form a new. Many concepts can be attributed to mixing of traditions, including syncretism, diasporic identity, transnationalism, and diffusion. Cultural mixing does not result in cultural homogeneity, but in the creation of new diversities. Music has been identified as an agent, avenue, or vehicle for mixing, where, for example, indigenous music is transformed or recreated by Western musicians. Yet in spite of all the mixing, one must treat the label globalization with care. For one, local life realities are produced locally. Secondly, the effects of globalization have little or no influence on certain parts of the world. Thirdly, there are large parts of the world, where the globalizing agencies hardly enter. Poverty, in this sense, serves as the anti-globalizing mechanism. The quadrants of similarity vs. difference and purity vs. mixing are not mutually exclusive ideas. They exist in tension and in practice. Cultural mixing is a reality of the world today, and is characteristic of globalization.[115]

Vulnerability. Globalization tends to blur or undermine traditional boundaries. With increased interaction and interconnectedness, globalization makes people more vulnerable to climate change, AIDS, terrorism, avian influenza, and SARS, because conditions or threats are often not locally produced or monitored. Researchers question whether certain forms of vulnerability or risk are purely natural. Rather, they argue that they are manufactured. For example, dense population in cities can make it easy for disease to spread, where many live in unsafe environments. There are also perceived risks. These are based upon anticipated consequences, where potential danger travels easily across geographic boundaries. Climate change can lead to significant consequences on a global scale. Because the world has become more interdependent, at least economically, climate change has tremendous global implications. The war on terror underscores global vulnerability, where the enemy is decentralized and deterritorialized. It is an example of a transnational conflict with global consequences. The response to global vulnerabilities is a difficult question to address. That is, how can

---

115. Ibid., 104–22.

the global community formulate common policies that address both security and sovereign rights issues?[116]

Re-embedding. Globalization shrinks and homogenizes the world at a superficial level by imposing a set of common denominators. It also expands the world by bringing to awareness the heterogenization of the world through the formation of new diversities from intense contact. In other words, globalization is also "glocal" in the sense that humans live in local contexts. Eriksen observes that "disembedding is always countered by re-embedding." Identity politics is a typical response to globalization, where "localization" engenders such phenomena as nationalism, separatism, ethnicity, religious revitalization, and interest groups. These recreate a sense of continuity and stability for regions that have experienced disembedding. Indigenous groups often seek political autonomy to preserve their identity in response to the forces of integration. Re-embedding, manifested in a variety of forms, also occurs with transnational migrants and their descendants, underscoring the human need for security and a sense of attachment. Through the processes of disembedding and re-embedding, the burning question for many is "what or who to trust." Interpersonal trust is still crucial despite many informal and formal networks that exist. The pressure to conform to social norms as well as the need to establish relationships is still very evident. Gangs are a prime example of this phenomenon.[117]

The concepts associated with globalization underscore "the compression of the world and the intensification of consciousness about the world as a whole."[118] Globalization must not be confused with Westernization, because poverty can deter globalization in those parts of the world, which are still relatively untouched by technological and economic growth. Certainly interconnectedness does entail homogenization to some degree, especially with reference to standardization and deterritorialization. However, as Eriksen argues, disembedding also entails re-embedding, with the latter creating heterogeneity.

Eriksen concludes that

> globalization does not entail the production of global uniformity or homogeneity. Rather, it can be seen as a way of organizing heterogeneity. The similarities dealt with , for example, in the chapter on standardization, are formal and do not necessarily lead to homogeneity at the level of content. The local continues

---

116. Ibid., 121–39.
117. Ibid., 141–54.
118. Ibid., 4.

to thrive, although it must increasingly be seen as *glocal*, that is enmeshed in transnational processes.[119]

Globalization and Culture

Several important implications can be drawn from the multi-dimensional nature of globalization and its impact on culture and religion. Firstly, one can infer from Giddens' definition of globalization that it is simply not helpful to refer to modernity simply as a period of time, presumably emerging in seventeenth-century Europe. Rather, the dramatic cultural changes that we see around the world today present a "radical" continuation of modernity, not a new phase commonly called "postmodernity."[120] Giddens observes that the "discontinuities of modernity" stem from powerful forces but were ushered in primarily through the processes, institutions, and spread of capitalism around the world.[121] Modernity, properly understood, refers to a process of social and cultural change induced by modernization.

Secondly, in the era of globalization, concepts of culture and religion are related yet remain distinct. They are clearly related in terms of Ninian Smart's seven dimensions of religion, including the ritual, narrative/mythological, experiential, doctrinal, ethical, social, and material.[122] One will notice that most of these elements constitute what we mean by culture as well.[123] As such, religion is closely linked with culture.[124] For example, Buddhism, as a religion, is distinct from Indian, Chinese, or Japanese culture, though it is closely related to all three. At the same time, one must not err by reducing a religion to its particular cultural expression, for there are significant gaps between a religion's ideals and its empirical expression.[125]

What is noteworthy is that culture and religion are not static and self-containing entities. They are fluid and subject to change. In the era of globalization, when cultures and religions around the globe interact with one another, both undergo transformation. Religion, evangelical Christianity in particular, is both a vehicle and a product of globalization.[126]

---

119. Ibid., 10.
120. Giddens, *Consequences of Modernity*, 1–3.
121. Ibid., 11.
122. Smart, *Worldviews: Crosscultural Explorations*, 11–22.
123. Netland, *Encountering Religious Pluralism*, 192–94.
124. Ibid., 194.
125. Ibid., 329.
126. Netland, "Introduction," 24.

Thirdly, globalization must not be equated with Westernization, though its institutions are derived from the West but now move in all directions. While acknowledging the patterns of globalization do move from the West to other parts of the world, Netland states, "the resulting institutions and processes are today genuinely worldwide, and their influences move in all directions simultaneously."[127] In reflecting on Asian evangelical critique of the inappropriateness of Western theology in Asia, Netland argues that it is simply not helpful to juxtapose "Western theology" and "Asian theology" in a globalizing world as if they were monolithic and static in nature.[128] Similarly, Roland Robertson notes that religions will continue to thrive in a globalizing world, but they are "increasingly subject to manipulation—indeed, to invention, largely because of relativization." In a word, they are "commodified."[129]

Giddens asks "Is modernity a Western project?"[130] The answer is "yes," if modernity refers to the institutional developments of the "nation-state and "systematic capitalist production," since both find their roots in European history. If, on the other hand, modernity is viewed from the standpoint of globalization, then it is not Western in nature. Beyond the spread of Western institutions and the eclipse of local cultures around the world, the process of globalization actually "introduces new forms of world inter-dependence" and "planetary consciousness."[131] One must take into consideration historical, cultural, economic, and political variations across the globe. The effects of globalization reach beyond economic and political realms to their influence on aspects of culture, such as the prevailing use of the English language and the spread of the "Western university model" of education around the world.[132]

Fourthly, although globalization does involve homogenization to a certain degree, it does not involve the eclipse of local identities. While local identities may appear more and more similar in different parts of the world, particularly in the nexus of East and West, they remain unique and will continue to thrive. This significant point is explained by social scientists who seek to unpack such complex phenomena.

---

127. Ibid., 21.
128. Ibid., 26–27.
129. Robertson, "Globalization and the Future," 68.
130. Giddens, *Consequences of Modernity*, 174.
131. Ibid., 174–75.
132. Netland, "Introduction," 21.

Religious Change

Indeed, the processes of modernization and globalization have important implications on religion, both as a vehicle and product of globalization. If modernity is inherently globalizing, as Giddens insists, how might one account for its impact on religion? Indeed, religion today has become globalized. The global nature of religion is underscored by Mark Juergensmeyer. To the extent that religious communities move, shift, and integrate with local traditions in an era of globalization, Juergensmeyer argues that religious boundaries become permeable.[133] As the world changes, so is religion transformed. Juergensmeyer explains, "The various forms of economic, social, technological, and cultural globalization at the dawn of the twenty-first century are the channels for new expressions of religion."[134]

In "The Four Faces of Global Culture," Peter Berger observes the phenomenon of economic and cultural globalization, where increasing worldwide interconnectedness has significant implications for transformation. He notes that evangelical Christianity, particularly in its Pentecostal expression, is both a product of and a vehicle for globalization.[135] There is no doubt that approximately 80 percent of the growth of Christianity in recent years can be attributed to the spread of Pentecostalism around the globe, according to Berger.[136] He writes,

> But the same variety of Protestantism has been rapidly growing in East Asia (with the notable exception of Japan), in all the Chinese societies, in the Philippines, the South Pacific, and throughout the sub-Saharan Africa. There are recent, as yet vague, accounts of an incipient growth in Eastern Europe. And while the origins of this religion are in the United States (the "metropolis"), its new incarnations are thoroughly indigenized and independent of foreign missionaries or financial support.[137]

The significant impact of evangelical Christianity, as it moves from place to place, is that it transforms society and culture, especially in terms of social relations, education, and traditional hierarchies. Moreover, Berger views the more significant impact of evangelical Christianity as it relates to Weber's "Protestant work ethic." Where evangelical Christianity is planted, there is

---

133. Juergensmeyer, "Thinking Globally About Religion," 4.
134. Ibid., 9.
135. Berger, "Four Faces of Global Culture," 23–29.
136. Ibid., 27.
137. Ibid., 27–28.

also the germination of modern capitalism—a disciplined, frugal, and rationally oriented approach to work.[138]

Recent sociological studies on Christian conversion focus on the global nature of Christianity as having an inherent "world-building" element within the tradition.[139] Researchers argue that the primary reason for the spread of Christianity in the era of globalization is that Christianity facilitates personal identity formation within the larger socio-political and economic arena.[140] Hefner states, "The most necessary feature of religious conversion, it turns out, is not a deeply systematic reorganization of personal meanings but an adjustment in self-identity through the at least nominal acceptance of religious actions or beliefs deemed more fitting, useful and true."[141]

That is, Christian conversion indicates not only a change in personal belief but also the acceptance of a new identity. Germane to Christianity is the new locus of self-identity found in Jesus' command "to make disciples of all the nations" (Matt 28:19). Christian identity in the age of globalization transcends local groups and cultural boundaries. Thus, religious rationalization involves several key processes: (1) the creation and intellectual systematization of doctrines, (2) the institutionalization of doctrines by certain social carriers, and (3) the socialization of doctrines in appropriate cultural forms and translation of ideas into action on the part of believers.[142] Polluck affirms this reason for religious conversion and argues that conversion in the era of globalization is more of a response to cultural and social change in terms of "culturally informed notions of person and identity" than to religious or cosmological crisis.[143]

Secularization and Religious Change

One important issue in religious studies is the relationship between religion and secularization. Postwar social science literature in the 1950s and 1960s examining the relationship between religion in the third world and modernization generally proceed along two lines of inquiry: (1) religion as an inhibitor of modernization and change, and (2) modernization inevitably

---

138. Ibid., 28.
139. Hefner, "World Building," 17.
140. Ibid., 3–45; Russel, *Conversion, Identity, and Power*, 148.
141. Hefner, "World Building," 17.
142. Ibid., 18.
143. Polluck, "Conversion and Community," 166.

leads to secularization.[144] The assumption is that as societies modernize, they become less religious. The corollary is that religions, such as Hinduism, Buddhism, and Islam, tend to hinder modernization. In *Religion and Modernization in Southeast Asia*, Von der Mehden rejects those prevailing premises and argues that religion is both an inhibitor and agent of change, though many social scientists prefer to draw on the negative role of religion in explaining modernization. According to Von der Mehden, the negative assessment of religion, particularly Hinduism, Buddhism, and Islam in third-world Southeast Asian countries, is posited on simplistic characterizations. The basic tenets of religions include otherworldliness and fatalism, which hinder innovation and progress. Religious practices and rites divert attention from productive endeavors. Resources used for religious practices can be better used for education and useful developments. Religious personnel, such as monks and priests, are not only unproductive members of society, but their parasitical role in society hinder productive endeavors. Moreover, religions are divisive that tend to contribute to political instability and social sectarianism.[145]

What is troubling about this body of postwar social science literature is that social scientists deal with modernization using broad understandings of rationalism and secularism.[146] Secularism, as an inevitable outcome of modernization, leads necessarily to the decline of religion. The course of modernization, involving urbanization, social mobility, secular education, and industrialization, inevitably leads to the weakening of religion in society. Von der Mehden laments that more balanced treatments by such sociologists as Robert Bellah were not carefully considered.[147] Bellah contends that modernization changed but did not eclipse religion. He writes,

> In conclusion, it seems worthwhile to stress that the process of secularization, which is part of what the transition from prescriptive to principal society is, does not mean that religion disappears. The function of religion in a principal society is different from that in a prescriptive society, but it is not necessarily less important. Moreover, in the very process of transition religion may appear in many new guises. Perhaps what makes the situation so unclear is its very fluidity.[148]

144. Von der Mehden, *Religion and Modernization*, vii.
145. Ibid., 5–7.
146. Ibid., 9.
147. Ibid., 10–11.
148. Bellah, "Religious Aspects of Modernization," 1–5.

Beyond the issue of secularism, the literature on modernization has come to view rationalism in a variety of ways. Firstly, rationalism is used in the Weberian sense of organization, bureaucracy, and decision-making. That is, the term is considered in a means-end schema to indicate planning and goal-oriented action. As such, rationality involves the use of deliberation, planning, and the best information available to make decisions aimed at achieving maximum economic ends. Weber's understanding of Protestantism and the rise of capitalism can be projected into other societies. This perspective presents a more favorable view of modernization because religion is not regarded as a negative factor.

Secondly, rationalism is also understood as privileging human reason. When cast against such light, reason reflects not only a scientific worldview, but necessarily entails the rejection of divine scriptures and the supernatural. In general, however, researchers of modernization view rationality "in terms of goal-oriented behavior, the use of human reason, a belief in science, pragmatic reasoning, and utilitarianism as against dependence on scriptures, magic, and traditional forms of legitimization based upon ascriptive, familistic, and prescientific considerations."[149] The crux of the argument is that rationalism negatively impacts religion. The rational attitude constitutes not only the core of the modernization process but rationalization necessarily entails the logical end of secularization.[150]

According to Von der Mehden, the latter perspective dominates the social science literature of the postwar era. As a result, literature on modernization predicts the decline of religious values, attitudes, and practices in the process of modernization toward human progress. All corollary attitudes and behaviors associated with traditional, irrational, and unscientific premodern society were undermined, while acceptance of modern foundations gave way to reason.[151] Von der Mehden observes that while researchers often failed to offer detailed explanations for their viewpoints, what seems implicit is that their arguments entailed some kind of negative depiction of the role of religion in modern society. Weber's negative view of Asian religions provides one such source, which contributed to the skewed views of social scientists in the postwar era. In *The Sociology of Religions*, Weber writes:

> For the various religions of Asia, in contrast to ascetic Protestantism, the world remains a great enchanted garden in which the practical way to orient oneself or to find security in this

---

149. Von der Mehden, *Religion and Modernization*, 11.
150. Ibid., 12.
151. Ibid.

world or the next, was to revere or coerce spirits and seek salvation through ritualistic, idolatrous, or sacramental procedures. No path led from the magical religiosity of the non-intellectual classes of Asia to a rational methodical control of life. Nor did any path lead to that methodical control from the world-accommodation of Confucianism, from the world-rejection of Buddhism, from the world-conquest of Islam, or from the messianic expectations and economic pariah law of Judaism.[152]

Over the course of five chapters, Von der Mehden defines religion primarily in terms of (1) basic tenets, (2) religious institutions, (3) popular beliefs, (4) popular practices, and (5) the power of religious symbols.[153] In his final chapter, Von der Mehden addresses the thesis that modernization necessarily leads to secularization or the disappearance of religion. Using Southeast Asian countries like Burma, Thailand, Malaysia, Indonesia, and the Philippines as his focal points, he rejects the two premises of postwar social science literature on modernization, namely, religion inhibits progress and modernization necessarily leads to secularization. With the exception of the decline of animist traditions, Von der Mehden concludes that belief in the supernatural and the maintenance of religious ritualistic practices remain strong in certain countries of Southeast Asia, while religion continues to play a significant political role in countries like Burma, Malaysia, and Indonesia.[154]

Indeed the study of religion, particularly in the broader context of modernization, involves the issues of secularization and religious change. The term "secularization" is notoriously difficult to define, especially in view of the elusive phenomenon of modernity. Proponents of "secularization theory" trace its roots to the Enlightenment and insist that "Modernization necessarily leads to a decline of religion, both in society and in the minds of individuals."

This definition of modernization, which correlates the decline of institutional religion with the erosion of individual religious consciousness, is widely discredited.[155] Peter Berger maintains that while modernization does have its secularizing effects, as evident in religious institutions having less influence, it should not be equated with the loss of individual religious consciousness. Moreover, if "modernity is inherently globalizing," as Giddens insists, it follows that globalization would lead the world to secular-

---

152. Weber, *Sociology of Religion*, 56.
153. Von der Mehden, *Religion and Modernization*, 53–174.
154. Ibid., 175–96.
155. Berger, "Desecularization of the World," 2–3.

ism and religion would become marginalized to twenty-first-century life. However, the opposite is unfolding. During the post-colonial era, the church outside the West has experienced tremendous growth, in spite of the effects of modernization and secularization. Peter Berger notes, "secularization theory is essentially mistaken" because "the assumption that we live in a secularized world is false." Berger goes on to say that the key assumption of secularization theory, which insists that "modernization necessarily leads to a decline in religion, both in society and in the minds of individual turned out to be wrong."[156] In fact, conservative religious movements are on the rise around the world today.[157]

Not only is secularization bound to particular assumptions of modernity, but it is also bound to how one defines religion itself. Given a "substantive" view of religion—as in beliefs, attitudes, practices, and institutions—secularization generally refers to the decline of supernatural beliefs. Bryan Wilson states,

> Secularization is the process in which religious consciousness, activities, and institutions lose social significance. It indicates that religion becomes marginal to the operation of the social system, and that the essential functions for the operation of society become rationalized, passing out of the control of agencies devoted to the supernatural.[158]

In other words, the secularization process does not necessarily entail the disappearance of religion but its transformation. The secularization process, which Weber calls "the disenchantment of the world," can be recognized throughout history in which one's observation of the natural realm is stripped of its religious meaning in favor of scientific or naturalistic explanations.[159]

The false bifurcation between the secular and the religious is underscored in *Rethinking Secularism*.[160] The editors argue, on the one hand, that the reality of secularization must be acknowledged. Something is happening around the world today. They explain, "The idea of secularization suggests a trend, a general tendency toward a world in which religion matters less and various forms of secular reason and secular institutions matter more. It is a trend that has been exposed at least since early modernity and has been given quasi-scientific status in sociological studies advancing a secularization

156. Ibid.
157. Ibid., 6.
158. Wilson, "Secularization," 8215.
159. Ibid., 8216.
160. Calhoun et al., "Introduction," 5.

thesis."¹⁶¹ In other words, the reality of secularization should be nuanced to indicate the increasing grounding of societal institutions in secular ideas. Explicit unbelief seems to be growing, and there is more compartmentalization of the various dimensions of religion. On the other hand, "demarcation does not mean disappearance."¹⁶² Rather, religions are transformed in ways that do not require followers to adhere to exclusive truth claims or participate in religious activities. Yet religious consciousness abounds. The problem with current discussions on the subject is the insistence that secularization necessarily means the disappearance of religion.

The controversial subject of secularization in Asia also relates to its purpose in society. According to Rajeev Bhargava, the original purpose of secularization as conceived in the West was "to check absolutism, religious bigotry and fanaticism, to ensure that values enshrined in particular religions did not trump other values, to manage religious conflicts reasonably."¹⁶³ Given the stratification and persecution of religious groups in India, he insists that such a purpose of secularization is not only desirable but "indispensable."¹⁶⁴ In the context of the modern state, Charles Taylor notes that "The origin point of modern Western secularism was the wars of religion; or rather, the search in battle-fatigue and horror for a way out of them."¹⁶⁵ Secularization, in that sense, is understood as government regulation of the public domain in order to ensure harmonious coexistence of conflicting religious truth claims. Taylor writes, "This is why secularism in some form is a necessity for the democratic life of religiously diverse societies."¹⁶⁶ As such, Bhargava defines "secularism" as "the separation of politics and religion" and "the separation of some religious and non-religious institutions."¹⁶⁷ For Bhargava, the secularism that he envisions "does not deny the difficulty of disentangling religious and non-religious practices." He concludes, "It follows that secularism is compatible with the view that the complete secularization of society is neither possible nor desirable."¹⁶⁸

In coming to grips with the complexity of secularization, Charles Taylor offers a helpful and perhaps more balanced view of the secular age as characterized by pluralism. He writes, "It is a pluralist world, in which

161. Ibid., 10.
162. Ibid., 11.
163. Bhargava, "Introduction," 1.
164. Ibid., 2.
165. Taylor, "Modes of Secularism," 32.
166. Ibid., 36, 46.
167. Bhargava, "Introduction," 488.
168. Ibid., 489.

many forms of belief and unbelief jostle, and hence fragilize each other."[169] As Peter Berger has rightly observed, modernity pluralizes viewpoints, so that the problem of religious faith begs "not only the question of why we should believe in God, but why we should believe in this God."[170]

The concept of secularization is indeed a complex issue, with seemingly conflicting results from different parts of Asia. The recent growth of Christianity in China, for example, reflects not only personal or micro-level factors of conversion but also the structural or macro-level factor of a modernizing and globalizing market economy under political repression. Yang writes, "In fact, the economic and political factors are intertwined."[171] Chinese people are turning to Christianity because it offers a sense of peace and security in the midst of economic uncertainty and political oppression. Christianity is attractive because people perceive it as a "universal" religion and symbolic of "modernity and cosmopolitanism." Younger, well-educated Chinese Christians favor meeting at McDonald's restaurants in urban cities in China, because McDonald's is a "symbol of modern cosmopolitan culture."[172]

Thus, the recent surge in Christian conversion in China reflects conversion not only as a process of identity formation but also the contextual and macro-level factors impacting that part of the world. That is, the growth of Christianity in China indicates what is happening on an individual or micro-level in terms of personal choices and responses to crises, but also reflects the "context of a globalizing market under political repression." People are converting because they perceive "Christianity as liberating, democratic, modern, cosmopolitan, or universal" in contrast to their perception of traditional Buddhism, Taoism, or Confucianism as "backward-looking" and "incompatible" with a globalizing world.[173]

Recent findings from Japan indicate, however, a decline in traditional religions. Buddhism, in particular, is in a state of "crisis" evident by the closure of temples and the growing negative perception of Buddhism in terms of funeral rituals.[174] Arguing against the so-called death of secularization theories, researchers find the exact opposite to be true and that secularization is a "growing force to be reckoned with in Japan today."[175] Moreover,

169. Taylor, *A Secular Age*, 531.
170. Berger, *A Far Glory*, 67, 146–47.
171. Yang, "Lost in the Market," 435.
172. Ibid., 438.
173. Ibid., 439.
174. Reader, "Buddhism in Crisis?," 233–63.
175. Reader, "Secularisation, R.I.P.? Nonsense!," 10.

"There are clear correlations between modernization, urbanization and higher levels of education (factors often cited as formative forces in the secularization process), and declining levels of religious belief and practice, whether individually or institutionally."[176]

Religions and Religious Change in Singapore

To be sure, the foregoing discussion on secularization, modernization, and globalization has important implications for traditional religions in Singapore. On the one hand, there seems to be a steady erosion of traditional Chinese religions and practices, particularly in terms of Taoism.[177] On the other hand, Singapore has vigorously promoted "Asian values" and witnessed a revival in religiosity in recent years.[178] How does one account for this tension? While Singapore rapidly industrialized and modernized between 1965 and 2000 in what Lee Kuan Yew, the first Prime Minister, proclaims as a transition "from third world to first," Singaporeans have reaped the benefits as well as the consequences of modernization.[179] Germane to the question of modernization is its impact on religion. In "Christianity and Social Context: Founding Principles," Lowe provides a very bleak assessment of the impact of modernization on Singapore in general and Christianity in particular. Modernization is characterized as the fountainhead of three processes: secularization, pluralization, and privatization.[180]

For Lowe, modernity and modernization processes indicate technological advancement, which, related to religion, necessarily entails secularization. The phenomenon of secularization take on two forms—theoretical rationalization and functional rationalization. The prior refers to naturalistic science and rationalistic philosophy, both of which deny the existence of God. As for the latter, functional rationalization refers to the development of systematic and structured controls manifested in organizations and modern bureaucracy, the result of which is a "managed" and "domesticated" God.[181] On the one hand, theological liberalism, the bastard child of theoretical rationalization, "denies God" and the supernatural. On the other hand, functional rationalization "manages him" and renders him "impotent."[182]

176. Ibid., 10–11.
177. Tong, *Rationalizing Religion*, 2–3.
178. Ibid., 2–9.
179. Lee, *The Singapore Story*.
180. Lowe, "Christianity and Social Context," 11–12, 12–20.
181. Ibid., 12–13.
182. Ibid., 15.

Moreover, modernity is antagonistic to not only Christianity but to all religions, because it either directly undermines religious faith and practice, or it indirectly creates a social context in which the supernatural is undermined. Whereas secularization marginalizes life away from the religion domain, pluralization relativizes religions by reducing the absolutes of each, and privatization restricts faith to the private realm as an occasion for self-fulfillment.[183] In view of the transformation of Christianity in the modernization process, Lowe concludes: "Modernity entails a modernized religion. A faith which has been secularized, relativized, and privatized bears little resemblance to historic Christianity."[184]

However, the religious landscape in Singapore does not seem to reflect the "gloom and doom" predicted by Lowe regarding the marginalization or eclipse of religions due to secularization. According to researchers, there is a religious revival taking place in Singapore in recent years due to religious competition and change. How does one account for these conflicting viewpoints? It is one thing to say that modernization transforms religion, but quite another that modernization inevitably leads to decline in religion.

While secularization is often recognized as a Western phenomenon, to what extent is "secularization"—a concept associated with Western Christianity—taking place in Asia?[185] That question can be posed in another way: "How useful is the concept when applied to religions such as Buddhism and Taoism, where the religion is diffused in society and in which the ideas of faith and beliefs differ from those of Christianity? How applicable is the secularization hypothesis to an Asian society such as Singapore?"[186]

If, on the one hand, the term is defined in association with urbanization and the "desacralization of nature" as a consequence of Western science, it may not be applicable to non-Western religions.[187] Highly industrialized, urbanized, and scientifically-minded countries like Singapore cannot be described as secularized, because people demonstrate a high degree of religious faith and practice. If, on the other hand, secularization denotes religious change, much religious transformation has occurred in Singapore in recent years. Religions in Asia do not always disappear, but are often transformed when confronted with a secular social system. There is a "dialectical relationship between social change and religious change."[188]

183. Ibid., 11–12.
184. Ibid., 20.
185. Clammer, *Sociology of Singapore Religion*, 4–5.
186. Tong, *Rationalizing Religion*, 12.
187. Clammer, *Sociology of Singapore Religion*, 112.
188. Ibid., 121.

The high degree of religiosity in Singapore appears "anti-secular." However, modernizing or secularizing effects are evident in the ways in which religious institutions reflect the characteristics of wider society.[189] The rationalization of religion can be understood both as a historical process (secularization) and an encounter with secular ideology (secularism).[190] In particular, the transformation of religion in Singapore is evident by (1) the prevailing Protestant work ethic throughout society, (2) the correlation of religion and ethnicity, (3) the privatization of faith, and (4) religious sectarianism.[191]

To be sure, the transformation of religion also relates to the use and impact of media on religion. For example, Kluver and Cheong examine the relationship between the use of the internet and religion in Singapore. Through interviews with religious believers, they conclude that technology shapes spirituality. Contrary to secularization theories, technology complements and reinforces religion. Religious believers perceive that the internet is helpful to disseminate religious content, to mobilize believers, and to encourage religious practice.[192]

The issue of religious change through technology is the subject of a collection of essays under the title: *Mediating Piety: Technology and Religion in Contemporary Asia*. Feng and Chen argue that in the context of Singapore, where religious information provided by the traditional media is often perceived as "manipulated" by the authorities, one's use of the internet as an "independent" platform by which to explore or "shop" religious options is becoming a popular medium. While the internet is a useful form of new technology, the authors caution on "the relative lack of control awarded to its users." They advocate, instead, for a combined use of traditional and new media technology with religious institutions in Singapore.[193]

The theme of religious change is underscored in Joseph Tamney's *The Struggle Over Singapore's Soul: Western Modernization and Asian Culture*. Tamney argues that no clash of Western and Asian civilizations is occurring despite the existence of vast modernization and globalization in Singapore.[194] The claim is tenable because the central ideology of Singapore is capitalism with an overlay of Asian culture.[195] In other words, through globalization,

189. Ibid., 122.
190. Wilson, "Secularization," 8216–17.
191. Clammer, *Sociology of Singapore Religion*, 114–16.
192. Kluver and Cheong, "Technology Modernization," 1–29.
193. Feng and Chen, "Shopping for God," 178–79.
194. Tamney, *Struggle Over Singapore's Soul*, 10–12.
195. Ibid., 19.

Western modernization processes and institutions are thoroughly planted in Singapore with their attending impact on religion, ethnicity, politics, family/gender, and the arts.

In the earlier 1980s, for example, the People's Action Party (PAP) instituted a religious knowledge program in Singapore's schools. All students were required to study one of several recognized religions. In such venues, religion was promoted as a moral ballast in society and as a way to foster discipline, diligence, and social harmony. The study of Confucianism was especially encouraged as its ethics were considered to be supportive of Singapore's quest for nation-building and economic prosperity.[196] Through the processes of modernization and globalization, Tamney observes that Confucianism has changed in Singapore. It would be difficult to define what Confucian orthodoxy means today in Singapore, "because religious beliefs, values, and practices are now resources being used to serve a variety of purposes." For Tamney, Confucianism conveys such ideas as national, cultural, and personal integrity.[197]

Today, religious and social identity transformations are taking place in the globalizing cultural context of Singapore. Two examples are notable. One, the Asian Civilisation Museum of Singapore interprets religious diversity "not as exclusive sets of beliefs but an ecosystem of diverse ideas bound by rich civilisations that are connected by centuries of trade and cultural exchange."[198] The museum offers instruction, research and publication opportunities, and, of course, guided tours. Two, the banner of "New Asia-Singapore" is touted by the tourist industry as a way to define the essence of a unique geographical location and to project an image of Asian identity—a *nouveau riche* or "new rich in Asia"—that is attractive to both tourists and local residents.[199] This "imaging" of overall Asian identity seems to give credence to Tong's characterization of Christian conversion in Singapore as a marker for educational, social, and occupational mobility.

What are some implications of the impact of modernization and globalization on religion in Singapore? Globalization tends to destabilize the embeddedness of social relations and creates many problems in particular cultures.[200] However, globalization does not necessarily lead to the clash,

---

196. Ibid., 25–27; Chang, "Nation-Building in Singapore," 761–73; Tan, "Re-Engaging Chineseness," 751–74.

197. Tamney and Chiang, *Modernization, Globalization and Confucianism*, 211–12.

198. Chin, "Seeing Religion," 192.

199. "Geographical Imaginations," 165, 169; Kong, "Negotiating Conceptions," 342–58.

200. Gille and Riain, "Global Ethnography," 271–95; Mutalib, "Singapore's Quest," 39–56.

convergence, or Westernization of cultures.[201] Instead, hybridization of religions is often the result.[202] Christianity, in the global era, will selectively interact with elements of other traditions. As these elements influence one another, they will appear "less like discreet entities."[203] In his discussion on religious diversity in Sinitic societies like Singapore, Tamney explains that the perception of Christianity as a Western religion identified with English-educated Singaporeans is still a hindrance to effective evangelism to Chinese-educated individuals. However, the long-term significance of such a perception "will cease" with globalization.[204]

---

201. Thompson, "Survival of Asian Values," 651–86; Guillen, "Is Globalization Civilizing?," 235–260.

202. Pieterse, *Globalization and Culture*; Zhang, *Singapore's Modernization*.

203. Cox, "Thinking Globally about Christianity," 252.

204. Tamney and Chiang, *Modernization, Globalization and Confucianism*, 177–78.

4

Christian Conversion and Identity in Singapore

RELIGIOUS CONVERSION IS AN important subject of inquiry in the social sciences, particularly, anthropology, psychology, and sociology.[1] In the field of sociology, religious conversion indicates the shift in personal belief and identity.[2] Conversion narratives are conceived as on-going biographical reconstructions, whereby one's personal stories are reinterpreted in the light of new understandings and experiences.[3] The study of conversion experience as an academic inquiry can be grouped into two distinct paradigms, including the human agency or the micro-perspectives and the structural or the macro-contexts of political, economic, and social factors of religious change.[4]

The scholarly literature accounting for why people change at the individual level is diverse and includes studies that focus on the psychological analysis of religious conversion,[5] the nature and function of language in constructing reality and directing religious performance as a ritual,[6] the convert as an active, seeking agent who undergoes a gradual rational rather

---

1. Rambo, "Theories of Conversion," 259.
2. Beckford, "Accounting for Conversion"; Balch, "Looking behind the Scenes," 137–43.
3. Snow and Machalek, "Sociology of Conversion," 167–90.
4. Woods, "Geographies of Religious Conversion," 442–44.
5. Rambo, *Understanding Religious Conversion*; Paloutzian et al., "Religious Conversion and Personality Change," 1047–79.
6. Stromberg, *Language and Self-Transformation*.

than an emotional conversion process,[7] and the appropriation of symbols, particularly sin and the need for repentance, in constructing "new selves."[8]

The second paradigm, often referred to as the structural approach, is more appropriate in examining Christian conversion in Singapore, because it considers the broader processes of modernization and globalization and their impact on social structures as key determinates of religious conversion.[9] That is, Christian conversion must not only consider the personal or micro-level factors, but also the structural or macro-level factors of modernization and globalization impacting conversion patterns. Max Weber's sociology of religion is a key example of such as an approach, in which he explains religious switching as a process whereby converts re-orientate themselves with emerging conscious thought, and that Christianity as a global religion represents a superior form of religious rationalization in comparison to traditional religions. Younger Chinese Singaporeans are converting from traditional Chinese religions to Christianity, because, in part, they perceive the latter as a more rational religion in contrast to the former, which are regarded as irrational. Religions are transformed as a result of modernization and globalization.

The Singapore Context

Why do research on Singapore, a relatively unknown island-state in Southeast Asia that just celebrated its 50th anniversary of independence? As one sociologist explains,

> In many ways Singapore makes an ideal case study for exploring certain social trends in Asia. The country is the most urbanized in the world, and that intense degree of urbanization is also associated with rapid industrialization, the building of a consumer society, and great openness to the influences of both East and West. These processes in turn are taking place against the back-drop of one of the world's most pluralistic societies in terms of ethnic, cultural, and religious diversity.[10]

This chapter reviews the domain of literature on Christian conversion theory in Singapore and analyzes the subject of religious change in the context of nation building, religious diversity, ethnic tension, and social change.

---

7. Popp-Baier, "Conversion as Social Construction," 41–61.
8. Priest, "I Discovered My Sin!," 104.
9. Woods, "Geographies of Religious Conversion," 442.
10. Clammer, "Singapore," 6.

The founding of Singapore in 1965 as an independent nation-state is a complex story of rapid industrialization from a "third" or "developing-world" country to a nation garnering "first-world" status.[11] Despite undergoing rapid modernization and urbanization, Singapore has witnessed steady growth in religiosity. In particular, Christians constituted 5 percent of the total population in 1920, when data were first collected, and grew to 14.6 percent in the 2000 census. According to the 2010 census, professing Christians constitute 18.3 percent of the total population.

Why have Singaporeans chosen to give up their family religion and convert to Christianity? This chapter examines studies by historians, anthropologists, and sociologists, accounting for religious change, especially among ethnic Chinese people. As a "state of the question" on Christian conversion in Singapore, this chapter addresses major theories, including kairos or divine timing,[12] religious educational and socioeconomic change,[13] anomie,[14] intermarriage,[15] transcendent solutions offered by Christianity,[16] religious switching among adolescents,[17] survey of churchgoing Protestants,[18] and the rationalization of religion.[19] The chapter also assesses the merits and deficiencies of these approaches and offer suggestions for further research.

Before one examines the major theories on religious conversion in Singapore, it would be helpful to analyze, first of all, the historical and social contexts of Singapore. Such an analysis involves studies from the fields of history, religion, and other social sciences. Key issues accounting for Christian conversion in Singapore seem to revolve around four questions. (1) How does the colonial heritage of Singapore influence Christian conversion? (2) What is the relationship between religion and ethnicity and language? (3) What characterizes Singapore culture and to what extent does the political process shape culture? (4) What is the nature of the interrelationship of religion and modernization?

Singapore, an island of approximately 225 square miles at the southernmost tip of the Asian continent, has several distinct periods in its

11. Lee, *From Third World to First*.
12. Sng, *In His Good Time*.
13. Sng and You, *Religious Trends in Singapore*.
14. Hinton, *Growing Churches Singapore Style*.
15. Tamney and Hassan, *Religious Switching in Singapore*.
16. Goh, "Rethinking Resurgent Christianity," 89–112.
17. Chew, "Religious Switching among Adolescents," 381–410.
18. Chong and Hui, *Different under God*.
19. Tong, *Rationalizing Religion*.

relatively short history.[20] First, Thomas Stamford Raffles, a representative of the British East India Trading Company, arrived in 1819 to develop the area as a British trading post. This development eventually led to Singapore becoming a British colony in 1826. After the Japanese occupation during WWII (1942–1945), British rule continued until 1959 when the People's Action Party (PAP) won a landslide victory in the general election, declaring Singapore as a self-governing territory within the British Commonwealth. This second phase witnessed the ascension of Lee Kuan Yew as Singapore's first prime minister, a post he held until 1990. The third phase commenced in 1963 when the Federation of Malaysia was founded, incorporating Malaya, Singapore, Sarawak, and Sabah. However, riots broke out in 1964 in an ethnic clash between Malays and Chinese, resulting in the killing of twenty-two people and the injury of hundreds of others.[21] These events caused not only tension and mistrust, but precipitated ideological differences between the ruling parties of Malaya and Singapore. The last phase occurred in 1965 when Singapore seceded to become an independent state.[22] Nation-building became a driving force for survival, modernization, and industrialization in the midst of insecurity and potential threats, both from within and without.[23]

Although governmental control has relaxed somewhat in recent years, thereby providing growing advocacy for more democratization, the general political climate in Singapore since 1963 has fostered movements which avoid social, cultural or political concerns. As a result, those engaged in religious ministries have often been restricted or closed down. Riots broke out again between the Malays and the Chinese in 1969, 1987, and 1996, threatening political stability. Those circumstances have limited both the writing and publishing of books on contextual Christian theology, despite the multiplicity of Bible colleges, seminaries, and Christian publishing houses.[24]

Since 1970, evangelistic and Charismatic movements have flourished, contributing to growth in both Roman Catholic and Protestant circles that in 1990 12.5 percent of Singaporeans were recorded as active Christians. The Christian population grew to 14.6 percent according to the 2000 census. Of all converts to Christianity, a high percentage of them (75.9 percent) are ethnic Chinese from Buddhist, Confucianist, Taoist, or some admixture

---

20. Fleming, "Singapore, Malaysia and Brunei," 81.
21. Sng, *In His Good Time*, 267.
22. Roxborogh, "Singapore," 879.
23. Fleming, "Singapore, Malaysia and Brunei," 95–96.
24. England, *Asian Christian Theologies*, 249.

of these religious backgrounds. People of Indian and Malay descent adhere to Hinduism and Islam. It would appear that religion in Singapore is intertwined with ethnicity.[25] This connection needs to be explained in terms of the sociology of religion in Singapore.

The main languages in Singapore include Malay, Mandarin, English, and Tamil. The major religions are Hinduism, Buddhism, Taoism—and traditional blends of these faiths—along with Islam and Christianity. Although English is the official language and has become the *lingua franca* of commerce, politics, and communications, it is observed that Singaporeans generally prefer to speak in dialects at the grassroots level, particularly in places of worship. What is the relationship between religion and language? Social scientists suggest that religion serves as a vehicle for the consolidation and perpetuation of vernacular languages.[26] How does language impact religion when the use of English in Singapore expands to secondary and university settings?

The population in Singapore today is approximately 5.7 million. The Singapore government uses a unicameral parliamentary system, with a constitution that calls for a representative democracy as the political system. Since independence was declared, the government has maintained controls on social, political, and religious life. This includes some restriction of democratic processes, imposition of censorship, and control of media and community organizations. Those measures also include careful monitoring of issues related to ethnic identity, social justice, and human rights.

What characterizes Singapore culture? Is it a unique blend of West and East as many insist? It is clear that historical factors, issues of ethnicity/race, economics, culture, and politics all contribute to the sociology of religion in Singapore. Historically speaking, Singapore's colonial heritage is significant, yet this perspective must be balanced with the fact that a major portion of its population is derived from migrant backgrounds. A tension exists, therefore, between a natural affinity toward Westernization and modernization and a desire to preserve Asian culture and values.

One of the defining characteristics of Singapore culture is its religious and ethnic diversity, an element which has not always contributed to a harmonious society. Here the question is how to develop harmonious multiculturalism while simultaneously promoting the cultural traditions of each of the main ethnic groups. In the midst of this diversity, there seems to be a great impetus to develop a national identity and to push the country toward modernization and economic growth. Within the confluence of all these

---

25. Yeow, *Doing Christian Theology*, 154.
26. Clammer, "Singapore," 18.

somewhat conflicting factors is the question of the role of government to organize and orchestrate an efficient and functional society.

Concerning the complexity of Singapore society, one researcher explains, "The whole arrangement then looks something like a functionalist's dream: a social system with a high degree of integration despite (or because of) its internal diversity and in which the function of any part is defined in terms of (and indeed politically only tolerated as) its contribution to the working of the whole." As such, he continues, Singapore culture should be characterized as a "political culture."[27]

Here, the government's role in defining the nature of "race" or "ethnicity" and the concomitant issue of religion is significant. Ethnicity and religion are perpetuated and mediated, for example, through public education. Secondary curriculum supports the study of Hinduism and Islam for those individuals from Indian and Malay communities. Traditional Chinese traditions are reserved for people from ethnic Chinese backgrounds. The only exception to these guidelines is Bible knowledge, which is in principle opened to people from any race. It is noteworthy that although in theory children may study another religion other than the one associated with his or her ethnicity, the reality is that only a few are allowed to so do. The government's intervention reinforces and perpetuates separate ethnic communities and identities. Religion, in this unique political system, is conceived primarily as "instrumental" to promote morality compatible with what the government deems as desirable to a harmonious society. There is then a push toward national unity and modernization, yet to do so without sacrificing the traditional Asian cultures and values, which are regarded as the cultural ballast of Singapore society.[28]

Given the government's central role in society, it may seem that it is the only source for the creation of cultural ideology. This, of course, is not entirely true. Although the government does play a significant role, it does not resort to overt or coercive force. Rather, competing ideologies are often culturally harnessed through social categories—ethnicity, language, education—so that the "folk" voices of the "heart-landers" agree with the "official" voice of the government. The citizens of Singapore acquiesce and legitimize the social system. Singapore, in this sense, is truly unique. But what makes this possible? What kind of over-arching ideology would support the creation and operation of this social system?

Sociologists of religion observe that the reintroduction of Confucianism—an integral element for economic growth in Japan and South

27. Clammer, *Sociology of Singapore Religion*, 13.
28. Ibid., 15–16.

CHRISTIAN CONVERSION AND IDENTITY IN SINGAPORE 87

Korea—is responsible for the central ideology in Singapore. This central ideology has three parts: (1) the necessity for economic growth, (2) the corollary of political stability and authority, (3) and the monopoly of the definition of Singapore culture.[29] Above all, what makes this possible is the so-called "Chineseness" of Singapore culture. That is, people from ethnic Chinese backgrounds will typically accept a strong government with a high degree of paternalism as long as the government is able to provide material wealth for its citizens. Also accepted, as part of this cultural mindset, is bureaucratic rule and the unwillingness to oppose the government unless the government is clearly in serious disorder or deemed incompetent. Moreover, it is also assumed that people from Chinese backgrounds will tolerate change and discomfort without voicing public discord. To this end, Singapore can indeed be characterized as a "Confucian" state. This is to say that the social system operates on the belief that the nation's core Confucian ideals express culture. Thus, any attempt to define Singapore culture apart from certain theories of economics, ethnicity/race, politics, cultural values, and religion, would not be helpful. Singapore culture, both in its theoretical and affective dimensions, is a carefully constructed and highly structured reality.[30]

With regard to the challenge of modernization, James Wong states,

> We see this in every segment of its national life. New factories are constantly built, the skyline keeps changing, economic growth keeps space of increased productivity and new pattern of social living are emerging. The church, finding itself in the midst of this dynamic society, should keep abreast of all these changes. Indeed, it should grow more rapidly and even outpace Singapore itself.[31]

Specifically, the processes of secularization, pluralization, and privatization account for Singapore's struggle with modernization.[32] In fact, one can argue that pressing social issues presented by communalism, ethnic tension, urbanization, and modernization have not been adequately considered by Christian thinkers.[33] Major issues unique to greater Asia, including poverty, suffering, social injustice, communism, and religious pluralism, have often been overlooked in preference for Western agendas.

---

29. Ibid., 18.
30. Ibid., 19.
31. Wong, *Church in the Midst*, 3.
32. Lowe, "Christianity and Social Context," 8–20.
33. Siew, "Theological Education in Asia," 59.

What chance for survival and advance does Christianity have given the challenges of modernization in Singapore? What is the phenomenon of modernization in relationship to religion? Concerning the nature of the relationship between religion and modernization, postwar social science literature has typically characterized religion as an inhibitor of modernization and change. Moreover, the overwhelming conclusion is that modernization leads inevitably to secularization, though the recent reality in Southeast Asia—resurgence of Islam in Malaysia, Buddhism in Thailand, and Christianity in Singapore—seems to counter that simplistic perspective.[34]

Recent research, however, demonstrates that no consistent pattern has emerged pertaining to the impact of modernization on religion in Southeast Asia. Perhaps, it may even be unhelpful to separate the concepts of "secularization" and "modernization," depending on how they are defined, into distinct categories.[35] Some facets of religion have declined. Animism, for example, has waned during the process of modernization. Malaysia, in recent years, has responded toward alien values related to modernization with efforts to stem their proliferation by expanding Islamic law to all aspects of society. Admittedly, this phenomenon is unique in Southeast Asia.

To the other extreme, there are indications that modernization may even spur the growth of religion. Many countries in Southeast Asia have given much attention to religious education by adding religion as part of the curriculum in state schools. As a result, an increase in knowledge of formal beliefs is quite evident in recent decades. Thus, the area where modernization may actually strengthen religious commitment is in the realm of ideology. Largely in response to Western influence and a consumeristic mentality, many religious groups have worked hard to intensify their adherents' understanding of the faith. The result is that more people are conscious of their beliefs, the nature of their religious cause, and the role in which their religion plays in society.[36] Now that a descriptive overview of the Singapore context is given, the following section surveys major theories on Christian conversion in Singapore.

---

34. Von der Mehden, *Religion and Modernization*, vii.
35. Clammer, *Singapore: Ideology, Society, Culture*, 109–23.
36. Von der Mehden, *Religion and Modernization*, 194–95.

Review of Conversion Theories

Bobby Sng (1980; 2003)

Having provided a brief history of Singapore, this chapter will now examine specific accounts of Christian conversion in Singapore. The first major account on Singapore is by Bobby Sng, the former General Secretary of the Fellowship of Evangelical Students. In his seminal study, *In His Good Time*, Sng selects a variety of sources to construct his perspectives on the history of the Christian church in Singapore from 1819 to 1978.[37] A revised edition, tracing Singapore's history to 2002 with analysis of data from the 2000 census of population, was later published.[38] According to the 2000 census of population, the percentage of Christians in Singapore reached 14.6 percent.

For many, the year 1978 represents not only the Billy Graham Crusade in Singapore but the culmination of a decade-long of successful evangelism. Sng's historical account is intertwined with his theological conviction that God is responsible for the growth of Christianity in Singapore. He writes, "The choice of the title *In His Good Time* is deliberate. It reflects the conviction of the biblical writers that in God's scheme of things, there is always the *kairos*—an opportune time (Ecc 3:1). God has had his timing for the church in Singapore too and part of the purpose of this book is to show how this has been so."[39]

Sng attributes Christian conversion to the phenomenon of nation-building beginning in 1965 and the Charismatic revivals beginning in 1972. Initially, the outlook of the Christian church in the nineteenth century was rather grim because Singapore was very much a transient society and Western missionaries did not take the region seriously as a mission field. Toward the second half of the nineteenth century, with the introduction of Methodist Mission schools and the influx of Christian immigrants from China, India, and Ceylon, the outlook improved dramatically, though the real surge did not take place until after WWII.[40]

Concerning nationhood, Sng notes that Singapore was transformed from a transient society, where people came to make money and returned to their home countries, to an independent nation which encouraged Christians to concentrate their financial and human resources on the island. Additionally, the emergence of a new generation of young people gave impetus

---

37. Sng, *In His Good Time*.
38. Ibid.
39. Ibid., 14.
40. Ibid., 319–20.

to a fledgling church once composed primarily of immigrants. Moreover, the government sought to relocate massive amount of people, who were segregated according to ethnic "enclaves," in an effort to promote a more integrated society. This ploy was ultimately aimed at stemming the tide of ethnic tension with the rhetorical slogan, "Who is Your Neighbour?" Sng notes that the move actually encouraged people to be more open to religious change.[41]

The second, and perhaps more significant, reason for Christian growth between 1965 and 1978 was the Charismatic revivals. Starting with several incidents at the Anglo-Chinese School in 1972, where a couple of young students experienced "a state of frenzy and hysterics," a spiritual revival broke out and blossomed into praying in tongues. The Pentecostal churches were the main recipients of this spiritual renewal in Singapore.[42] According to Sng, the ministry of the Holy Spirit spread across various denominations, where scores of people experienced deliverance, healing, and conversion. Thus, the Charismatic movement was quickly launched, in spite of hesitation from church leaders. In a 1979 "Christian Profile Survey," the report indicates that 36.4 percent of the 2,321 respondents have attended charismatic meetings at one time or another. More importantly, Sng notes that spiritual revivals in Singapore exceeded those in Pentecostal and Charismatic circle to include traditional churches as well.[43]

If there was a particular factor that characterized this period of growth, it was the focus on evangelism. Sng calls this period the "decade of evangelism," culminating in the Billy Graham Crusade in 1978.[44] The five evenings of meetings yielded the fruits of 11,883 new converts and attracted 337,000 in attendance.[45] What was even more remarkable were the thousands of Christians who were mobilized to invite non-believers, conducted follow-up and home visitations, provided counseling, as well as support requisite to the success of the event.[46]

A major strength of the book is Sng's insistence that a story of the church in Singapore cannot be told without due consideration to the sociopolitical events that helped produce it. However, similar to the Book of Acts, Sng's historiography is an apologetic—an interpretation combining history and theology—of God's favor and timing on Singapore. The strategic aim

41. Ibid., 303–5.
42. Ibid., 288–89.
43. Ibid., 291–95.
44. Ibid., 296–303.
45. Ibid., 302.
46. Ibid., 299.

for writing is to instill the church with strength, faith, and resolve to press forward to a promising, yet uncertain future. Sng concludes by stating his purpose for writing about Singapore,

> It is to urge ourselves to perceive that the story of a nation always has two levels of reality—the human level where man makes decisions and acts, and the divine level where God works out his own purposes. History, therefore, is more than just the simple record of the movements of men and nations; it provides the stage on which the unobstrusive sovereign hand of the God of the universe is actively at work.[47]

Thus, the history of the church in Singapore is ultimately God's story, according to Sng. As a historical account, however, Sng' interpretation is broad, a bit anachronistic at times, and reflects his selective use of data and theological perspectives.

Bobby Sng and Poh Seng You (1982)

The theme of church growth or Christian conversion is extended in Bobby Sng and Poh Seng You's *Religious Trends in Singapore*. This study, which is based on a government document, "Census of Population 1980: Singapore Release no. 9 Religion and Fertility," uses a survey questionnaire and provides statistical analysis and discussion on the "strengths and weaknesses of the Christian community."[48] The first part of the book—statistical analysis—lists a number of demographic variables measured with relation to the phenomenon of religion.[49] The second part—discussion—interprets the quantitative results.[50]

The book's findings show that in 1980, there were 203,517 Christians in Singapore, which accounted for 10.3 percent of the total population. Of Chinese people who constituted 76.9 percent of the population, 10.6 percent considered themselves as Christians. Of Indian people who constituted 6.4 percent of the population, 12.4 percent considered themselves as Christians. According to the authors, these figures show a marked increase compared with 2.8 percent and 6.0 percent, respectively, the last time when a person's religious belief was asked in a census exercise in 1931. The total

---

47. Ibid., 320–21.
48. Sng and You, *Religious Trends in Singapore*, 1.
49. Ibid., 4–43.
50. Ibid., 45–64.

number of Christians in 1931 was not available, because Malays were not surveyed then on the assumption that they were all Muslims.[51]

Sng and You then go on to discuss the reasons for Christian conversion. The chief reason is a higher level education, which can be explained on two levels. They argue that, on one level, the influence of a Western style of education contributed to growth. In particular, Chinese people had received education based upon an "antiquated Confucianist syllabus which dated back to the Han dynasty."[52] However, as time passed, Chinese parents preferred to send their children to vernacular schools, using the English language as the primary medium of instruction. This shift undermined the overall traditional Chinese values and outlook of students. The implication is that Westernization of particular education systems facilitated the transformation of Christianity in Singapore to take on a more Western appearance in form. According to Sng and You, "The same trend may also be noted in the Tamil and Malay schools."

On a deeper level, education in the form of church or mission schools, in particular, facilitated Christian conversion. According to Sng and You, these schools existed in Singapore as early as 1819 with the arrival of the first resident missionary, Rev. Samuel Milton. These mission schools, especially those from the Methodist church, played an important role over the next several decades, facilitating conversion and church growth. When some denominations tended toward theological liberalism in the early to the mid-twentieth century and evangelism waned, para-church organizations were established to continue the work of evangelism.

During the period of 1956–66, Youth for Christ and Inter-School Christian Fellowship managed to set up over one hundred school groups. Sng and You conclude that between 1950 and 1980, the para-church organizations actually surpassed the mission schools in terms of their influence on students and winning them over to Christ.[53] The authors note, however, that the focus on education as the primary reason for Christian conversion does not preclude socio-political developments that worked concurrently with it in Singapore during this period. They note, in particular, the independence of Singapore as a republic and massive relocation of its population as contributive factors to religious change.[54] The overall salutary effects of moral and religious education, urbanization, and modernization contributed to Christian conversion. An important implication is that the prospects for

51. Ibid., 45.
52. Ibid, 46.
53. Ibid., 49.
54. Ibid., 50.

continued church growth appear good, if these mechanisms continue to be in place.[55]

A major contribution of this study is the authors' focus on educational changes in Singapore, particularly the role of the church or mission schools, contributing to the growth of Christianity. Although there is a correlation between education and conversion, the number of Singaporeans who attend mission schools is relatively small.[56] It is questionable that religious education and socioeconomic change alone can account for the steady growth in the number of Christians in Singapore.[57] Perhaps religious education in Singapore represents a unique, contextual factor of conversion. The study can benefit from considering broader and macro-level factors as well.

Keith Hinton (1985)

The vast changes in Singapore, ushering in a growing nation-state, modernization, and urbanization, took its toll on the residents of this small nation-state. Keith Hinton's study, *Growing Churches Singapore Style*, argues that "anomie" was the main reason for Singaporean's conversion to Christianity.[58] Although he acknowledges that Christian growth is ultimately the work of the Holy Spirit, Hinton argues that God uses both conducive and non-conducive factors to grow people.[59] As such, Hinton maintains that it is necessary to identify church growth factors in order to facilitate effective evangelism and discipleship.[60] He states his purpose for writing, "Our aim is to identify those growth factors which are significant for the church in Singapore, in order that they may be used by church leaders as a basis for developing strategies and programmes that will increase the harvest. Growth factors may be positive stimuli or negative retardants; it is important to perceive the traps as it is to recognize the triggers to growth."[61] Having studied under Peter Wagner in Fuller Theological Seminary's church growth program, his analysis of the Singapore context is derived from the perspective of church growth theory.

Hinton explains that Christian conversion and church growth in Singapore can be attributed to both contextual and institutional factors. What

55. Ibid., 61–62.
56. Tong, *Rationalizing Religion*, 77–155.
57. Ibid., 3.
58. Hinton, *Growing Churches Singapore Style*, 101–8.
59. Ibid., 4–5.
60. Ibid., 5.
61. Ibid., 6.

then are some contextual factors for Christian conversion in Singapore? A primary contextual factor is the short history of Singapore. The period between the 1950s and 1980s, characterized by Christians as "harvest time" in Singapore, is marked by independence and nation-building. Germane to Singapore's history is her positive experience as a former British colony. This experience contributed to Singapore's openness toward the West, allowing her citizens to accommodate Western Christianity more readily than most other Asian countries with a colonial past. Additionally, when a large number of Western missionaries left communist China and took up residence in Singapore in 1949, the sudden surge in resources stimulated enthusiasm and church growth. Chinese churches, in particular, which could no longer import Christian workers from China, focused instead on training its own laity. This shift, which was evidenced by the founding of Bible colleges and seminaries, further contributed to growth. Para-church organizations were also founded during this formative period.[62] A second contextual factor includes the tenuous religious background of the Chinese people. Citing the research of Vivienne Wee, Hinton concludes that religion for Chinese people surrounds the concept of "fate," an impersonal force that cannot be altered during the course of one's life time. One cannot help but feel resigned to living out his or her fate, though "luck" may fluctuate considerably within the boundaries of one's fate. The nature of religion for the Chinese, according to Hinton, is to discover how to circumvent bad luck and to take advantage of good luck.[63] Moreover, Chinese religion is basically a folk religion, highly eclectic, combining aspects of Confucianism, Taoism, and Buddhism.[64] It can be characterized as highly pragmatic, problem-solving oriented, this-worldly and materialistic, individualistic, and action-based.[65]

One can only surmise from the above that Chinese folk religion is very pragmatic, action-oriented, and lacking a clearly defined system of beliefs. People would follow it so long as they feel luck is going their way. It does little, however, to offer a satisfactory explanation of worldview questions that educated people would ask in a modern society. Moreover, it does not require much commitment that would challenge its adherents of the temporal nature of their materialistic worldview, nor to transform their identity in a transitory society.

From this summary, Hinton then enumerates implications for church growth. While his discussion is appropriate and helpful, Hinton could

---

62. Ibid., 23–28.
63. Ibid., 31.
64. Ibid., 30–32.
65. Ibid., 33–34.

provide more in-depth discussion on the relationship between the "diffused" nature of Chinese folk religions and Christian conversion. In addressing the question, why would Chinese Singaporeans be open to religious change, Hinton provides a short section exploring "influences in conversion." He notes that respondents typically explained three factors for their conversion: (1) searched for a true religion, (2) attracted to the corporate life of Christianity, and (3) faced a life crisis. Hinton concludes that it is no wonder that many Chinese young people, who are educated with modern scientific understanding, often question the credibility of traditional religions. Hinton believes that Christianity offers an authentic, relational alternative, one that is more consistent with a modern worldview.[66]

A third contextual factor for Christian conversion is the harshness of life in a modernizing and pluralistic society. Hinton refers to sociologists, such as Durkheim, who explain city life as a breeding ground of anomie.[67] What exactly does Hinton mean by the anomic conditions of Singapore? He describes anomie in terms of social pathologies, resulting from living in a highly competitive society. These include the rising divorce rate between 1974 and 1983, dense living conditions, government pressure on its people to achieve economic success, and emotional stress. As a result, anomie refers to "The disruption of long term social relationships through urban renewal that has produced probably the most serious social pathology."

Pointing to the Chinese, in particular, for their inability to build relationships, Hinton explains, "People under stress are tending to withdraw into their own private worlds where they do not meet others. They become inward looking, impersonal, individualistic, apathetic and increasingly insecure."[68] Hinton points out the irony in the Singapore story is that the country has been able to meet the physical needs of its people, but the psychological needs constitute a greater challenge for the foreseeable future. As a prescription to this social pathology, Hinton suggests that the only solution to anomie is the building of community. This is exactly where the church can offer help and facilitate change, because Christianity is essentially a communal religion.[69]

Institutional factors for Christian growth include clear denomination structures, healthy democratic forms of church government, the existence of church or mission schools, the contributions of para-church organizations,

66. Ibid., 119–20.
67. Ibid., 59.
68. Ibid., 106.
69. Ibid., 107.

good preaching and teaching, strong efforts for evangelism, formation of cell-groups, as well as able Christian leadership.[70]

Hinton rightly observes that Christianity is rapidly growing among the English-educated Chinese people of Singapore, and that their values and lifestyle are becoming more alike with those of society. One wonders, however, if this trend reflects Christian influence on Singapore society, or if Christians are assimilating with societal values. This point needs clarification, though the latter is probably true.

Nevertheless, Hinton provides a clear compelling case for the growth of Christianity due to anomic conditions. Hinton maintains that in Singapore, anomie is on the rise, as people withdraw into their private worlds. This, in turn, creates social pathologies, which often prompt people to search for transcendence in life. This is indeed a plausible explanation. However, Hinton does not provide adequate empirical evidence, whether quantitative or qualitative, that anomie is on the rise. He also does not provide evidence, explaining why people, if they are anomic, would turn to Christianity. In fact, data do not show an increase in anomie in Singapore.[71] Most previous sociological studies have also found that anomie is not an effective indicator of religiosity or religious participation.[72] Additionally, a church-growth model to Christian conversion seems limited because it merely assesses whether one is a Christian or not. It does not adequately explain for the processes of conversion, which are not always evident in terms of church growth.

Joseph Tamney and Riaz Hassan (1987)

Sociologists Joseph Tamney and Riaz Hassan argue in their brief study, *Religious Switching in Singapore: A Study of Religious Mobility*, that cultural crisis in general and interethnic marriage in particular account for religious conversion in Singapore.[73] The authors make their argument based upon data sets derived from interviews with university students and the 1980 Singapore census on married couples.

Germane to the authors' thesis of interethnic marriage is the assumption that religious conversions "represent dissatisfaction with the values, norms, or beliefs associated with the culture in which a person was

70. Ibid., 125–55.
71. Tong, *Rationalizing Religion*, 3.
72. Carr and Hauser, "Anomie and Religion," 69–74; Photiadis and Johnson, "Orthodoxy, Church Participation," 224–48.
73. Tamney and Hassan, *Religious Switching in Singapore*, 44.

raised."[74] Thus, the theory of anomic cultural conditions predicts religious conversion, which is related to several factors, including "being young, unmarried, mobile, relatively friendless, educated, and urban."[75] Two groups of people—college students and married couples—are examined to test this hypothesis.

Concerning the phenomenon of interethnic marriage, the authors cite studies in the United States that attribute religious conversion to interethnic marriage. They then cite studies in Singapore on the same subject and make a couple of observations. (1) Of all interethnic marriages in Singapore, over 70 percent occur among adherents of Islam and Christianity. (2) Of the interethnic marriages, 60 percent are intra-religious and 31 percent are inter-religious[76]

The sample results from university students show that the religious retention rates are as follow: Muslim—99 percent, Catholic—98 percent, Protestant—86 percent, Buddhist—30 percent, and traditionalist—16 percent. The authors observe that, since Singapore is predominately Chinese who are from traditionalist religious backgrounds, the figures provide some support their thesis.[77]

Additionally, seven case studies of fifteen interethnic marriages are analyzed. They authors observe:

> In ten out of 15 cases both partners were found to have the same self-reported affiliation. In six of them one or both partners had converted to their partner's religion or to a new religious identity and in one case a couple changed from a religious to a non-religious identity—no religion. The fact that seven out of 15 interethnic marriages involved religious switching by at least one of the partners provides considerable support for the intermarriage explanation of religious.[78]

Tamney and Hassan conclude that the findings show religious conversion occurring primarily among Chinese Singaporeans. The flexibility on the part of Chinese people to switch their religion is best explained by the observation that there is a clear disjuncture between religion and their cultural identity as Chinese Singaporeans. On the other hand, the Indians and

---

74. Ibid., 11.
75. Ibid., 12.
76. Ibid., 10.
77. Ibid., 13–15.
78. Ibid., 36.

Malays are much less likely to switch their religions due to the closer connection between religion and ethnic identity.[79]

Indeed, Joseph Tamney and Riaz Hassan offer a unique perspective that religious change is caused by cultural crisis and intermarriage in Singapore society. However, the authors' sample cases for intermarriage seem too small. This limitation weakens the study for an apparent lack of evidence. More importantly, the authors do not provide actual figures of interethnic marriages in Singapore. In fact, the rate of interethnic marriage in Singapore is low, and like Hinton's claim on anomie in Singapore, there is little data to support the cultural crisis hypothesis.[80]

Daniel Goh (1999)

Daniel Goh argues in his essay, "Rethinking Resurgent Christianity in Singapore," that Christianity, fueled by Charismatic renewal, has surged since the early 1970s. As a professor in the department of sociology at the National University of Singapore, Goh is aware that the surge has attracted sociological interest. He evaluates several explanations, including: rationalization of religion,[81] meeting practical needs,[82] and providing meaning and community.[83]

Goh is critical of Tong's thesis that the perception of Christianity as "more rational belief systems" is responsible for Christian conversion. He proposes instead that "the most popular option for Singaporean converts is Charismatism, a religious system combining 'rational' (Protestant fundamentalism) and 'mystical-magical' (Pentecostalism) beliefs and practices,"[84] What is actually happening today, in terms of Christian conversion, is the "re-enchantment" or the "anti-rationalization choices of many modern individuals in Singapore."[85] Moreover, Goh thinks that Tamney makes the same mistake as Tong and contradicts himself in his observation that the growing segment of Christianity in Singapore is associated with "healing and exorcism," but argues that Christianity has modernized and moved beyond elements of folk religion.[86] Concerning Clammer, Goh judges that he is biased

---

79. Ibid., 44.
80. Tong, *Rationalizing Religion*, 3.
81. Tong, "The Rationalization of Religion in Singapore," 206–7.
82. Tamney, "Religion in Capitalist East Asia," 56.
83. Clammer, *Sociology of Singapore Religion*, 3.
84. Goh, "Rethinking Resurgent Christianity," 89, 90, 98.
85. Ibid., 90.
86. Ibid.

in his assessment of Charismatism as a "superficial and foreign" response to modernity, and that a relevant religion must provide "ethical injunctions in the political, economic and social dimension."[87] Over against these theories, Goh argues that the growth of Christianity is best explained by the ability of Christianity to provide transcendent solutions for individuals.

According to Goh, the challenge of life in the Singapore context is "an increasing distantiation of individuals from rationalizing societal and cultural institutions." In other words, due to pervasive modern technocratic order and rationality governing society, interpersonal relationships have become increasingly impersonal and controlled. Goh maintains that "This process is experienced phenomenologically by the individual as the *transcendentalizion* of one's consciousness. Social reality becomes one that is beyond the individual's grasp, understanding, and control." The result is a social pathology characterized by intense self-consciousness and loneliness.[88]

To substantiate his claim, Goh provides a historical analysis of modern life in Singapore from 1965 to the 1990s. He notes, in particular, the consequences of national independence by which individuals were mobilized, pushed to achieve, and atomized from traditional allegiances to local communities and to national commitments. The result is a "corporatist communitarian ideology based on multiculturalism" articulated by the government. The hastening of the process of industrialization by the People's Action Party (PAP) in the late 1960s to integrate the Singapore economy with the world economic system further exposed individuals "to transcendental and impersonal structures of relationships."[89]

A third significant development is the national educational system, which represents "the state's cultural instrument for atomizing and detaching individuals from primary relationships, integrating them progressively into the polity and economy." The English language is privileged and becomes the *lingua franca* of commerce, politics, and communications. The Western detached sense of self is now imposed over traditional concepts. Most importantly, the locus of intimate relationship shifts from an allegiance to kinship groups to friendships defined by transcendent categories.[90] As a result, people exhibit existential doubt by asking, "Who am I? What is the meaning of life?" They could also experience anger, asking, "Are relationships real?"

87. Ibid., 91.
88. Ibid
89. Ibid., 92–93.
90. Ibid, 94.

According to Goh, the resolution to these challenges is twofold: transcendence and transience. On the one hand, transcendence refers to the adoption of an identity derived from a coherent set of cultural meanings that can make sense of the existential self and its relations to subjective reality. On the other hand, transience refers to the felt unity of the existential self with subjective reality achieved through the active experience of being. The Charismatic form of Christianity in Singapore best provides for both transcendence and transience.[91] These are accomplished by a variety of means. Pentecostal and Charismatic commitment to biblical inerrancy, for instance, facilitates a transcendent narrative in which self-identity is formed. Within such a narrative, a premillennial theological framework also explains the presence of a rather pessimistic outlook for the future. However, the transcendent is reinforced by deep transient experiences, facilitated by expressive worship experiences, speaking in tongues and other sign gifts, and the inter-subjective relationships of ministry, fellowship, and evangelism.[92] Thus, the dialectic of transcendence—mediated by sermons, Bible study groups, testimonies, quiet times—and transience—mediated through the worship experience, tongues, fellowship, spiritual warfare, service—reinforce each other in powerful ways, which provide a "coherent worldview of self-in-world that helps the embedded existential self to deal with transcendent reality."

Goh points out that the Charismatic renewal is particularly appealing to "lower-middle class Chinese Singaporeans," who experience social alienation the most. Regarding its overall success in Singapore, Goh concludes that "Charismatism is inherently modern because it advocates a this-worldly transcendent activism reinforced by transient experiences that seeks to transform the transcendent world into a modern Christian one."[93]

Goh's essay offers empirical data and a sustained argument that religious change in Singapore is due to the ability of Christianity to provide transcendent solutions for individuals. Methodologically, however, the scope of his study is limited to Charismatic churches in Singapore. Moreover, Goh's study is limited to the growth of Charismatic churches in Singapore, occurring between the 1980s and 1990s. Thus, it cannot explain the dramatic growth of Christianity from 1950s to the 1980s, before the arrival of Charismatic movements in Singapore. The major shortcoming with the transcendent argument is that while it may conceivably explain the growth of Christianity for a smaller sector of the population at a certain period

---

91. Ibid., 96–97.
92. Ibid., 97–107.
93. Ibid., 107.

in time, it cannot account for the growth of the Christian population as a whole. Furthermore, Goh does not really explain why Singaporeans would suddenly experience a need for transcendence, and why only those from Chinese backgrounds.[94]

Robbie B. H. Goh (2005)

The social impact of the growth of Christianity in Singapore is examined by Robbie B. H. Goh in a chapter on Singapore in *Christianity in Southeast Asia*.[95] Noting that the percentage of Christians has increased to 14.6 percent according to the 2000 Census of Population, Goh maintains that "the statistical figure does not really capture the broader influence of Christianity in Singapore."[96] Rather, the introduction of Christianity to Singapore in 1819 as a part of British colonialism has exerted a significant "social influence."

This influence was mediated primarily through the establishment of various well-respected "mission schools," such as the Anglican St. Margaret's School (est. 1842), St. Andrew's School (1862), and the Methodist Anglo-Chinese School (1886) just to name a few.[97] Goh observes that educational ministry became a very effective tool for churches to bridge the initial gap between British colonizers and immigrant people.[98] Those schools not only provided reputable and affordable "Anglophone" education but opened the door to employment opportunities for locals under the colonial government.[99] Consequently, a natural association was made between Christianity, education, higher income, and middle class identity.[100]

Statistics certainly bear out these claims. In fact, 33 percent of college graduates claim to follow Christianity, the religion with the strongest representation of degree holders. This is followed by Buddhism, which is represented by 23 percent college degree holders.[101] In terms of income and housing, Christians accounted for 34.3 percent of the most expensive housing scheme in Singapore, while Buddhists accounted for 30.1 percent. Additionally, among households who spoke English at home, Christianity dominates at 39.8 percent, whereas Buddhism accounts for 24.8 percent.

94. Tong, *Rationalizing Religion*, 3–4.
95. Goh, "Singapore."
96. Ibid., 35.
97. Goh, "Mission Schools in Singapore," 362–63.
98. Goh, "Singapore," 38.
99. Ibid., 39.
100. Ibid., 35.
101. Ibid., 41.

The English language has become the *lingua franca* in Singapore and is commonly associated with "cosmopolitan" social identities.[102] It is no wonder that Goh claims: "Christianity is often perceived as the religion of English-speaking, middle-class cosmopolitans who studied at a good school (if not specifically a mission school), had the opportunity to study in a university (possibly an overseas one), and who are now in a professional or managerial position with a comfortable middle-class lifestyle."[103] Goh concludes that the *de facto* identity of Christianity as a group of Anglicized middle-class professionals is reinforced by an authoritarian government that restricts the church from engaging social, societal, and political issues. This trend has certainly changed somewhat in recent years when the church began to voice their concerns on issues including gambling, homosexuality, and bioethics.[104] Nonetheless, the pro-establishment mentality has entrenched the perception of Christianity as an Anglophone middle-class religion. Given its strategic location, prosperity, and openness, Goh predicts that Singapore will continue to serve as the "hub" for Christian organizations and ministries in Southeast Asia.[105]

What key implications can be drawn from those observations? Mission schools provided a distinctly Christian influence during Singapore's nation-building period, and continue to exercise moral influence today.[106] Christianity exists in Singapore within the tension of national impulses and globalized networks.[107] On the one hand, Christianity, like all religions in Singapore, is regulated by and conforms to state policies under the "Maintenance of Religious Harmony Act" in terms of religious space, practices, and multiculturalism. Under Singapore's multicultural policy, race and religion are conflated with government definition and control of those boundaries.[108]

For example, all Singaporean students are required to study a "mother tongue," such as Tamil, Malay, or Mandarin, according to racial categories imposed by the government. This simplified way of categorizing citizens extends to the domain of religious practices as well, where ethnic Chinese are identified as practicing Chinese religions, Indians identified as Hindus, and people of Malay ethnicity are identified as Muslim. As one social scientist notes, "The policy thus has the effect of reinforcing a simplification of race

---

102. Ibid., 42.
103. Ibid.
104. Ibid., 43.
105. Ibid., 45.
106. Goh, "Mission Schools in Singapore," 374.
107. Goh, "Christian Identities in Singapore," 1.
108. Ibid.

into official categories; racial identity is pegged on cultural practices (in this case, the learning and use of a 'mother tongue'), so that to be Chinese is to speak Mandarin, and to speak Mandarin is 'Chineseness.'"[109]

Beyond racial and religious identities, socioeconomic factors also play a significant role in shaping identity. In the geography and culture of Singapore, Christianity is "strongly correlated with better lifestyle, more expensive types of housing, and university-level education. Thus, Goh observes:

> Christian Chinese form a distinct grouping among the Chinese, exhibiting what might be called "elite" modernized qualities which tend to segregate them from other Chinese who speak Mandarin or Chinese dialects, live in the public housing in common with the majority (about 80 percent) of Singaporeans, and accordingly practice the "traditional Chinese religions" of Buddhism or Taoism cum traditional Chinese practices such as ancestor worship.[110]

On the other hand, Christianity, unlike religions that are ethnically correlated (i.e., Islam, Hinduism, Buddhism, and Taoism), is perceived by many in Singapore as a Western religion, one which is obliged to expand itself at the expense of ethnic or race-based religions. With its roots in colonialism, Christianity, along with concomitant association of Western values and ways, is resisted out of fear of cultural "deracination."[111] The perception of Christianity as a Western religion associated with "elite" social status and English-education is thus perpetuated by non-English speaking Singaporeans.[112] A class divide is thus created with the perception of "Anglophone Christians" in Singapore associated with university-education, English-speaking, social class elitism, and "cosmopolitan" in identity.[113]

This awkward positioning, according to Goh, compels Christianity in Singapore to constantly rationalize and adapt its processes on two fronts. On the one hand, Christianity in Singapore identifies itself as a rooted aspect of the national community, which preserves the uniqueness of Chinese identity and the "hegemony of the state."[114] On the other hand, it associates with Western languages and cultures, capitalizes on its global networks and its affinities to capitalist modernity, and segregates from traditional religious

---

109. Ibid., 2.
110. Ibid., 3.
111. Ibid., 9.
112. Ibid.
113. Ibid., 10–11.
114. Ibid., 13.

practices.[115] As such, Singaporean Christians adopt a "flexible identity" by preserving the social bonds with the Singapore "heartland" and channeling the bulk of their evangelical energies outside of Singapore's shores, thus avoiding inter-faith tensions at home, which might be construed as a violation of the Maintenance of Racial Harmony Act. In this way, Christianity creates a "modernity without deracination," holding in tension the "cosmopolitan" and "heartland" identities.[116]

Phyllis Ghim-Lian Chew (2008)

In "Religious Switching and Knowledge Among Adolescents in Singapore," Phyllis Ghim-Lian Chew argues that 60.1 percent of those who "switched" from traditional Chinese religions, such as Buddhism and Taoism, to Christianity were adolescents or students of ages twelve to eighteen.[117] Using quantitative questionnaire analysis and qualitative case studies, Chew attempts to show nuance on the "push" and "pull" factors on the dramatic shift in religious affiliation among adolescents in Singapore. The "push" factors or negative aspects, which tend to drive younger people away from Buddhism/Taoism, include their "disenchantment with the practice of rites/rituals and the lack of knowledge of these faiths either from the temple or their parents."[118] Switchers from Buddhism/Taoism to Christianity characterize their former religion in terms of obligation to rites and practices, which are "meaningless," "illogical," and "irrational."[119] Buddhist and Taoist groups have typically responded by providing a more "canonical context" and doing away with the more "superstitious elements of their faiths." Additionally, these groups in recent years have put up internet sites, formed clubs in schools, and utilized music as ways to appeal to youths.[120]

What are the "pull" factors unique to adolescent conversion? Recent research cites peer influence and personal support as prime reasons.[121] What is interesting about adolescent converts is that conversion to them "is almost always an 'emotional' rather than an 'intellectual' one."[122] In other words, they converted not so much because they were on a personal quest

115. Ibid., 20.
116. Ibid., 14.
117. Chew, "Religious Switching and Knowledge," 389.
118. Ibid., 406.
119. Ibid., 399.
120. Ibid., 406.
121. Ibid., 398–99.
122. Ibid., 406.

for truth but because of "peer-influences" and receiving emotional support in solving life-problems.[123] This observation attempts to differentiate between adolescent conversion from conversion among "older youths," who converted based more upon intellectual and economic factors.[124] Beyond the positive aspects of peer influence and crisis intervention, other contributing factors for conversion include missionary and evangelistic efforts, and the perception of Christianity as an "acultural," "modern," and "global" religion of choice. Lastly, in comparison to other religions in Singapore, Christianity is regarded as "the best organized and has networks which allow youths to develop personal relationships with unusual speed."[125]

Terence Chong and Hui Yew-Foong (2013)

Noted as "the first substantial, comprehensive and scientific analysis of Christianity in Singapore," *Different Under God: A Survey of Church-Going Protestants in Singapore* is not so much of a study on conversion as it is an exposition of Singaporean Christians. Based upon a major survey done between December 2009 and January 2011 of 2,663 respondents from twenty-four churches, consisting of Anglican, Methodist, Bible-Presbyterian, independent churches, and megachurches, the study aims to provide a profile of the demographic as well as certain attitudes of Singaporean Protestants.[126] Although the book is not strictly a study on Christian conversion, the findings are highly suggestive of conversion and shed light on such topic as why people attend their church of choice, their attitude toward money and finance, politics, sex and sexuality, and perceptions of religions and religious others.

Written by social scientists and for a popular audience, the authors' findings reinforce previous scholarly conclusions regarding the profile of Christians in Singapore. For example, 95.1 percent of the people surveyed identified themselves as ethnically Chinese, with 0.1 percent as Malay, 2.8 percent Indian, 0.3 percent Eurasian, and 1.8 percent as others.[127] This confirms the correlation of ethnicity and religion in Singapore. Education is another defining characteristic of Singaporean Protestants with 52 percent indicating university-level education compared with 40.9 percent from the

---

123. Ibid.
124. Ibid., 407.
125. Ibid.
126. Chong and Hui, *Different Under God*, 10.
127. Ibid., 38.

2010 census.[128] Respondents between eighteen and twenty-nine years of age constituted for 36 percent of people surveyed, with higher age brackets represented by lower percentages of people surveyed.[129] The findings on the types of housing Protestants dwell also reveal that they are, by far, the most affluent communities in Singapore.[130] The demographic profile of Singaporean Protestants in this study corresponds with the one provided in Tong's study.

The primary focus of the study concerns the rise of the megachurches in Singapore. Here, one is made aware of the limitations of Tong's earlier research, as the authors attempt to account for the rise of the megachurch population in Singapore. Largely neglected in Tong's study, Chong and Hui define "megachurch" as one with at least two thousand members in attendance.[131] The largest megachurches in Singapore include City Harvest Church at nearly twenty thousand in average attendance, and New Creation Church with an average of thirty thousand in weekly attendance. Given that many members are first-generation converts from a variety of social, educational, and religious backgrounds, the growth of Protestantism in Singapore has occurred mainly in megachurches.[132] The authors conclude that respondents from mainline and independent churches are generally better educated and are more apt to use English as the preferred language than those from megachurches, who represent more working class people from Chinese speaking backgrounds. Chong and Hui state, "In other words, we can characterize megachurch respondents as the aspiring or emergent middle class that has achieved upward social mobility."[133]

Concerning the choice of church attendance, megachurches have experienced higher rates of conversion compared with those from mainline and independent churches.[134] However, the reasons for why respondents from megachurches attend their choice of church are not different than those from mainline or independent churches. The typical reasons include "praise and worship," "exciting church," "people care for me," and "small group ministry."[135]

128. Ibid., 40–41.
129. Ibid., 39.
130. Ibid., 42.
131. Ibid., 32.
132. Ibid., 133.
133. Ibid., 60–61.
134. Ibid., 67.
135. Ibid., 67–68.

The survey does reveal manifest differences between members of new megachurches and those of traditional mainline churches. For example, those from mainline churches are more inclined to take part in civil society activities and give more attention to public discourse on matters of moral and political concern. Megachurch members are typically more reticent about such matters and show a distinct tendency to limit these discussions to private spheres.[136]

The question of money and finance also stands out as a contrasting matter between mainline, independent, and megachurches. For the authors, there seems to be a more acute awareness on the part of megachurch attenders of the connection between spirituality and material prosperity. This is due, in part, to the use of marketing strategies as an integral part of the theological discourse on the part of megachurches. There is, by extension, a corresponding tendency to correlate church growth with group as well as personal upward mobility.[137]

Perhaps the most interesting finding relates to Christian relationship with religions and religious others. While respondents across denominations insist that Christians should interact more with non-believers, respondents from megachurches seem "more likely to have friends from other religions, especially those from the Buddhist and Taoist community, as well to more likely to spend their leisure time with them."[138] Moreover, megachurch attenders demonstrate more sensitivity when doing evangelism or sharing the Christian faith with religious others. The authors posit that this is probably due to the fact that many of them are first-generation Christians and "are more likely to have parents of Buddhist or Taoist backgrounds." The seeker orientation of megachurches also encourages Christians to interact more with religious others, thus closing the gap between the two groups.[139]

Different Under God reveals interesting insights. However, as it demonstrates limited interaction with prior scholarship, the findings leave the reader needing more explanation. The substantial research by Tong is curiously not mentioned at all. Chong and Hui's study offers what is happening with the Protestant church in Singapore but fails to adequately explain why and how. In terms of sociological inquiry, Tong's 2007 study remains the benchmark for scholarship on Christian conversion in Singapore, though it lacks engagement with the rise of megachurches in the last decade. The two texts should be read in tandem, each complementing one another, as a way

---

136. Ibid., 84–90.
137. Ibid., 81–83.
138. Ibid., 133.
139. Ibid.

forward for exploring the nature of Christian conversion in Singapore and its missiological implications.

Rationalization of Religion in Singapore

While the foregoing review describes the variety and richness of Christian conversion theories in Singapore, the major theoretical framework for this research is Chee Kiong Tong's *Rationalizing Religion: Religious Conversion, Revivalism and Competition in Singapore Society*.[140] It is, by far, the most scholarly and comprehensive study on Christian conversion in Singapore.

Thesis

Tong's central thesis argues that the process of rationalizing religion is responsible for religious conversion, revival, and competition in Singapore. In particular, Tong explains that many have converted to Christianity over the years because Christianity is rationalized and perceived as an "intellectual" religion in contrast to the traditional Chinese religions, such as Taoism or Buddhism, which are largely characterized as "illogical," "irrational," and "superstitious." According to Tong, it is the perception of Christianity as a "rational, modern, ethnically neutral religion that partly explains its attractiveness to younger Singaporeans, who are themselves socialized into an English-stream western oriented educational system."[141]

The process of rationalizing religion is described by Tong in terms of six concepts. By "intellectualization" of religion, Tong refers to "a process where individuals shift from an unthinking and passive acceptance of religion to one that they regard as systematic, logical, and relevant."[142] He observes that certain people perceive traditional Chinese practices as "illogical" and "irrational" and prefers a belief system that they regard as more "rational." By rational, they mean a religion of the "book," whereby one can study it systematically. The textual basis of Christianity, in particular, is favored because coverts favor critical, rational, and thinking processes that reflect the Singaporean educational system.[143] Thus, the emphasis on the intellectual aspect of religion underscores the "rationalization" process. For

---

140. Tong, *Rationalizing Religion*; Tong, "Rationalization of Religion," 198–212
141. Tong, *Rationalizing Religion*, 82.
142. Ibid., 4.
143. Ibid.

Tong, "Rationalization involves the clarification, specification, and systematization of the ideas which men have concerning their reason for being."[144]

Concomitant to the process of rationalization is the "demystification" of what some perceive as certain "irrationalities" of religious beliefs and practices. Tong observes, in particular, the filtering out of "folk beliefs." Converts from traditional Chinese religions to Christianity will probably approach their newfound faith with "a more philosophical, and critical view of religion."[145] Moreover, "There is a process of questioning or at least, an attempt to locate justification for the beliefs and rituals of the religion, a search for verifiable truths."[146] As traditional Chinese religions, such as Taoism and Buddhism, have lost members to Christianity, they have modified their beliefs over the years to be more rational in order to compete for their market share. This is what Tong means by religious "competition."[147] As religions become more rational, a process of "differentiation" is also evident among traditional religions, whereby they become more distinct from their former amorphous or eclectic manifestations.[148] In this milieu of religious differentiation and competition, Christianity is often stigmatized by adherents of traditional Chinese religions as "Western" in orientation and associated with the English-educated population.[149] Lastly, Tong points out that "the co-existence of so many religions in close proximity has also resulted in a degree of hybridization of religions." Religious rituals have also been modified and adapted to local culture.[150]

For Tong, rationalization does not indicate the decline of religion in Singapore but rather its transformation and the role religion plays in the human lives.[151] He observes in Singapore a couple of important trends: (1) a rationalizing of Christianity among its adherents; and (2) a conversion process where rationalization plays an important role in religious switching. Perhaps the converts themselves are unaware that the intellectualization of the Singapore population and its impact on the overall social structure of society actually play a significant role in determining one's religious choice.[152]

144. Ibid., 5.
145. Ibid.
146. Ibid., 6.
147. Ibid., 7.
148. Ibid.
149. Ibid., 8.
150. Ibid., 9.
151. Ibid., 5.
152. Woods, "Geographies of Religious Conversion," 442–43.

Tong's study is significant because it examines data on conversion first collected in 1920 to recent times, and indicates major religious shifts in Singapore. However, findings on the social structural and organizational aspects of Christianity in Singapore began to emerge as early as 1988 in governments reports prepared for the Ministry of Community Development.[153] What accounts for the decrease in adherents of Chinese religions from 72.8 percent in 1920 to 51 percent in 2000? What accounts for the increase in the number of Christians, especially among younger Chinese Singaporeans, from 5 percent in 1920 to 14.6 percent in 2000? In contrast to previous theories that tend to focus on transcendent faith as the reason for Christian conversion, Tong offers a sociological analysis of religious change in Singapore.

The basis of Tong's notion of rationalization is the Weberian thesis that one of the main features of a modern society is the process of continuous rationalization. Society as a whole tends toward *zweckrational* organization, whereby traditional and affective actions as determined by habits and emotions are replaced by rational actions shaped by emerging conscious ideas. According to Weber, "One of the most important aspects of the process of rationalization of action is the substitution for the unthinking acceptance of ancient custom for deliberate adaptation to situations in terms of self-interests."[154] Tong explains, "As conscious ideas emerge in the orientation of action, society tends towards rational action."[155]

Moreover, rationalization is intricately connected to religion. As modern societies are transformed structurally, religions are also transformed to meet the new ethical and intellectual challenges of modernity. In that sense, rationalizing religion involves the "clarification, specification, and systematization of the ideas which men have concerning their reason for being."[156] Thus, modernization precipitates religious conversion from traditional or so-called inferior religions (e.g., animism and ancestral worship) to superior rational religions (e.g., Christianity).

An important assumption of Weberian rationalization of religion is the concept of the "disenchantment of the world," in which he insists that in the modern world "there are no mysterious incalculable forces that come into play, but rather that one can, in principle, master all things by calculation. One need no longer have recourse to magical means in order to master

---

153. Tong, *Trends in Traditional Chinese Religion*, 21–13; Tong, *Religious Conversion and Revivalism*, 32–33.

154 Weber, *Economy and Society*, 30.

155. Tong, *Rationalizing Religion*, 5.

156. Ibid.

or implore the spirits, as did the savage for whom such mysterious powers exist."[157]

Tong's argument that traditional Chinese religions are being replaced as a result of the rationalization of religion is supported by several observations. One, the uniqueness of the Singapore context demonstrates that religion and ethnicity are closely correlated, with Hinduism and Islam confined respectively to Indian and Malay communities. People of Chinese descent, which constitute about 75 percent of the total population, are the most heterogeneous of the three major ethnic groups and follow one of three trends: (1) conversion to Christianity, (2) shift to no religion, and (3) rationalization of traditional Chinese religions. Taoism and Buddhism are transformed over the years from "non-proselytizing" to outreach-oriented religions.[158]

Two, the rationalization of religion in Singapore is also evident by the observation that those who convert to Christianity are primarily from a specific socio-demographic sector—young, Chinese, English-educated, and affluent.[159] The major reason for conversion among this group is their perception of Christianity as a rational religion in contrast to the perception of Chinese religions as irrational. Thus, Christian conversion is an identity marker for educational, social, and occupational mobility. Taoism and Buddhism, in particular, are increasingly rationalized and transformed in order to compete for religious followers. This, in turn, spurs intellectual competition among religions in Singapore.[160]

According to Tong, Christian conversion is very complex, and involves both emotional and intellectual elements. Germane to the discussion on the perception of Christianity as a rational religion, Tong notes that intellectual conversion is more prevalent in Singapore, because converts are more exposed to the critical and scientific mode of analysis characteristic of Western systems of education.[161] In contrast, traditional Chinese religions are renounced because they do not offer codified systems of belief, nor authoritative scriptures.

The third important reason why younger Chinese Singaporeans are converting from Chinese religions to Christianity is due to the modernization of society. Tong argues that the Christian conversion process is facilitated by Singapore's modern social environment, which emphasizes

157. Ibid., 114.
158. Ibid., 13.
159. Ibid., 9–10.
160. Ibid., 6–7.
161. Ibid., 113.

voluntarism in decision-making, exposure to various religious options, and an educational system that emphasizes scientific and critical thinking.[162] Traditional Chinese religions, "based upon the principles of obligatory-ness and duty," are fading away because modern Singapore is steadily characterized by voluntarism.[163] In the environment of modernity, ideas and religions are contested, as alternative options are made available. As the modern world undergoes the process of rationalization, traditional religions are transformed from largely habitual practices to actions shaped by conscious ideas. The crux of Tong's argument is that religious conversion does not involve the total denial of one's religious past but often results in the hybridization of religious beliefs and practices.[164]

Tong cites the process of "McDonaldization" as an example of rationalization in which education, occupation, health care, politics, family life, and religion are impacted. The principles of rationalization on society include efficiency, calculability, predictability, increased control, and the use of nonhuman technology. For Tong, rationalization refers to the functional aspect of religion in society as opposed to the philosophical or theological reflection of religion. He states, "It is important to note that rationalization does not mean the decline of the significance of religion, rather that there are changes in the nature of religion and the role of religion in human lives."[165] Simply stated, the rationalization of religion attempts to explain the what, why, and how of religious change in the throes of modernization. Tong concludes that the processes of industrialization and modernization have not led to extreme secularization. Religious involvement remains very high in Singapore.[166]

Beyond the fact of the rationalization of religion, Tong observes that conversion to Christianity in Singapore occurs primarily among people of Chinese descent. Thus, he assesses the relationship between religion and ethnicity, and the way in which religion functions in ethnic identity formation. The strong correlation between ethnicity and religion among adherents of Hinduism and Islam means that there is a greater cultural resistance for both Indians and Malays to convert to another religion. People of Chinese descent display the greatest heterogeneity of all the major ethnic groups in Singapore.[167] Social scientists observe, on the one hand, that tradi-

---

162. Ibid., 5.
163. Ibid., 115.
164. Ibid., 78.
165. Ibid., 5, 114.
166. Ibid., 265.
167. Ibid., 62.

tional religions are less of an ethnic identity marker for the Chinese. Hence, there is less resistance to convert to another religion.[168] On the other hand, there seems to be a strong relationship between religion and social class among Chinese Singaporeans, which is reflected in education, language, and upward mobility as factors for conversion.[169] The latter point needs to be examined more carefully in terms of accounting for Christian identity formation in Singapore.

For example, does becoming a follower of Jesus Christ necessarily negate one's ethnic (e.g., Chinese) and national (e.g., Singaporean) identities? Tong argues "that a switch in religion does not always necessitate a denial of the previous religious outlook. There is a cultural element involved here. Conversion to another religion does not mean the denial of one's own culture."[170] Dissatisfaction with one's parents' religion is identified as a typical reason for a Chinese to convert to Christianity.[171] However, the fact that many Chinese Christians in Singapore are not baptized indicates their continued respect for their parents' religious traditions and the assumption of accepting baptism as tantamount to giving up one's culture.[172] Conversion to Christianity, thus, involves "a modification in the theology of the religion to fit the local historical and environmental factors."[173] Tong concludes, "Thus, in Singapore, conversion does not mean the total denial of a past identity and the acquisition of a completely new one. Rather, there is an accommodation between the new religious identity and the cultural forms from which the individual is socialized from young."[174] In other words, religious conversion often results in a hybridization of beliefs and ritual behavior.

Religions in Singapore

Traditional Chinese religions are receding in Singapore, and have been for a number of years. It can be surmised that one of the reasons for the growing negative perception of traditional Chinese religion is that its nature, history, and role in Singapore society are still relatively undocumented, at least on a scholarly level.

168. Ibid., 65.
169. Ibid., 74, 82.
170. Ibid., 10.
171. Ibid., 110.
172. Ibid., 11, 117.
173. Ibid., 11.
174. Ibid., 117.

Those who are less-educated and who represent the lower socioeconomic groups tend toward Taoism.[175] As early as 1988, qualitative and quantitative research findings reveal that only 7 percent of the Chinese with Chinese-education became Christians, while 25 percent of those with English-education were converted to Christianity.[176] Researchers also note that Chinese-educated individuals reject Christianity for two main reasons: (1) the exclusivistic truth claims of Christianity, and (2) the perception that Christianity is a Western religion, and, thus, more suitable to the English-educated young people Singapore. The implication is that religion is divided on "social-structural differences between Christians and non-Christians."[177] Chinese-speaking individuals opt on remaining in Chinese religion. But what exactly constitutes as traditional Chinese religion?

In a review of past studies on Chinese religions in Singapore, Tong notes that anthropological works have primarily been descriptive of ritualistic practices, failing to provide comprehensive and systematic studies on Chinese religion in Singapore. The shortcoming of these initial studies is that they only provide "snapshots of ritual life in Singapore."[178] For example, Marjorie Topley's seminal study, *Vegetarian Houses in Singapore*, focuses on the activities of a group of intentionally celibate women dedicated to operating vegetarian houses in order to provide security for one another in old age. In doing so, Topley argues that these houses served as "death benefits" for "arranging funerals, maintaining burial grounds and looking after the soul tablets."[179] Leon Comber's *Ancestor Worship in Malaya* describes the functions of Chinese funerary rituals from the preparation for the journey to the journey itself, paraphernalia of the departure, and mourning rites.[180] Maurice Freedman's study focuses on the relationship between religion and kinship, arguing that the practice of ancestor worship is essentially "the ritualization of filial piety."[181]

Beyond the limitation of these initial descriptive studies, more recent sociological studies have attempted to relate religion to Singapore society. For example, Tong's 1989 study on Chinese rituals focuses not on belief or practice per se, but how they reveal the nature of the relationship between power and knowledge in Chinese society. That is, the notion of power is

---

175. Tong, "Religious Trends and Issues," 28.
176. Tong, *Traditional Chinese Religion*, 12.
177. Ibid., 13.
178. Tong, "Religion," 380.
179. Ibid., 375–76.
180. Tong, "Religion," 376.
181. Freedman, *Study of Chinese Society*.

linked to the control of rituals relegated to the religious specialists who have insight of sacred knowledge.[182] Also notable is Vivienne Wee's 1976 study on Chinese religious beliefs and rituals. Using canonical Buddhism as a base-line for comparison, Wee argues that the form of Buddhism practiced in Singapore is not consistent with prescribed Buddhist literature but reflects a syncretized religion, combining elements of Buddhism, Taoism, Confucianism, ancestor worship, and folk religion.[183]

By way of conclusion, two points can be made regarding the study of Chinese religion in Singapore. Firstly, with the exceptions of Wee and Tong, most of the studies are descriptions of Chinese rituals and practices but do not attempt to connect them to the larger contexts of Chinese religion, culture, and society.[184] An important question that needs to be addressed is whether the negative perception of Chinese religion in Singapore could be nuanced had there been more comprehensive studies made available on the subject, detailing its nature, history, and role in the shaping of Singapore society. Secondly, most of the studies on Chinese religion focus primarily on its manifestation in Singapore but do not attempt to explain if and how they were transformed from their founding days in China.[185] In other words, the relationship between Chinese religion in Singapore and Chinese religion in China—in terms of their continuities and discontinuities—need to be examined.

As Singapore is comprised of people from immigrant origins, Chinese religion was transplanted from China with the arrival of Chinese migrants beginning in the early nineteenth century. Numerous temples, representing different Chinese dialect groups, were founded during that time.[186] Little research, however, has been done to account for how Chinese religion was transformed since being transplanted from China.[187] In its Singapore manifestation, the nature of traditional Chinese religion is highly "eclectic" to say the least.[188] Of all major ethnic groups represented in Singapore, the Chinese population is most heterogeneous when it comes to religious affiliation.[189] The label, "Chinese religion," is a generic category used to indicate

---

182. Tong, "Religion," 381.
183. Ibid., 382.
184. Ibid., 383.
185. Ibid., 384.
186. Ibid., 29.
187. Ibid., 384.
188. Tong, "Religious Trends and Issues," 31.
189. Ibid., 40.

the various beliefs adhered to by Chinese people, including Buddhism and "Shenism" (神教).

According to Tong, different researchers have used various nomenclatures to describe traditional Chinese religion, including "Shenism," "anonymous religion," "religion of the masses," and "Chinese folk religion."[190] Citing the 1976 study by Vivienne Wee on Chinese rituals and beliefs, which uses Buddhism as a basis for comparison, Tong characterizes Chinese religion in Singapore as a variation of "non-canonical" Buddhism in contrast to "canonical" Buddhism expressed in the Theravada and Mahayana traditions. The syncretistic nature of non-canonical Buddhism in Singapore can be further delineated as "Shenism" or "baishen" (拜神).[191] By far, Shenism—a syncretized religion comprising elements of Taoism, folk religion, worship of gods and deities, and ancestral worship—best characterizes traditional Chinese religion along with canonical Buddhism.[192]

A national survey was conducted in 1988 to ascertain the kinds of Chinese rituals practiced by typical Chinese Singaporeans.[193] They include the following: (1) Chinese festivals (including New Year, All Souls Day, Lantern Festival, Rice Dumpling Festival, Hungry Ghost Festival, Mid-Winter Solstice Festival, Double Nine Festival, and Reunion of the Seven Fairy and Cowherd Festival), (2) worship at home of popular deities (including *Guan Yin* [觀音], *Dabe Gong* [大伯公], Buddha [佛], and *Guan Gong* [關公]), (3) birth rituals, (4) wedding rituals, and (5) death rituals.[194]

Research indicates that younger Singaporeans abhor the practice of Chinese rituals for various reasons or trends.[195] (1) They are meaningless to the educated, English-speaking person because they are essentially promulgated through duty and imitation.[196] (2) Chinese-speaking individuals, who favor Shenism or Buddhism, are more likely to practice customs and rituals.[197] (3) The general attitude toward Chinese rituals is that they are too complex to understand and are largely the products of "old-fashioned superstitions." Moreover, they are too expensive to maintain and are in need of

---

190. Ibid., 31.
191. Ibid.
192. Tong, *Traditional Chinese Religion*, 3.
193. Ibid., 19.
194. Ibid., 19–30.
195. Ibid., 30.
196. Ibid., 31–33.
197. Ibid., 33.

simplification or eradication.[198] (4) Beyond religious meanings, Chinese rituals are significant primarily because they signify cultural identification.[199]

As researchers have pointed out, the religious landscape in Singapore has shifted in recent decades. A noticeable trend is recognized in the substantial increase in the number of Christians and the corresponding decline in the number of people who adhere to traditional Chinese religion.[200] The percentage of adherents of traditional Chinese religion in Singapore in 1988 was 78.8 percent.[201] That percentage has since declined to 51 percent in 2000.[202] If this trend persists, it will no doubt spur further competition among religions, where respective religions will have to address boundary issues.

Structurally, the switch from Buddhism/Taoism to Christianity occurs within a particular socio-demographic sector of Singapore society, indicating an intertwining of social class and religion. Researchers point to the consistent correlation between adherents of Christianity and social class indicators, such as age, education, language, income, and occupation.[203] While Christianity is still considered as a minority religion in Singapore when compared with tradition Chinese religions, what is significant regarding the emerging influence of Christianity is its success in reaching the younger, predominate Chinese population, affluent, and better-educated sector of Singapore.[204] In other words, the success and potential of Christianity's influence in Singapore must not be measured by the number or percentage of religious adherents alone, but the kind of people the church is attracting.

Sociologists surmise that religious conversion will continue to manifest a "demographic structure," if current trends persist. On one level, the strict correlation of ethnicity and religion in religious conversion could continue to be a source of tension, "where the population is differentiated along ethno-religious lines." On another level, the correlation of social class and religion, with Taoists representing lower socioeconomic status and Christians representing higher socioeconomic status, will have to "take into account the strong emotional sentiments that can be attached to religion."[205]

198. Ibid., 38–39.
199. Ibid., 40.
200. Tong, "Religious Trends and Issues," 49.
201. Tong, *Traditional Chinese Religion*, 3.
202. Tong, "Religious Trends and Issues," 37.
203. Ibid., 49.
204. Ibid., 50.
205. Ibid.

These are indeed important matters, because they involve complicated issues related to the nature of religion, religious change, and conversion. The boundaries between religion and culture are distinct, yet fluid. Proper understanding of these and related matters will have to involve not only further research but require Christians to involve themselves in inter-ethnic and inter-religious dialogue going forward.

Markers of Christianity as a Rational Religion

Since the central research question of the book focuses on the extent and the ways in which Christianity is perceived as a rational religion that is attractive to the aforementioned socioeconomic sector of the population, it is appropriate to delineate the markers of Christianity as a rational religion. Specifically, how and in what ways is Christianity perceived as a rational religion? Why do Chinese Singaporeans find Christianity so attractive? The following discussion of markers of Christianity as a rational religion is drawn primarily from Tong's 2007 study.

Intellectual Dimension. The intellectual dimension or doctrinal aspect of Christianity is an important marker of Christianity as a rational religion. Converts characterize Christianity as rational because it "provides the truth," or "I cannot prove Christianity wrong." University students, in particular, accept Christianity because it is perceived as a rational religion.[206] Thus, in probing people's perception of rationality, it is important to ascertain what they mean by "truth" and the criteria used in adjudicating competing truth claims.

By using the term "rational" to describe their religion of choice, what Singaporeans really mean is that they prefer a religion which they can actively evaluate its validity for themselves. In the gradual course of conversion, this evaluation process involves both intellectual and affective aspects of Christianity.[207] Moreover, Christianity's emphasis on Bible study, whereby individuals can explore for themselves the validity of its truth claims, indicates a modern preference for "active" evaluation rather than "passive" acceptance of faith.[208] As one is confronted with religious options, he or she shifts from passive acceptance to active search for meaning. Notably, the decision to convert involves not only a view of religion as a "problem solving mechanism," but indicates one's attempt to align religion with self-identity

---

206. Tong, *Rationalizing Religion*, 104.
207. Ibid., 105.
208. Ibid.

and worldview or as an avenue to facilitate identity transformation.[209] In contrast to Taoism, for example, Christianity is regarded as a rational religion because it encourages followers to cognitively and affectively evaluate religious truth claims. The conversion process is a "sequential trying out of new beliefs and identities in an effort to resolve felt difficulties."[210]

Meeting Spiritual Needs. While the intellectual aspect of conversion is noted, a common reason for conversion is the spiritual dimension of Christianity, according to Tong.[211] In contrast to Chinese religion, which focuses on performance of rituals as one's duty, Christianity is favored because of its focus on knowing God, who, in the person of Jesus Christ, died for the sins of the world and sent the Holy Spirit to indwell believers. Believers attest to the reality of sin in their lives. By accepting Jesus, they believe their sins are forgiven and enter into a relationship with Christ.[212] With its emphasis on a relationship with God, Christianity is appealing because it is "intrinsic experience" as opposed to "extrinsic performance" characteristic of Chinese religions.[213] Through the person and reality of the Holy Spirit, Singaporeans experience God in a dynamic and personal way.[214] Singapore's religious diversity, where people routinely encounter the spirit realm, the emotional or experiential dimension of Christianity is very significant.

In a sense, the intellectual aspect of Christianity is affirmed and validated by personal experience with God. Christianity is attractive because it offers the promise of eternal life, providing converts with a sense of security in the future life.[215] In facing the challenges of everyday life, converts experience answered prayers, miracles, and their spiritual needs are met.[216] Christianity's emphasis on the spiritual dimension of religion is favored because it serves the all-important purpose of helping people to cognitively and affectively make sense of the world in which they live.

Christianity is perceived as a rational religion because it provides meaning of life in a world filled with trouble, suffering, and uncertainty.[217] As a modern religion, Christianity serves as a framework through which people can interpret the events of everyday life and find meaning out of

209. Ibid.
210. Ibid.
211. Ibid., 110.
212. Ibid.
213. Ibid., 110, 119.
214. Ibid., 103.
215. Ibid., 118–19.
216. Ibid., 119.
217. Ibid.

apparent chaos. It explains problems of humanity and gives power for endurance within a troubled world. Christianity also offers moral boundaries without which a society cannot exist or function. In sum, "Religion provides man with the cognitive, affective, and moral capacity to deal with the world he lives in."[218] Christianity's emphases on the individual, active faith, and personal experience indicate the modern quality of religion in Singapore.

Social and Relational Benefits. In contrast to traditional Chinese religion, which tends to be amorphous, unstructured, and private in nature, Singaporeans favor Christianity because religious faith is validated and lived out in community. It can be argued that Christianity is a rational religion to the extent that it facilitates socialization, which, in turn, shapes identity formation, particularly through the social and organized events. The social and relational benefits of organized Christian ministries are perceived as relevant because Christian converts were socialized in Western-oriented educational systems.[219] In qualitative interviews, informants who converted to Christianity often credit their decision because of peer influence. In fact, the majority of those converted made their decision based upon the influence of friends or family members, who care for and love one another.[220] Without a doubt, peer influence and the social benefits offered by churches are immeasurable, where people experience community life and mutual care and concern.[221] Converts note the social benefits that promote a "sense of belonging," along with fellowship groups and other ministries that meet a variety of needs.[222]

Holistic Orientation. Lastly, Christianity is a rational religion to the extent that identity formation takes place when people involve themselves in comprehensive activities. The church plays an important role in mobilizing people to integrate religious and non-religious activities to meet the holistic needs of all its members and potential followers. Such efforts as outreach, mission and evangelism meet not only spiritual, physical and social needs, but serve to reinforce religious belief and continuous socialization.[223] Singaporeans who convert to Christianity from Buddhism and Taoism do so because they find Chinese religion amorphous. Christianity, as expressed in its social and organizational dimensions, offers a much more attractive

---

218. Ibid.
219. Ibid., 114, 123.
220. Ibid., 100.
221. Ibid.
222. Ibid., 120–21.
223. Ibid., 111, 120–23.

alternative. Religion serves its purpose best when it "provides man with the cognitive, affective, and moral capacity to deal with the world he lives in."[224]

Markers of Chinese Identity

Now that markers for Christianity as a rational religion have been identified, how would one determine if those are Western in derivation or uniquely Asian in nature? In rejecting traditional Chinese religion, are Singaporeans opting for a Western form of Christianity as depicted in missiological literature? In addressing these pertinent questions, one must keep in mind that Singaporeans who convert to Christianity rationalize their behavior by insisting that they reject Chinese religion but not Chinese culture or identity.[225] One way to hold Christian faith and Chinese identity in tension is "an accommodation between the new religious identity and the cultural forms from which the individual is socialized from young."[226]

In Tong Chee Kiong and Chan Kwok Bun's "Once Face, Many Masks: The Singularity and Plurality of Chinese Identity," the authors observe that Chinese ethnic identity in Singapore is "in flux."[227] Singaporeans, whether from Chinese-speaking or English-speaking backgrounds, disagree on the extent to which language, territoriality, and religion play in ethnic identity formation. Despite fragmentation and multiplicity, there is a growing consensus that "ascriptive elements," such as phenotype, bloodline, and lineage, are becoming the "core features" of ethnic identity[228]

Ritualistic Practices. A primary factor concerns the negotiation of traditional Chinese religions and practices. Once viewed as the "homogenizing" factor for Chinese identity, religion—encoded in terms of filial piety, duty, and family lineage—is fading in influence.[229] One main concern, on the part of Chinese parents, is that their children would not neglect to provide proper funeral rites for them if their children converted to Christianity.

In a recent survey on Protestant clergy's attitude toward non-Christian rituals, the findings show that clergy found many practices unacceptable. These include: (1) following a funeral procession led by a Chinese medium or Buddhist monk, (2) bowing to a deceased family member during a

    224. Ibid., 119.
    225. Tong and Chan, "One Face, Many Masks," 375; Tong, *Rationalizing Religion*, 117.
    226. Ibid.
    227. Tong and Chan, "One Face, Many Masks," 364.
    228. Ibid., 384.
    229. Ibid., 372.

funeral service, (3) eating food offered to family idols, (4) holding joss sticks as a funeral rite, and (5) placing a flower at an altar in honor of one's ancestors. Among the two practices which received highest disapproval include the use of joss sticks or religious artifacts.[230]

The central question concerns how to decide between acceptable and unacceptable forms of ritualistic practices. In teaching their church members, those pastors explain the need to separate cultural expressions from religious practices. Those practices which are clearly cultural forms are negotiable, while religious rituals are forbidden. Sociologists point out the demarcation between those is not easily distinguishable and there is little or no consensus as to how they go about determining it.[231] The general rule is to ask Chinese religious leaders for their understanding of particular practices to determine the distinction between cultural and religious boundaries.[232] There is an attempt on the part of pastors to negotiate the tension of the particularity of Christianity and the need to live harmoniously with religious others in a multi-religious state. What seems clear, at least from a sociological point of view, is that Christians in Singapore consciously "draw symbolic boundaries" between themselves and religious others and their practices in order to create religious tension. The exclusivity of Christianity in Singapore is responsible for giving its "vitality in a competitive religious economy."[233]

While Singaporean clergymen view participation in ritualistic practices in a more restrictive sense, the general attitude among Chinese Protestant Christian Singaporeans toward ritualistic practices seems much more relaxed. Jeremiah Goh, in his study of seventeen itemized ancestor ritualistic practices, concludes that informants considered eleven practices as acceptable for Christian participation.[234] In particular, the five rites considered unacceptable include burning incense and paper money for the deceased, preparing ritualistic items and setting the altar at a funeral, chanting and holding joss sticks around the coffin, erecting family altars in the home, and offering sacrifice and burning incense at the grave or columbarium.[235] One item was considered undecided. Goh explains that the main reasons for Christian acceptance can be attributed to spiritual maturity and the

---

230. Mathews, "Negotiating Christianity," 590–91.
231. Ibid., 594.
232. Ibid., 595.
233. Ibid., 596.
234. Goh, "Practice of Ancestor Rites," 221.
235. Ibid., 167.

fact that Singaporean Christians considered the acceptable rites as cultural, while denouncing the five rites as religious in nature.[236]

Filial Piety. At the heart of Chinese culture is the doctrine of filial piety, which can be expressed in various ways. In fact, one can argue that ancestor worship is the "ritualization of filial piety."[237] On this point, English-speakers view filial piety primarily as a cultural rather than a religious element. Concerning the role religion plays in identity formation, Chinese-educated individuals insist that one must follow Chinese religious customs, rituals, and practices. Predictably, the English-educated Singaporeans deemphasize those as defining markers but regard filial piety and observations of key rituals, such as Chinese New Year or Mid-Autumn Festival as "core values."[238]

Language. Chinese-educated individuals view the Chinese language—written and spoken—as an indispensable element to defining identity, while the English-educated tend to deemphasize the role of language as a marker for identity.[239]

Lineage. In addition to filial piety, both the Chinese-educated and the English-educated agree that descent—the perpetuation of the family name through sons—also constitutes a core Chinese cultural value.[240] With regards to territoriality, the Chinese-educated Singaporeans still consider China as their homeland, while English-educated Chinese individuals insist on "disembedding" of space for defining their Chinese identity. For them, there is a clear demarcation between a "Singaporean-Chinese" and a "China-Chinese," while allowing Singaporean-Chinese to identify with the Chinese community world-wide.[241]

Ascriptive Features. With such divergent or multiplicity of markers of identity, one wonders how Singaporeans reconcile those ambiguities. Tong and Chan observe that Chinese Singaporeans tended to use "ascriptive features" to define Chinese identity. Phenotype, lineage, and bloodline serve to create strict sociological boundaries. In other words, people are "born Chinese" and cannot become "un-Chinese," though some may be regarded as "inferior" Chinese if they do not fulfill all the markers of Chinese identity. Moreover, people from other races cannot become Chinese, even if they speak Chinese or adopt "Chinese cultural values."[242] There is a strong sense

236. Ibid., 221–22.
237. Tong, "Religion," 378.
238. Tong and Chan, "One Face, Many Masks," 380.
239. Ibid.
240. Ibid.
241. Ibid., 384.
242. Ibid.

of exclusion and inclusion within the Chinese community in Singapore, while members struggle to accept diverse and multiple concepts of what it means to be Chinese.[243]

Summary

From the foregoing discussion on Tong's discussion on the "rationalization" of religion in Singapore, it is necessary to clarify how that term is used and understood in the context of Singapore, and how it compares with the missiological critique of Western theology in Asia as too "rational." To be sure, Tong's usage of the term "rationalization," at least in its Weberian derivation, refers to the process of religious change rooted in modernization and globalization. In that sense, the term must not be confused with the critique of "rationalistic" theology as in preoccupation with intellectual concerns. However, Tong argues that rationalizing religion in the Singapore context refers to the transformation of how people perceive the validity of religion as systematic, logical, and relevant in contrast to the so-called irrationality of traditional Chinese religions. In that sense, Tong's notion of "rational" does indicate the intellectual dimension of religion.

On the one hand, Tong's thesis—that people are converted due to their perception of Christianity as a rational religion—does seem to counter the prevalent criticism of rationalistic theology as inappropriate for Asia. On the other hand, the preference for rational religion among younger Chinese individuals as a factor for Christian conversion experience may be unique to Singapore because of the country's colonial experience and Western educational system. Certainly, Singaporeans who are not afforded such an experience may view Christianity as a Western religion—too rationalistic, alien, and irrelevant for their life experience. Such a stigma will hinder effective evangelism and conversion to Christianity. In that context, the missiological criticism of the inappropriateness of Western, rationalistic theology in Asia will certainly find its champions. What the Singapore context does demonstrate is that missiologists can no longer offer a general criticism of Western Christianity in Asia without giving due consideration to the rationalizing effects of modernization and globalization on religion.

---

243. Ibid.

5

Research Methodology

General Procedure

THE PRESENT STUDY EXAMINES the extent to which the perception of Christianity as a rational and/or Western religion serves as a factor in Christian conversion among younger Chinese people in Singapore. Recent sociological research on religious conversion in Singapore appears to challenge the common missiological assumption that Western rationalistic theology is inappropriate for Asia because it contributes to the perception of Christianity as a Western religion. Tong, in particular, argues that religions in Singapore are undergoing a process of rationalization in response to the effects of modernization and globalization. In the process of transformation, religion is intellectualized, as one's acceptance of religious faith is based upon active reflection and thinking as opposed to passive acceptance based upon oral tradition characteristic of traditional Chinese religion.[1] The research focuses on Singaporeans' perception of Christianity as a more "rational, systematic, and intellectual religion" as a key factor for their conversion from Buddhism and Taoism, which, in contrast, are perceived as irrational and illogical.[2]

The research methodology involves reviewing three domains of literature, including (1) contextualization of Christianity in Asia, (2) modernization, globalization, and religious change, and (3) Christian conversion and identity in Singapore. The purpose of literature reviews is to determine what writers are saying about the nature of the missiological problem in Asia, the subject of religious change in the midst of modernization and globalization, and how these processes impact Christian conversion and identity in

1. Tong, *Rationalizing Religion*, 267,
2. Ibid., 115.

Singapore. With these domains of literature as the backdrop, the present study seeks to address the central research question: *To what extent and in what ways is the perception of Christianity as a rational and/or Western religion a factor in Christian conversion among younger Chinese people in Singapore?*

In addressing the research question, the study uses the mode of qualitative research—in-depth interviews—to investigate why Singaporeans are converting to Christianity in recent decades. Qualitative research is primarily about exploring issues, interpreting phenomena, and answering questions. It seeks to answer the "why" as well as the "how" of its topic through analysis of gathered information.[3] Concerning the methodology of qualitative research, one writer states, "Many qualitative researchers follow a naturalistic approach, often guided by a social construction approach that focuses on how people perceive their worlds and how they interpret their experiences. These researchers argue that people construct their own realities based on their experiences and interpretations."[4] Various data-gathering methods exist. Common ones include participant observation, narrative analysis, and interviews. Qualitative interviews can be conducted in various formats, including focus groups, internet interviews, and informal and structured interviews.[5] This book uses primarily qualitative interviews for data-gathering. In doing so, in-depth interviews seek to reconstruct events, challenge long-held assumptions, explore social processes, describe change diachronically, and examine the complexity of lived experiences in the real world.[6]

A particularly helpful method in conducting interviews is narrative analysis. This form of analysis focuses less on the content of conversations and more on how or the ways in which people tell narratives or stories.[7] Narrative inquiry seeks to address the complexities and subtleties of human experience that people tend to organize into narratives. As a research method, it provides a framework through which to examine the ways humans experience the world through their stories.[8] Special attention is given to the descriptions of human experiences, how interviewees make sense out of their experiences, how those experiences are interpreted, and how those experiences are conveyed. The ways in which narratives are told can reveal

---

3. Rubin and Rubin, *Qualitative Interviewing*, 3.
4. Ibid.
5. Ibid., 25–30.
6. Ibid., 3–5.
7. Ibid., 28–29.
8. Webster and Mertova, *Using Narrative Inquiry*, 1.

much about one's emphases, blind-spots, moral values, and cultural beliefs.[9] In that sense, narrative inquiry does not attempt to explain objective life experiences, but seeks to give an account of how life is perceived in a holistic manner.[10] This distinction underscores the differences between "positivist" and "constructionist" paradigms of research. The prior assumes the human search for objective universal truth, while latter assumes that people construct perceptions of reality.[11]

Interview Process and Data Analysis

The research involved private qualitative interviews as the basis for information gathering. To ensure that the research question was adequately addressed and high quality data were gathered, it is imperative that informants offer recent, first-hand, credible, thorough, and nuanced accounts of their experiences.[12] Specifically, thirty-five interviews were conducted with an interview protocol on Chinese Singaporeans who converted to Christianity from Buddhist and/or Taoist religious backgrounds. The general sequence of the questions posed to informants include: (1) personal information such as age, educational background, occupation, date of conversion, and church or denominational affiliation, (2) Christian conversion experience, describing key events or turning points, along with people who influenced them, (3) view and attitude toward their religious background in Chinese religions such as Buddhism and or Taoism and their practices, (4) reasons for conversion to Christianity or why they regarded Christianity as the true religion in comparison to Buddhism and/or Taoism, (5) perception of Christianity as a Western religion in Singapore, and (6) personal journey in Christian faith and identity formation, marking continuities and discontinuities with their religious past.

The thirty-five informants were selected on the following criteria: (1) individuals of Chinese ethnicity roughly between fifteen and thirty-five years old; (2) converted to Christianity from non-Christian homes and traditional Chinese religions within the last ten years or so; and (3) educated in English systems from either local or foreign institutions representing various levels of academic achievement. Preference was given to those who were converted to Christianity within the last five years, as their first-hand

---

9. Rubin and Rubin, *Qualitative Interviewing*, 29.
10. Webster and Mertova, *Using Narrative Inquiry*, 3.
11. Rubin and Rubin, *Qualitative Interviewing*, 15–17.
12. Ibid., 60.

experiences were still relatively recent and fresh.[13] Individuals who were trained in technical or scientific fields were especially appropriate.

The individuals interviewed included twenty males and fifteen females, and were selected from churches across denominational lines, including those from Charismatic and Pentecostal backgrounds. The researcher initially approached church leaders and pastors via email correspondence to identity suitable informants. However, this method did not prove effective, as it yielded no response. As a recourse, the researcher contacted friends and acquaintances to help identify potential interviewees. Upon their recommendation, the researcher contacted potential informants to gain their consent to be interviewed. A letter was then sent out, followed by telephone calls, to explain in detail what the research project entailed. Informants under the age of eighteen were not interviewed without permission from a parent or legal guardian. When necessary, on-site visits were arranged in order to further explain the nature and importance of such a study. The thirty-five interviews were conducted in a variety of venues, including private offices and open public places. When interviewing female informants, the researcher primarily used public venues, such as restaurants and coffee houses, to avoid making them feel uneasy.

It must be noted that while the researcher prescribed a set of criteria for selecting informants, there were occasions when contacts set up interviews with people who deviated a bit from certain criteria in terms of age and date of conversion. For the most part, however, most of the people interviewed were between the ages of fifteen and thirty-five. Additionally, the researcher often found it inappropriate at times to ask female informants for their age as part of the interview process. Moreover, only a few people interviewed represent mega-churches in Singapore. Perhaps due to the on-going trial of a prominent mega-church pastor on charges of misappropriation of church funds, mega-church members were reluctant, if not resistant, to be interviewed for fear of revealing information that may impact public opinion of the church along with the pastor and his wife.

All interviews were recorded and transcribed.[14] In probing human experiences, the interviews aim for detail, depth, vividness, and nuance, and richness. Detail refers to the "fine points" or the "particulars" of a subject. Depth can include history, context, and contrasting points of view. The quest for vividness refers to descriptions and word pictures that elicit emotions. Nuance refers to subtlety that goes beyond stark contrasts and right or

---

13. Ibid.
14. Ibid., 100–101.

wrong categories. Lastly, the quality of richness refers to extended descriptions or stories that have multiple themes.[15]

Computer software was used to code the data.[16] A written introduction was read to each informant before the start of an interview. No time limit was placed on interviews, though each ranged approximately between forty-five to seventy-five minutes in duration. Interviews were conducted with utmost discretion. The information gathered was held in strict confidence in order to protect the anonymity of the individual informant and the reputation of the church represented by the informant.

Once the qualitative data were collected and coded, the study engaged both theological and social science literature to underpin and interpret gathered information. The study then proceeded to analyze the research findings derived from qualitative interviews that probed the extent to which Chinese Singaporeans converted to Christianity because they perceived Christianity as a rational and/or a Western religion. This was determined by comparing markers of Christianity as a rational religion as perceived by Chinese Singapore and the notions of rationalistic Christianity as depicted by missiologists. What are the continuities and discontinuities between what Singaporeans perceive of Christianity as a rational religion and what missiologists view as rationalistic theology and Western Christianity? By clarifying issues, the study seeks to provide a more nuanced understanding of Christianity as a rational religion in relation to its impact on shaping Christian identity in Singapore.

For the purpose of this study and consistent with the claims of social scientists, the markers of "rational" Christianity can now be summarized. They include the following elements: (1) an overall dissatisfaction with Chinese religious rituals as irrational, (2) a spiritual relationship with God, (3) an intellectual, textual, thinking religion that is systematic, logical, and relevant, (4) social and relational benefits derived from organized activities, and (5) a holistic view of the reality.

For missiologists, the markers of rationalistic and Western theology include: (1) dependence upon Enlightenment rationalism, dualism, individualism, (2) a naturalistic or scientific worldview, (3) detachment from human lived realities, (4) emphasis upon reason, logic and systematic consistency, (5) and focus on abstract ideas that are disconnected from pastoral or spiritual concerns. Ability to speak Mandarin or dialects, practice of Chinese religious rituals, territoriality, and ascriptive features are typically used as markers for Chinese ethnicity or identity. The present study also

15. Ibid., 101–7.
16. Ibid., 192.

probes how Chinese Christians in Singapore contextualize Christianity by reinterpreting traditional Chinese birth, marriage, and death rituals in accordance with biblical teachings, while at the same time seeking to preserve Chinese identity.

Criteria for the Selection of Informants

The criteria for the selection of informants were based upon data of census of population and Tong's quantitative and qualitative data collected over the last twenty years, which depicted a distinct profile of those converting to Christianity. Since the 1950s, religious switching in Singapore occurred primarily in favor of Christianity.[17] According to the 1990 census of population, only 46.3 percent of Christians were born into the faith, while 53.7 percent converted to Christianity from other religions.[18] More significantly, the total number of Christians who converted to Protestant traditions from other religions was 65.9 percent.[19] If Christianity is the primary religion experiencing growth in Singapore, from what religions did it receive its converts? The data from the 1990 census indicate that 45.7 percent of converts came from Taoism and 44 percent came from Buddhism.[20] Converts to Christianity from other religions, including Hinduism (3.1 percent) and Islam (0.5 percent) were fairly minuscule in comparison.[21]

Three key observations can be enumerated with regards to conversion to Christianity. One, Christian conversion takes place within a specific socioeconomic sector of the Singapore population.[22] Indicators of socioeconomic status (SES) include ethnicity, age, gender, education, occupation, and income. The second observation is that this group of people—younger educated affluent Chinese—demonstrates a marked shift in their attitude toward traditional Chinese religion and ritualistic practices as "illogical" and "irrational" in preference for Christianity, which they consider as more "rational."[23] Thus, there seems to be a clear correlation between education and religion, where those who received their education in English-speaking and Western-based environments were more inclined toward Christianity

---

17. Tong, *Rationalizing Religion*, 78–79.
18. Ibid., 79–80.
19. Ibid., 80.
20. Ibid., 81.
21. Ibid.
22. Ibid., 82.
23. Ibid.

than those who were educated in Chinese-speaking schools.[24] Thirdly, religious switching in Singapore is related to social mobility, as those who were better-educated with higher economic status were more inclined to convert to Christianity from traditional Chinese religion. A social class gap, though not always acknowledged, is becoming more apparent between Christians who hold higher social status and those who remain in traditional religions.[25]

The socioeconomic profile of Christians includes such indicators as ethnicity, age, gender, education, income, and occupation. According to the 1990 census of population, conversions to Christianity occurred primarily among people of Chinese descent (14.8 percent), while the percentage of Indians (2.9 percent) and Malays (0.2 percent) were very small.[26] The explanation for this trend is that the heterogeneous nature of traditional Chinese religion is less of a marker of cultural identity. Thus, Chinese Singaporeans are more susceptible to conversion than Indians and Malays, whose cultural identity is intricately bound to Hinduism and Islam respectively.

In terms of age, there seems to be an optimal window of conversion for those between the ages of ten and nineteen (40.0 percent) and twenty and twenty-nine (32 percent). The data indicate that the majority of people converted to Christianity between the ages of fourteen and nineteen (66 percent). Conversely, as people increased in age, there was a corresponding decline in the percentage of conversion. Notably, the conversion rate for people who are sixty years old and above is only 2.2 percent.[27] One can surmise that people between the ages of fifteen and twenty-nine are in a period when they are in secondary, undergraduate or post-graduate educational programs, and are still relatively open to changing their views and convictions.

Gender also seems to be a significant indicator for religious conversion. While the percentages for conversion between male (10.2 percent) and female (12.8 percent) are rather even, the slightly higher percentage of women converting to Christianity is significant. This is especially revealing in view of the fact that in typical Chinese families, ritual practices are generally carried out by women and not by men.[28]

The strong correlation between education and religious conversion is also very apparent in Singapore. Statistics indicate that 40.6 percent of those

24. Ibid.
25. Ibid., 82–83.
26. Ibid., 83.
27. Ibid., 84–85.
28. Ibid., 87.

with university degrees converted from one religion to another, while 28.9 percent of those with upper secondary and polytechnic education switched religions.[29] The percentage for conversion steadily declines for those with corresponding lower levels of educational attainment. The appeal of Christianity, for example, is that Christians perceive it a "rational" religion in contrast to Buddhism and Taoism, which are perceived as "irrational" and "illogical." Tong maintains, "It is this perception of Christianity as a modern, English-based, ethnically neutral religion that partly explains for its attractiveness to the younger generation in Singapore, who are themselves socialized into an English-stream western-oriented educational system."[30]

Other important indicators of socioeconomic status include occupation and income. Researchers point out that there is a distinct correlation between religious conversion and occupation. According to the 1990 census, of all those who converted to Christianity, 28.7 percent represented professional/technical occupations, while 19.0 percent of those in administrative/managerial occupations made the switch.[31] Moreover, the data indicate a drop in conversion rate corresponding with the decline in occupation and income status. In fact, the highest percentage of conversion (21.3 percent) occurred for those with the highest income bracket of S$6,000 and above monthly salary.[32] In sum, religious conversion—mostly from traditional Chinese religion to Christianity—"tends to occur within a particular sector of the population: the younger, better educated, and those from the more prestigious and higher income occupational groups."[33]

The aforementioned discussion highlights the observation that Christian conversion occurs primarily within a specific socioeconomic sector of Singapore society, for those between the ages of fifteen and twenty-nine, and indicates a strong correlation between education and religion. Thus, in selecting informants, the writer of this book sought individuals who not only converted from Buddhism and/or Taoism but those who represent a certain age bracket (roughly between fifteen and thirty-five) and received their education in an English-stream environment.

29. Ibid., 88.
30. Ibid., 91.
31. Ibid., 82.
32. Ibid., 93.
33. Ibid.

6

Research Findings

CURRENT LITERATURE ON CHRISTIAN conversion experience suggests that this phenomenon involves much more than a mere reorientation of personal religious belief. Rather, the process involves the redefinition of self in relation to others.[1] In an effort to gather information about people in social settings, this researcher used the method of qualitative research to explore their opinions, feelings, and beliefs about particular aspects of their lives. The method involved asking questions, listening to the responses, and then asking clarifying questions. The interviews aimed for depth and nuance of understanding as people discussed about their experiences and understanding in specific individual and group situations.[2] This chapter presents the findings or results of the thirty-five interviews conducted with Chinese Singaporeans on their Christian conversion experience in Singapore. The nature of the work is primarily descriptive, summarizing some of the key themes and concepts from discussions with the informants.

Views and Attitudes Toward Chinese Religions and Rituals

In interviewing the thirty-five Chinese Singaporeans who converted to Christianity, the interviewer typically began by probing the informant's view and attitude toward his or her background in Chinese religions and rituals.

---

1. Beckford, "Accounting for Conversion," 253–58; Balch, "Looking behind the Scenes," 137; Snow and Machalek, "Sociology of Conversion," 167–90; Hefner, "World Building," 17; Woods, "Geographies of Religious Conversion," 440.
2. Rubin and Rubin, *Qualitative Interviewing*, 2.

The respondents reported a variety of religious backgrounds from which they converted. A total of thirteen converted from Taoism, six from Buddhism, five from ancestral worship (a form of Taoism), one from Confucianism, eight from some eclectic mixture of those traditions, and two simply said they converted from "Chinese religions." Prominent deities mentioned in the interviews that informants used to worship included *Guan Yin* (觀音) or "goddess of mercy," *Tian Gong* (天公) or "heavenly grandfather," and *Shang Ti* (上帝) or "supreme god." *Guan Yin* is a Buddhist Bodhisattva depicted as a Chinese female deity, placed on altars as a statue, and worshiped in private homes. She is presumably a "sinicized version of the Indian male god, *Avalokitsvera*."[3] She is also revered by Taoists. *Tian Gong* is another name for the Jade Emperor, the highest ranking of the Taoist gods. Because he represents the whole of the heavens, he is not depicted in the form of a statue but by burning incense.[4] *Shang Ti* is generally regarded as the most supreme god in Chinese religious traditions.

For the average Chinese Singaporean, particularly the common working-class "heart-landers," those designations are undefinable. One informant simply said, "They refer to abstract, unidentifiable, and impersonal powers, spirits, or gods." When asked to clarify, one Chinese Singaporean insisted that she would simply repeat the *Hanyu Pinyin* (漢語拼音) and describe their religious connotations, which can vary greatly from person to person. The average Singaporean, who believes in and worships those deities, would typically express awareness of their spiritual reality and power. They worship or pray to them primarily for material blessings, success, fortune, protection, health, and peace, though their identities are largely unknown.

Various religious rituals were practiced by the people interviewed. Most, if not all, informants talked about burning incense, joss sticks and paper, and offering of prayers, as common rituals practiced prior to their conversion. Reportedly, those rituals were practiced both at home and in public temples, though with varied frequency. Food offering to deities and ancestors in the form of statues, idols, and pictures of the deceased set up on altars at home is another common practice characteristic of those from Taoist and ancestral worship backgrounds. In addition to consuming food offered to idols and ancestors, a few mentioned that they drank water containing burnt joss paper. The practice of chanting, which was reported by three informants, was noted as more characteristic of Buddhism. Respondents also observed annually various religious events, including the Hungry

---

3. Tong, *Trends in Traditional Chinese Religion*, 21.
4. Ibid., 21; Tong, "Traditional Chinese Customs," 161.

Ghost Festival, *Qing Ming* (清明節), Mid-Autumn Festival, and the auspicious Chinese New Year celebration.

Moreover, many informants reported that they often visited monks to receive stamps on their clothes for protection. It was not uncommon for people to wear amulets for protection and talismans for good luck. As expected, many informants who experienced a death in his or her family would have participated in Chinese funeral rites to send off their family members with adequate materials and safe passage to the next world. The common funeral rites reported by informants include burning of incense, joss sticks and paper, paper symbols representing material goods sent to the next world, chanting, food offerings, and taking part in the funeral procession. Informants discussed participation in funeral rites as one of the most important and common practices for those from Chinese religions.

Findings on the views and attitudes of the thirty-five interviews are summarized and organized in four main areas, (1) including lack of knowledge or understanding, (2) respect for and obedience to Chinese parents and culture, (3) religious practices in exchange for blessings and results, and (4) compelled by fear for protection. The following quotes of informants' views and attitudes of Chinese religions and practices reflect their opinions prior to Christian conversion, though many statements were expressed in the present tense.

Lack of Knowledge or Understanding

What is significant about the thirty-five interviews is the emergence of an overwhelming consensus that informants did not know or understand their religious beliefs and practices. Moreover, they did not have access to sacred texts or sources as the basis for them, except for a few. One informant said he read the Buddhist scriptures, but did not understand them because they were in ancient Chinese (Transcript #16, 8). Another said he read the *Analects* by Mencius, which he characterized as "humanistic" and "non-transcendent" (Transcript #19, 12). Recalling the years when she did much chanting of Buddhist Sutras in Japanese, a young mother said, "Our whole family, I don't think, has any idea during that time. We just know that by chanting, you will bring good life" (Transcript #7, 2).

As if speaking for everyone regarding his ignorance of Chinese religions, one informant opined, "I think basically you don't really understand and also don't go and find out, but you follow because, you know, we are Asian" (Transcript #29, 6). Asked if he can explain about Buddhism and Taoism, a teacher said, "Not really—like you don't do bad things. You do good to benefit the results. It's a lot more cause and effect" (Transcript #1, 6). When asked whether she understood much about Buddhism, a college student, who came from a Buddhist family, retorted, "Not really. I actually treated it like folklores and stories" (Transcript #12, 9). A computer science student was very candid about her view of going to temple and praying. She said, "Back then, I would just go through the motions. I guess I wasn't really convinced behind the significance of doing things. It always felt like a series of stories or legends that, for example, *Guan Yin* would be watching over me and bless me. And I never understood the basis for it" (Transcript 17, 5–6).

A few informants voiced their perceptions of Chinese religions as irrational, illogical, or something that does not make sense. When asked about her view of Buddhism and Taoism prior to her conversion, one teacher said, "Of course I don't believe in what they teach. I don't believe all these teachings. They don't make sense to me, and some people think it is very logical, but to me no, I don't think so. I cannot accept it" (Transcript 6, 8). She continued, "It is difficult to imagine god as being in so many forms, in form of a kitchen god, in the form of something else. To me, it doesn't make sense. It is not logical either. It is not logical for the god to be so divided in his identity" (Transcript #6, 14).

Another informant voiced his critical opinion of Chinese religions prior to his Christian conversion. Trained as an engineer, he said that his education in the sciences contributed to his view of Chinese religions "as a bit backward, irrational, very much superstitious rather than something that is rational, something that can be explained" (Transcript #4, 4). Much of his skepticism regarding Chinese religions was that people practiced rituals out of fear. They have never read sacred texts on their meaning and that "a lot has to do with trying to appease the unknown" (Transcript #4, 5). An accountancy student noted that he was a "practical" and "very logical" person. As such, he would always consider "whether things make sense or not" (Transcript #32, 7). So when it came to consulting the Chinese zodiac, burning joss sticks, paper houses and other material goods to ancestors, he regarded the rituals as "illogical" (Transcript #32, 7).

A few even snidely remarked that what little they learned about Chinese religions was mediated through watching popular movies or television programs. "I guess my influence was more of the shows on the TV, you know, this is the monkey god," offered one informant (Transcript #3, 2). Another said, "Sometimes we learn what to do from TV and movies, that we burn incense so it's like their food; they smell if they need food" (Transcript #9, 10). When asked if he thought Chinese religions are to be followed or practiced and not to be understood, one informant agreed: "Yeah, that is right. And in fact, a lot of the value systems can be seen in the movies or shows on TV" (Transcript #1, 9). Given the lack of knowledge and understanding of Chinese religions and practices, what motivated informants' participation in Chinese religions and rituals? The following three themes explain their views on the roles and purposes of religions.

A few informants expressed frustration about being offered as god-sons or god-daughters to deities at an early age. For example, one informant talked about his family's strong involvement in Taoist practices and having over one hundred and thirty idols in his home. He recalled that his home was turned into a "home temple," whereby people would come to offer incense and other gifts to the idols. He was brought up in that kind of environment, and people saw "spiritual potential" in him. "It was a very spiritual environment," he said. He was only ten years old and did not understand much at the time but he sensed that he was being groomed. He recalled, "I was the eldest grandchild, so I was supposed to take over the entire temple. I was actually made the god-son of many different deities. I was really into it" (Transcript #2, 2).

Recalling his experience in Buddhism at a young age, another informant said his mother "brought him to the temple all the time." He continued, "We ate vegetarian food, drank burnt talisman water, and I was even offered up to be a god-son to *Guan Yin*" (Transcript #23, 3). "That is my past," he said rather disparagingly. His parents became very angry when he started going to church. "So I was termed as like a traitor, you know, because who is going to carry the ashes when one of them dies" (Transcript #23, 3).

One woman said, regarding her family's background in Taoism, "So my parents were more Taoist. I was frightened at those temples and of the mediums who cut themselves, because I couldn't stand blood." She continued, "Those experiences really haunted me and it was very difficult for me to relate to that religion and I just couldn't believe I was given away by my parents to some temple god where they chop my T-shirt and say I'm becoming one of their god-child. I didn't like to be given away like that" (Transcript #34, 6).

Respect for and Obedience to Chinese Parents and Culture

A correlation exists between the lack of religious understanding and viewing the practice of Chinese religions as obligatory duty. In fact, twenty-two informants discussed performing religious practices for the sake of their parents, in spite of not knowing or understanding them. For those informants, Chinese religions and practices were inherited from their parents and performed out of duty and obligation. In other words, "they just follow" because they were told to do so. Acceptance was merely passive in deference to parental expectations or conformity to being ethnic Chinese. A few notable examples can be cited.

A successful engineer said, "I think they spread by so-called oral tradition, what you follow, what your parents would be doing. There is nothing I could read about. I just follow the customs and their practices" (Transcript #4, 3). A correlation also exists between education and religious views. Asked if he thought his education influenced his view of Chinese religions prior to his conversion, the engineer continued, "Yes, I think I see them as a bit backward, irrational, very much of superstition rather than something that is rational, something that can be explained" (Transcript #4, 4).

A graduate student recalled his "frustrations" with Buddhism because he did not think it answered his questions regarding the origin of the universe and life. He recalled asking his mother and other relatives many questions. Yet, to his dismay, they refused to answer him. When asked to describe his feelings, he said, "Frustrated by the fact that they cannot answer my questions. And they dismiss me, oh, children don't know so much. You just accept what I tell you. Yeah, and they didn't bother to find out. And it was not important to them" (Transcript #16, 5–6).

While some informants were inquisitive in seeking answers, most, however, expressed passive obedience to their parents' expectations. This so-called passive acceptance is evident among many informants who were very good students in top universities. When asked about how they reconciled their education and religious practices, such as praying to idols for favor, one said, "Yeah, it was easy for me to live in two worlds. There are many smart people who continue going to temples. You know, you can be more pragmatic, don't disturb the harmony in the family. So for me in both literature and political science, maybe it made me more critical in the way I thought, but it wouldn't make me, like, reject my parents. Because actually in the end it's about them" (Transcript #11, 10). A National University of Singapore (NUS) student explained her passive acceptance of worship as follows: "I was a bit like my parents were doing it so I'm just following it at the time. I mean, it didn't hold. I wasn't really thinking about what I was doing" (Transcript #24, 4). Another NUS student summarized her view of Buddhist practices: "My heart really wasn't into it but the reason why I did it was because out of respect for my parents or my grandparents. Yeah, so it's more like a cultural thing." She regarded Chinese religions as "myths" and "folklore" and attributed her religious skepticism to her studies in math and science, which were "very logical" (Transcript #12, 8).

Passive acceptance of Chinese religious practices was also evident among informants from varied backgrounds. When asked to explain why she participated in rituals, a teacher answered, "I think I just trusted what my parents tell me to do, and I sincerely believe when I went to the temple to pray that I would be smart, I would get good results. I prayed earnestly. I feared the spirits actually because like my mother always tell me about hungry ghosts" (Transcript 10, 3).

An English teacher insisted that she did not believe in the religion of her upbringing. She said, "I don't think I had strong belief. I felt it was just a lot of legends and folklores. None of that is really the truth. So although I took part, I just did it out of obedience, not because I believed in what they (parents) believed in" (Transcript #6, 5). When asked if her parents believed in Chinese religions and practices, she said, "My grandmother I am not very sure, but my mother, she said, this is our tradition, our family religion, so we all have to follow; it's kind of a duty" (Transcript #6, 5).

A medical doctor claimed no strong feelings toward worshiping ancestors, but did it out of respect for them (Transcript #18, 5). It is obvious that many worshiped ancestors out of obligation. An executive asked rhetorically, "I mean, if I have to do it, it's because I was asked to do it, right?" (Transcript #21, 6) Asked if he understood Buddhism or Taoism, an engineer said, "No. I was following my parents as a child. Of course, subconsciously, I didn't feel comfortable. I never felt comfortable walking into a temple" (Transcript #23, 6).

Ancestral worship for one student was a form of filial piety. Although not understanding the nature of worship of *Guan Yin*, a young lawyer connected it to Chinese culture. He continued, "It's almost hard to see it as a separate thing from our identity as a Chinese." For him, being Chinese meant filial piety and deference to parents (Transcript #28, 7). Concerning why he went to temple, another informant said, "Yeah, I think it was like all Chinese people do that. So to me it was like pretty normal" (Transcript #32, 5).

A young woman shared about not understanding Taoist practices. She recalled having to kneel on numerous occasions for hours at a time in front of an altar at home to ask for protection or when she did wrong things. She practiced and endured the excruciating ritual "Because I need to obey my mom, like my parents" (Transcript #30, 16). Due to weak health, one informant was offered as a god-daughter to deities for protection. When asked if she understood the significance of that action, she said, "Actually, I don't really understand the significance but I know it's sort of a tradition to me, rather than something spiritual. It's more of a formality that I need to go through to respect my ancestors" (Transcript #33, 9).

Religious Practices in Exchange for Blessings and Results

A second perspective on Chinese religious can be described as performing religious practices in exchange for material blessings and success. Beyond placating parental wishes and expectation, it is clear that many informants viewed Chinese religious practices as doing good deeds, as an "exchange" or a "transaction." On this theme, informants reported a spectrum or continuum, ranging from more neutral to pejorative statements on thirteen occasions. Several examples can be cited to illustrate the more neutral opinions. After noting his lack of understanding of Chinese rituals, a manager said, "They only taught me one lesson, to be good, do no harm, and help others. So that is religion to me, even in Taoism" (Transcript #5, 3).

More than performing good deeds, one informant explained her view of religion was for the purpose of attaining success. She said, "My mum had always seemed to be more religious than my father. She was the more dominant influence in my early religious life. She would make the point to bring me to temples to pray for my studies, for my health and for my overall success as a person. She would teach me to pray to the sky to what she called *tian*" (Transcript #13, 2). A young woman talked about coming from a dysfunctional and abusive family, and working at a very early age to help support the family. When asked about her understanding of praying to *Guan Yin*, she said, "Yes and no. I knew we had to go through it because for blessings. Yeah, it's really for blessings and for peace supposedly" (Transcript #20, 10).

When asked why she chanted and prayed at least five times a day, she said, "Because my parents believe that praying will make me smarter." She continued, "What I know is that Buddhism teaches people to be good. So my pressure was that you chant to have a better life kind of thing. Then for the Chinese side, it is for me to pray so that I will be smarter" (Transcript #10, 2). They performed the rites because she trusted in her mother's instruction (Transcript #10, 3). Another young woman shared about "going through the motions" when performing rituals. When asked about what she felt, she explained, "Okay, my heart was not in it. Maybe it's a way that I can understand it like, oh if I need a favor, if I'm sick, yeah I'll just light the joss stick and then I'll ask that I'll feel better. It's kind of asking the gods, oh whatever things that I need and just by using the joss sticks" (Transcript #30, 19).

The relationship between the performance of religious rituals and money emerged in several interviews. One young woman referred to practicing Buddhist rituals in monetary terms. She said, "I only know that you have to be good and then you kind of have it (good karma). If you do good and it banks into the system, then maybe when you reincarnate, the next life, you will be better" (Transcript #26, 9). One lawyer began his discussion by stating that he was from a poor background, where his parents pressed him to do well in school so he can earn a good living. As he grew older, he became "disillusioned" about his career path and the trajectory of the life, where the "number one goal in life is to earn money." He concluded that "money itself is meaningless," which prompted him to search for meaning in life and for a "moral code" (Transcript 25, 2). For him, Chinese religions were not viable options. He explained, "It's because from my version of Taoism and Buddhism is a very blessings-based religion. It's like you only go to them because you want to receive blessings from then and they don't talk to you, and you do not feel the connection at all" (Transcript #25, 4).

A young accountant understood the significance of offerings and burning joss sticks as an exchange for favors. He explained, "It was like when we burn the joss papers and everything like the money, then my granddad will receive it in heaven. And like offering him joss sticks and in front of the altar it is like talking to him like as a way of communication and to ask for things and stuff like that" (Transcript #32, 4). When asked about his view on making offerings and sacrifices to deities and idols, a lawyer bluntly said, "food sacrifices in return for, let's say, kind of a blessing or protection" (Transcript #27, 3).

Given the varied and questionable motivations for performing religious rituals on the part of informants, one wonders how they felt about the deities representing Chinese religions. On this topic, several responses were quite critical to say the least. The question of the possibility or the nature of a relationship with *Guan Yin* was posed to a science teacher. He characterized Chinese religions as a "cause and effect" and about being a "good person" (Transcript #1, 6). Then he explained, "Like all the deities cannot be offended or I would get punished. If I do bad things like get mad at my mum, I would get scolded. Then I go to my room to pray to *Guan Yin* or Buddha and promise to not do anything bad again. Then my mum would be very nice to me. So it is kind of like tit-for-tat relationship" (Transcript #1, 7). When asked about his opinion or view of *Guan Yin*, one informant responded, "He is to be feared, to be respected, someone to bless me, but not someone that I would have a relationship with me. Buddhism is a way of life. Maybe Taoism is the fear of a particular deity, but I can't say to monkey god do you love me" (Transcript #2, 12).

During the course of interviewing informants, one realizes that Chinese funerals in Singapore constitute a huge business venture, which is a source of resentment among many Chinese consumers. In expressing his dissatisfaction of Chinese religions as it relates to money, an engineer recalled, "When my grandfather passed away, we spent a lot of money. What I think about Chinese funeral is we spent a lot of money. Very expensive! It's about S$20,000. Then after funeral finish, like a few months later, they called and said your grandfather come to the street and said he is suffering below. Then he needs more things. So the end of their request is that they need more money from us. But the real money which to pay, about S$10,000, this is a lot" (Transcript #9, 8–9). Regarding the funerary advisors—particularly Taoist and Buddhist priests—the informant concluded: "They are cheaters. They just want to earn money. They use their charities, thinking about getting rich of it" (Transcript #9, 9).

Lastly, one woman recalled her disgust about making burnt offerings in order to fend off evil spirits, and how she went to different Taoist specialists to receive help. She complained, "I didn't have to burn S$100.00 worth of fake money or some something to get protection. You know if you are haunted by some spirit, you go to that black and white guy, right? And if you need help in your studies, then there is a different kind of specialization. Taoists have specialists. It's very commercial. It's like a transaction—like going to a specialist to get your thing fixed" (Transcript #34, 11–12).

Compelled by Fear for Protection

From the thirty-five interviews, it is clear that fear motivated many Singaporeans to find refuge in Chinese religions and rituals for protection from evil spirits or to keep from going to hell. Informants talked about experiences of fear and the need for protection on ten separate occasions. A teacher recalled going to temple to ask for good results and for protection. She said, "I fear the spirits actually, because my mother always tells me about ghost, hungry ghosts, so we burnt them offerings" (Transcript #10, 3).

An engineer recalled growing up in a poor family background when he experienced much hardship. As a result, he turned to the monkey god for protection from hardship, danger, and evil spirit. Concerning this monkey god, he said: "My personal impression is that the monkey god is someone with a lot of power. When my mum goes to work, sometimes comes back late. It's pretty scary. Sometimes at night we just need all kinds of protection" (Transcript #3, 2). Yet when asked if he experienced protection from the monkey god, he said, "There is no encountering with him in terms of spiritual power but it just helps me to feel at least we are protected when we are alone" (Transcript #3, 3). Although he did not encounter the monkey god, he did acknowledge the spiritual reality and power underlying Chinese religions. He elaborated, "I think there is some form of spiritual forces out there. I have no doubt that they are spiritual. The mediums trying to slash themselves in blood, but it always comes out okay. We now know those are forces of darkness behind them just trying to draw us away" (Transcript #3, 5).

A young mother experienced spiritual attacks at home when her brother suffered from sleep-walking and incontinence. The mother brought him to see a Taoist medium and he was later cured. Upon meeting the medium for the first time, she recalled the entire experience as frightening. She stated: "And then my mum was freaking out. Everyone was just afraid. The medium just confirmed the problem, saying that he had to go down to hell to negotiate with people in Hades about the problem. So I saw my brother was in a trance. After the consultation with the medium, he was brought back to normal" (Transcript #20, 11). Looking back, she characterized those occurrences as demonic and attributed them to the "works of evil forces" (Transcript #20, 12).

A fourth report of feeling the need for protection from evil spirits involved a young girl. Growing up in a Taoist background, where her home contained an altar with idols, she remembered that they served as protection from evil spirits. She referred to the idols as "The policemen, the protectors from evil spirits" (Transcript #30, 13). In addition, her mum brought her to temples to consult mediums, receive stamps on her clothing, and drink water with burnt offerings for protection or as remedies for health problems (Transcript #30, 14).

Beyond the fear of evil spirits, a few informants reported about fear of the unknown, death, or hell. An engineer characterized his experience in Chinese religions as succumbing to fear. When asked to explain, he said, "I think a lot has to do with trying to appease the unknown. When I gave up Chinese religions, it was not an immediate thing because it was a transition trying to bid farewell to these unknown gods, so that they will not harm me when trying to swing over to the Christian God. So it was like a transition. It is not an immediate cut. So it is all this fear" (Transcript #4, 5–6). When asked to discuss the nature of his fear, he said, "I think the strongest fear would be death. When I was a non-believer, I mean there is something frightening when attending a funeral. It is something that is not clean, something that can actually harm you" (Transcript #4, 6).

The concept or reality of "hell" was also an important theme gleaned from the interviews, particularly described in terms of a dragon boat ride descending into the so-called "eighteen levels" of hell in a theme park near the Haw Par Villa MRT stop. A teacher reported his feelings concerning all the Buddhist and Taoist rituals he performed. He said, "I guess one of my feelings that I can remember is fear. When my mother died, when we were going through the rituals, one of these things is you cannot do this, you cannot do that. If not, bad luck will follow you—like you cannot look at the coffin. When I slept next to the coffin, you must watch out for cats. Once the cat jump over the coffin, the dead person will wake up. That was so scary" (Transcript #1, 5). He was also warned that if he lied, terrible things would happen to him. Recalling his visit to Haw Par Villa, he said, "So I saw sculptures of demons tied to a pole, pulling out his tongue and like cutting it off. I was so scared." He continued, "Okay, I'd better not lie. I'd be good. If not, you will be in hell and there are eighteen levels that you can go down" (Transcript #1, 5). Chinese religions and rituals to him can be characterized as "cause and effect."

Another informant recalled his experience at Haw Par Villa as follows: "They have this dragon boat ride and you go down a dragon's mouth, and it takes you through the course of hell. If you are a liar, your tongue gets cut off. If you steal, your hands get chopped off. I was convinced after I finished life, because of so much wrongdoing, I would go to hell limb-less. I mean Haw Par Villa scared the daylights out of me. I was so afraid" (Transcript #2, 4). Although Haw Par Villa can be appropriately considered as a "theme park," nonetheless, he regarded Chinese religious rituals as "deeply spiritual" (Transcript #2, 5). In particular cases involving mediums when they inflicted pain upon themselves in performing rituals, he said, "The pain is real, the act is real, the devotion is real, their commitment to what they are called to do is real" (Transcript #2, 6).

Chinese religions, as motivated by fear, is expressed in another account involving a visit to Haw Par Villa. When asked about her view or feelings of rituals, a teacher said, "I think at that time was when I believed in another world, because I didn't want to go to the eighteenth levels of hell. At Haw Par Villa, my mother will point out you cannot lie or your tongue will look very grotesque. So it is always the images of eighteen levels of hell actually planted or rather taught to me. So I believed that hell was a reality" (Transcript #10, 4). Obviously, for her, Chinese religions and rituals involved many "do's and don'ts."

The cause and effect view of Chinese religions is clarified by a young woman. Describing her sense of fear upon seeing the demons or people in hell, she said, "Yeah, black and white faces. So they were so scary and like, these are the people I will see when I die? I really don't look forward to it" (Transcript #26, 10). She recalled seeing their faces every time she had to carry out her rituals and offerings. On one occasion, she asked her mum for an explanation on why bad things happen. Her mother replied "its basically to stop this people from doing bad things. When they do bad things, bad things will happen to them" (Transcript #26, 10).

Looking back when she performed religious rituals and being prepared to become a "medium," one informant complained about how Chinese religionists capitalized upon fear as the motivating factor. She pointed out, that through the process of her training, she experienced personal bondage. Referring to the rituals, she said, "But that's where they find protection. Yeah, you have to do something in order to get something in return. To get the protection of not going to hell or not to be fried in oil, you know" (Transcript #34, 5). She continued, "Because that's the outcome. And there's no end to how many of these you have to do. So you almost have to be respectful for so many of them. And it's like there's endless. In everything you do, you lost that freedom" (Transcript #34, 5).

In retrospect, Chinese Singaporeans, who converted from Chinese religions, viewed them as traditions for becoming a good person and its rituals as ways of finding protection in a world filled with capricious spirits and lurking dangers. Perhaps with the exception of one woman who became a devout Buddhist and experienced peace, though she later realized that she had to "lose her identity to reach Nirvana" (Transcript #34, 8), all other informants essentially expressed negative views of Chinese religions. For many, Chinese religions and rituals were not to be understood *per se* but something to be performed, usually as an exchange for good results or material blessings. For a few, Chinese religions and their leaders were viewed as manipulative, even deceitful, because rituals involved the nexus of spirits, religions, and commercialism. For the very secular-minded, Chinese religions and practices appeared as illogical, superstitious, or simply as ways to solve life problems. If any positive reflections were given by informants regarding Chinese religions, they were discussed in association with filial piety and Chinese ethnicity. Chinese Singaporeans practiced religions, for the most part, out of obligation, duty, and respect to their parents and ancestors.

Christian Conversion Experience

The following section summarizes the process through which the respondents became Christians. It seeks to narrate a number of key themes, including informants' personal crises, initial search for life's meaning, significant experiences and events, and influential people involved. Of the thirty-five people interviewed, most informants reported a rather drawn-out process of struggling with personal issues, searching, reading the Bible and other Christian literature, and coming into contact of believers in Christian communities, who helped to facilitate the conversion process.

Crises and Search for Meaning and Purpose in Life

Given that many, if not all, informants reported some degree of dissatisfaction with their religious background in Chinese religions and rituals, it is not surprising that fifteen out of thirty-five informants shared about their initial conversion process as an inner search for meaning and purpose in life precipitated by various crises. Due to confusion or some breakdown of the worldview in which they were nurtured by their parents, informants typically asked questions that need to be addressed. With the exception of one informant, who talked about his conversion stemming primarily from intellectual dissonance or curiosity (Transcript #2, 2), all others were sparked by personal crises.

For example, a chemistry teacher discussed about his tumultuous upbringing, a period in his life filled with violence, vulgarity, and personal struggles. Having been exposed to Christianity from his sister who attended a mission school, he attended church but was rather disinterested. However, his life was unchanged until a pastor from church challenged him about his misbehavior. He recalled her saying, "Your behavior is not changed because inside you it is not changed" (Transcript #1, 3). From that point on, he felt he needed "to make a drastic change in life from all the fights and naughty things I have done. That was when I begin to stop using all the vulgarity and the fights and all these things" (Transcript #1, 3).

An engineer, who experienced much difficulty growing up in his family of origin, shared about being afraid and the need for protection. He recalled, beginning in secondary six, that he was rebellious, doing poorly in school, and sensed the need "to make a big change" (Transcript #3, 3). He attributed his personal struggles not only to his difficult upbringing but to not having a purpose in life. Consequently, his sister brought him to her Christian school club. He said, "I was still rebellious in many ways, because I don't have a purpose of life. I was really struggling with a lot of hardship. My sister then brought me to her school club, and I kinda enjoy the messages and they shared the gospel with me. I said, sure, why not, there is some meaning in there" (Transcript #3, 4).

An executive manager with an MBA degree referred to his formative years as "looking for a purpose for living" (Transcript #5, 1). Having come from a Taoist background, which did not make much sense to him, he was primarily concerned about pursuing academics. When he dated a Christian girl who told him that he had to be a believer before they could marry, he struggled greatly before converting to Christianity. He said, "I was struggling at least more than 6 months to a year, before I finally said, okay, she is the lady I want to marry. And to do that, I have to be a Christian. So I became a Christian" (Transcript #5, 2).

One informant, whose conversion is an exceptional case in that it was prompted by positive circumstances, talked about the process as an intellectual journey. After spending more than six years in a mission school (ACS), he had lingering questions about religious faith. Meeting a Christian girl he liked, they engaged in "serious discussions" about purpose and truth. Although, "she could never really answer my questions," he recalled, she gave him *More Than a Carpenter* by Josh McDowell to read. Coming from a Buddhist background, which he "never really understood what it meant," reading the book really helped him (Transcript #8, 2).

Another informant shared about being afraid at an early age and experienced somewhat of an intellectual break-through. Having studied the solar system in primary school, she wondered about who or what was responsible for it. She recalled feeling "terrified because of this idea that I don't know who made all this happened and felt this cold dread" (Transcript #11, 1). Then, she recalled, some Christian relatives shared the gospel with her. She recalled just the thought that there is a creator God and a reason for her life "comforted me and that cold terror just slowly turned into a warmth." Just looking back, "I felt as though it was a divine intervention at that point, just this thought entering to my head that it's okay" (Transcript #11, 1).

A young student who attended a mission school (ACS) shared about his "decade-long struggle with depression and the meaninglessness of life" (Transcript #13, 6). He came from a Buddhist background but concluded that not only did it not make sense but it also did not work for him. Sharing his sense of "despondency," he recalled, "I went to temple only because my parents brought me there and told me to do those things by praying, burning joss paper and it's okay" (Transcript #13, 6). However, it was one incident, which changed his life. He said, "It was the fact that pastor Joseph Prince was telling me about Jesus Christ was central to my life, and how he offers the blessings and the grace of God which can transform and save me from hell" (Transcript #13, 8).

When asked about how he became a believer, a young university student talked about being exposed to Christianity at various stages of his upbringing. He was, for example, brought to a Christian kindergarten. Although he did not know God, he remembered the "spirit of love within the community." He went to a primary school, which had no Christian influence. It was not until his time at Anglo-Chinese Junior College, a mission school, that he sensed the "preachers were preaching based on life lessons." However, "It was not until university that, I mean, you start thinking about questions of life" when he felt "dissatisfied" (Transcript #14, 2). He was given a Bible at the time, which really helped, because he was reading many self-help books at the time.

Coming from a family whose parents divorced, a young college student talked about his conversion experience as a process of discovery. Meeting with Bible study leaders, he recalled his experience in weekly sessions as like "everything really makes sense" (Transcript #15, 4). What helped him, in particular, was "that this Christianity explained a lot of things in my life, you know, why we are here and how we should live" (Transcript #15, 5). Prior to his exposure to Christianity, he had to define his own meaning and purpose. And growing up in a Chinese religious background and remembering one occasion when his mum got very ill, he became worried and wondered about the meaning of life. He said, "Yeah, and following that time, I kind of felt, so this is what life is about and possibly there's no explanation. So, yeah, I think I began searching for that answer" (Transcript #15, 6).

Also coming from a family with divorced parents, a teacher talked about his adolescent years as filled with many questions regarding his Buddhist religious background. He attended a mission school, and was thus exposed to Christianity. The two naturally collided, however, and he recalled feeling quite "frustrated by the fact that they [his mother and relatives] cannot answer my questions" (Transcript #16, 5). He admitted that Buddhism "fits well" with the "darkness in my life" at that time (Transcript #16, 11–12). In Buddhism, "Life is very difficult. It's full of pain. There is no hope. There's no way of getting out. There's no purpose. No meaning," he lamented (Transcript #16, 12).

A female college student explained her conversion experience as a "build-up over the years." When asked how she became a Christian, she explained, "But it's more of little things that happened over the years that got me to question what the meaning of life was, what life really is about. And I think part of that would be the deaths of close ones, as well as a surgery that I had to go through that was almost life changing. So after all those experiences at a very young age, it kind of got me to think about what life is about" (Transcript #17, 2). Given her lack of understanding of Buddhist practices, it is clear that religion was not much of a factor for her in her adolescent years while growing up. She said, "I was just going through the motions" when it came to observing religious rituals (Transcript #17, 5).

A civil servant, who identified himself as a Confucianist and a successful student in school, discussed at length about feeling "alienated" while growing up. As a presidential scholar who studied in the UK, he studied physics, chemistry, mathematics, and literature. Recalling his junior college days, he said, "I had become incredibly alienated within the school. People would write horrible things about me. I felt completely rejected" (Transcript

#19, 3). In fact, he was so despondent that he "was actively suicidal" (Transcript #19, 3). While "searching for a new worldview," he "stumbled upon Buddhism" while abroad, because it "at least has an explanation for suffering" (Transcript #19, 4). It was not until he was involved in a biking accident and Singaporean Christians reached out to him that he began to reflect more deeply. He said, "I was bleeding from my head and had a concussion for three days. And during that period of time, I started to ask myself about the meaning of life" (Transcript #19, 4).

An IT engineer said his life "hit rock bottom" in 2009 after eight years of feeling "pressurized, because I, at the time, slowly see my friends doing very well" (Transcript #22, 9). For him, "It seems like they're getting better and better, you know. Some of them doing business. Some of them getting married. Or some got kids. Then it seems like I don't have anything" (Transcript #22, 9). Then he recalled a good friend from secondary school met up with him and seemed very concerned about his condition. He said, "I felt like he's very concerned about my life" (Transcript #22, 9). Upon the invitation from his friend, he started attending church, and it has been a very good experience for him because the preacher, according to him, "He's like talking about my life" (Transcript #22, 11).

When asked about how she became a Christian, a college student remembered receiving a gospel tract from a close friend back in secondary two. She said, "But back then, I didn't receive it. I mean it's actually like a good story and it didn't touch me. I mean, I didn't feel connected with it until like when I was in secondary three. There was an incident that happened at home that cause me to think about the meaning of life and whether there is life beyond death" (Transcript #24, 2). Reflecting upon her Buddhist background, she said "I was a bit like my parents who were just doing it. So I'm just following it at the time. I mean, it didn't hold. I wasn't thinking about what I was doing" (Transcript #24, 4).

A young lawyer discussed about life growing up in a poor family, where his conservative and religious parents emphasized diligence and earning money. For him, he "did not really understand" the religious rituals and felt they were "obligatory" (Transcript #25, 2). During his National Service, right before he was about to enter university, he reexamined his life. He recalled, "I had a lot of time to think about life and I felt that I need to have a worldview to sort of arrange my life around it, sort of like a compass. I was disillusioned with his current belief system, where the number one goal in life is to earn money" (Transcript #25, 2). Moreover, even though he did not personally embrace Taoism, he insisted that he had a "moral code." He also admitted that "he did certain things which I'm not proud of and I realized that I cannot live up to my own standards and I wanted to find a moral compass" (Transcript #25, 3).

A social worker shared her conversion experience as precipitated by a painful breakup from her boyfriend. Lamenting about not having one single friend in school until university, she shared about meeting a Christian girl in NUS who went through some Navigators materials with her. She recalled being "open to Christianity" at the time but was not converted yet (Transcript #30, 3). Although she attended campus groups, it was not until her last year of school when she became despondent over the breakup from her boyfriend that stirred her thinking. She said watching the movie, *The Matrix*, with the virtual world, made her reflect more deeply about herself. She said, "And I started to really ask myself what exactly is the thing, the meaning for me, the meaning of life" (Transcript #30, 6). She was later converted at a major Christian event in the Singapore Indoor Stadium, where she experienced spiritual deliverance and tongues (Transcript #30, 8–9).

Meeting Needs, Answered Prayers, and Signs

It must be pointed out that not all informants reported conversion narratives spurred by active search for meaning and purpose in life. While that approach to faith is a prominent theme among the thirty-five interviewees, signifying more intellectual or cognitive engagement, many informants came to faith through other means, including signs, answered prayers, and meeting of felt-needs. In those instances, the perception of Christianity as an intellectual or rational religion may not be overt, though Christian faith was conveyed in very relevant and personal terms.

Two informants, in particular, talked about feeling afraid, which led them to consider the truth claims of Christianity. One remembered about going through the dragon boat ride at Haw Par Villa and "was terrified about hell." He recalled, "Haw Par Villa scared the living daylights out of me. I was so afraid, and then that was the first time I thought about eternity" (Transcript #2, 4). Feeling distraught, he went to his father and told him, "Papa, I don't want to die. I went to hell today and I don't want to go there." He was later converted at a Christian camp when he responded to the gospel because of Christ's offer of eternal life (Transcript #2, 5). The other individual who reported about being afraid is an engineer. Reflecting upon his background in Chinese religions, he said, "I think Chinese religion held a very strong grip on me in the sense of fears of the spirit, fears of the unknown." When he later received a Bible and began reading it, he got the impression that the Christian God is "a more rational God" and he sensed "the need for the Savior" (Transcript #4, 2).

Prayer, sometimes offered out of desperation, seemed to have played a key role in a few conversion narratives. A young university student was going through a "rough patch" with her then boyfriend. Because he was a Christian and she was not, she attended Bible studies to "find out more about what he believes." In comparison to Taoism, which she regarded as "folklore and myths," Christianity gave her a more positive impression. She said, "Christianity to me is like really based on the truth like the Bible itself is a piece of documentation that has been passed down for so many years" (Transcript #12, 3). When asked about how her struggles with her boyfriend led her to become a believer, she said, "So during one night I was really emotional. I just tried like a little prayer. And immediately I felt like a peace, a sense of calm. And I knew that the prayer wasn't talking to the air but it was really someone listening to you" (Transcript #12, 4).

A young mother, who attended a mission school from an early age, recalled her experience growing up in an abusive, dysfunctional family. Of course, she had been exposed to the gospel and prayer while attending school, though she did not embrace them due to her family background in Buddhism. She and others in her family endured "prolonged beatings" by her father. Feeling distraught, she often prayed to *Guan Yin* at home when the father got drunk and beat her or her mother. But then she said, "Because I think I was at school every day, the influence I had was probably more subtle because I was exposed to praying to another person; there's another God I can pray to" (Transcript #20, 2). As she recalled, it was through a long series of difficult experiences at home in which her Buddhist parents abused her, and one time her mother even threaten to "throw her out the window," that she stopped praying to *Guan Yin*. She said, "God, she almost made a mistake by throwing me. I remembered that my uncle came and he read a Bible and my mother just blacked out." She continued, "So after that, but before I already knew that this is Christian God that I could pray, it was also about that time that I actually stopped praying to *Guan Yin* at home" (Transcript #20, 4).

Another case where prayer played a decisive role in Christian conversion involved a mother who was going through a major struggle with her son. She regularly went to a Buddhist temple with her son to pray to *Guan Yin*. Because she never experienced answered prayer before, on one particular occasion in the temple when feeling desperate about her son, she somehow prayed to the Christian God instead. She said, "This time I don't pray to *Guan Yin* anymore because I prayed to her and there's no result. So I said, God please help. If you want me to be a Christian, if you answer my prayer and help my son, I will become a Christian" (Transcript #21, 3). Later, she felt her prayer was miraculously answered (Transcript #21, 4). And in response to her "vow" made to God, she became a Christian and has since attended church "to pay back, you know, what God has done for me" (Transcript #21, 4).

A couple of informants also mentioned about receiving "signs" from God as a major factor leading to Christian conversion. In telling their amazing stories, those informants did not express inner tension, nor intellectual incredulity. Miraculous occurrences seemed like second-nature to them. Christianity, in this sense, may not seem like a very rational religion. A stay-home mother recalled, "I was actually at the crossroad to make a decision on which course I should study in my university, when I was really confused which I course I should take. Then, I think my only Christian sister just said a very simple prayer. So she prayed for me and after that, the journey to submit my application, yeah, I heard something from the Lord. I mean, as I reflect back, it's actually the Lord's voice. He spoke to me through a very big signboard about my education" (Transcript #33, 3). The sign was so powerful that she changed her course on the spot and experienced peace as a result. Her sister later invited her to church and she "received Christ" (Transcript #33, 5).

An engineer discussed about "saying the sinner's prayer" during a chapel while attending a mission school. However, it was some time after that "the truth sank in of what Christianity is all about" (Transcript #23, 1–2). He insisted that Christianity is "feeling-based," and that he was not sure when he became a believer—at the time of hearing a message and saying the sinner's prayer, or when he "experienced" God (Transcript #23, 2).

When asked about his "experiences," he said he was actually prevented from going to church for a long time after saying the sinner's prayer because his parents were devout Buddhists. He was even "offered up to be a godson to *Guan Yin*," he recalled (Transcript #23, 3). However, he later heard an "inner voice" that "reinforced" his faith—to ask his mother to allow him to go to church. The request was miraculously granted by his mother (Transcript #23, 4).

Questioning whether this was indeed from God, he asked for a second sign. He said, "So immediately that night, I was thinking, 'God, I prayed and you said yes through my mom like that? I didn't believe it. Can you show me another sign?'" The second sign involved God prompting a particular girl in his school to invite him to her church. He continued, "I said, God, if you allow me to see this girl and making it in such a way that I cannot run away from her, she will run to me and she will ask me about church, then I'll go" (Transcript #23, 5). The sign from God was given when the girl invited him to church the next day during lunch time. To this day, he is undecided about when he became a Christian—when he said the sinner's prayer or when he received the two signs from God.

The theme of experiencing a felt-need met as contributing to conversion was expressed by several informants. A medical doctor talked about growing up in a large family, feeling very lonely, lost, and needing love (Transcript #18, 2). Recalling her undergraduate days as being bombarded with people from campus ministries trying to reach out to her, she said, "I was attracted to them, like they were a clique in the way they related to each other, you know. There was a lot of warmth and joy" (Transcript #18, 3). She explained about her conversion experience as follows: "My classmates, they will come to me and they say they are interested in me and, yeah, they want to talk to me about Christianity. So I just feel that having known them, I could trust them for what they have to offer. I have the need in myself of wanting to be loved and so I thought it goes together" (Transcript #18, 3).

Similarly, another college student shared about feeling lonely and needing love as a major impetus for Christian conversion. Having attended a mission school, she remembered responding during an "altar call" one day in school. When asked to explain what compelled her to become a Christian, she said, "Yeah, so it was during one of those chapels they had an altar call. And I remember I accepted it, but the initial reason why I became a Christian was because my best friend was a Christian. It wasn't really like I wanted to be one" (Transcript #26, 3). Obviously, her friend meant much to her, and she said, "And then she said this God could help her when she's in need. So because of that, then I thought, since I'm feeling lonely and that nobody loves me at home anyway, maybe I would just try this God, because I didn't really felt the religion that I grew up with was somewhere where I could find love" (Transcript #26, 4–5).

The theme of loneliness and the needy receiving care from someone is expressed in a banker's conversion account one year before she got married. Coming from a very devout and sometimes intense Buddhist background in which she received training to become a medium, she spoke about having financial problems. While going through her university days, she took out loans and had to work to pay for tuition. Consequently, she never made friends. She recalled one day when an Indonesian girl reached out to her in the library. "And we started talking," and discovered that "she was a Christian in spite of her Muslim name," she said (Transcript #34, 2). Feeling impressed with the girl's testimony about her faith, she ultimately turned to Christianity when she met her eventual husband. She said, "But when I sat down and hear her struggle in a country and yet she was holding really fast to this religion, it's like, wow, okay, against all odds, you still want to believe in Christ. And she said, 'yeah, gives me the peace.' I didn't quite comprehend what kind of peace she gets anyway. So that was that. And then I got to know my husband. After school, I didn't really date, and he's a Christian" (Transcript #34, 4). She later met his family and started attending church.

Beyond the aforementioned narratives, a couple of informants discussed about coming to faith almost serendipitously. An accountant talked about his exposure to Christianity while he was in secondary two when his sister brought him to attend Youth for Christ. Because his parents were devout Taoists or Buddhists and strongly objected Christianity, he never pursued it. Now married to a woman from Taoism, he found the "temple environment with the rituals very intimidating." Feeling that "everyone needs a religion," he started attending City Harvest Church and was later converted (Transcript #29, 3). When asked to explain what happened, he said, "Yeah, we feel very touched. We feel like, you know, we are being welcomed. Now we see the Holy Spirit working, but at that time we may not know that" (Transcript #29, 4).

Lastly, a business woman who worked in the corporate world for a number of years said she was exposed to Christianity and attended church at an early age. However, when she married her Taoist husband who objected, she refrained from Christianity for a long period of time (Transcript #35, 2). When asked what happened next, she said, she felt a need for God and asked her husband if she could go to church. The husband gave her permission, and she started attending City Harvest Church. She conveyed her conversion experience in the following statement: "So one day, I told myself, why do I need God now? Why is it that I'm thinking of him now? So I told my husband, that one day, I will step into this church. And my husband said, go ahead with what you want to do" (Transcript #35, 2). She later made the decision to convert to Christianity in an Alpha course.

Encounters and Interactions

In interviewing the thirty-five informants, a variety of experiences were reported about why and how they converted to Christian faith. In particular, fifteen informants characterized the conversion process as a search for meaning and purpose in life precipitated by personal crises. The remaining twenty informants, however, did not characterize their conversion as an active cognitive process. Rather, they reported about experiencing answered prayers, receiving signs from God, or the meeting of felt-needs as the impetus for conversion. With a few exceptions, most informants endured a prolonged process before making a clear decision to convert. A few never noted a decisive moment or event of conversion, but simply reported going to church as a demonstration of faith.

What seems clear about the thirty-five interviews is that every informant reported about having some kind of contact or interaction with Christians somewhere during the conversion process. In other words, people did not make a decision to convert in isolation but was aided, encouraged, informed, or evangelized by others. During a period in his life when he struggled with personal issues, informant #1 was introduced to Christ by his sister, who attended a mission school. He later attended a church and was converted there. Informant #2 attended a mission school as a non-believer. However, coming out of a background steeped in Buddhism/Taoism, he was later invited to a church campus and was converted there. Having experienced much personal struggles and turning to the monkey god for protection, informant #3's sister brought him to her Christian school club where he was converted to Christianity.

Informant #4 received a Bible from his brother and began reading it at a time when he was seriously questioning his Chinese religion as irrational. Informant #5 was dating a Christian woman and agreed to become a Christian before they got married. Having attended a Roman Catholic convent school, informant #6 was eventually converted through friends who invited her to their Christian campus club meetings. Informant #7 lived much of her life, practicing "meaningless" Buddhist chants at home. She later became attracted to a Christian man and was invited to attend his church, where she became a believer. Informant #8 attended a mission school as a non-believer. He later got reacquainted with a friend from that school and the two engaged in serious discussions about Christianity. He started to attend her church, where he was converted in an Alpha class.

Reared in a very religious Buddhist family and feeling skeptical about his religion, informant #9 was exposed to Christianity when he attended church with his friend from school. Informant #10 attended a mission school as a non-believer and later attended inductive Bible study meetings at her university campus. Struggling with fear, informant #11 was exposed to Christianity through Christian relatives who talked to her about the creator God. After dating a Christian boyfriend for a period of time, informant #12 was later converted in a campus Bible study meeting. After attending a mission school, a friend from university invited informant #13 to hear a message presented by Joseph Prince. He was converted when pastor Prince prayed for him to receive Christ toward the end of the service. Informant #14 attended a mission school as a non-believer, where he heard many chapel messages. During his time in university, a Christian gave him a Bible to read. He also read a book by Lee Strobel, which convinced him about the truth of Christianity.

Coming from a broken family, informant #15 was converted in a campus Bible study group. Informant #16 attended a mission school as a non-believer, and was later invited to church by friends. He found the preacher and messages helpful and became a Christian. Informant #17's conversion experience was a slow process, when she questioned the purpose and meaning of life. She was converted in a university campus Bible study fellowship. As a self-professing lonely undergraduate student, informant #18 was befriended by Christians on campus who witnessed to her.

Studying overseas as an undergraduate student, informant #19 was involved in a biking accident. During the recovery, fellow-Singaporean students at the university reached out to him with the gospel. Informant #20 was exposed to Christianity in her mission school. She learned to pray to God in school and later prayed to God for help when she encountered physical abuse in her family. Informant #21 started to attend church after she experienced an answered prayer to God for help. Believing she was a Christian at the time, she started to attend church. Hitting a low point in life, a friend, sensing his need for help, invited informant #22 to church where he was converted.

Having been exposed to Christianity in a mission school, informant #23 received a sign from God when a classmate invited him to her church. A friend shared the gospel with informant #24 in secondary two. Although the message did not immediately impact her, she was exposed to the gospel to which she later accepted in secondary three. Informant #25 attended church as a non-believer and later joined a Bible study. Having attended a mission school as a non-believer, informant #26 claimed that her best friend, who was a Christian, encouraged her to faith in the Christian God. Informant #27 was exposed to Christianity through a seminar on creationism, and later attended a seeker's class in his university, which got him to consider Christianity more seriously.

A teacher at school invited informant #28 to attend church with her, where he prayed to receive Christ. After his conversion, he attended a believer's class in his current home church. Exposed to Christianity in secondary two in a Youth for Christ meeting, informant #29 later accepted Christ after his wife became a Christian. In her last year at university, a friend invited informant #30 to Navigators meetings on campus. She later received Christ in a large Christian event. Informant #31 reported about hearing a Christian who donated his liver to a needy patient. Impressed with that act of sacrificial love, he started to attend church.

Informant #32 dated a Christian girl as a non-believer. She later invited him to her church, where he was converted. While facing a difficult decision in life, informant #33's sister prayed for her. She received a sign from God and was later converted at her sister's church. As an undergraduate student, informant #34 met a girl at school, who talked to her about Christianity. She later met her husband-to-be, who invited her to his church. She became a believer one year before they got married. Feeling a need to return to church since her early childhood exposure, informant #35 asked her Taoist husband for permission. After her husband miraculously acquiesced, she started to attend church and was converted in an Alpha class.

Another important theme derived from the thirty-five interviews, though not as prominent as the previous in terms of frequency, is the report about reading the Bible and other Christian literature as instrumental in facilitating the process of Christian conversion. Here, on this point, eight informants talked about the benefits from reading the Bible and other Christian literature. One informant attributed his decision to convert to Christianity on two key factors: (1) a pastor admonishing him of his misbehaviors, and (2) reading the Bible. Concerning the latter, he said, "And then I begin to read my Bible very, very regularly until my sister noticed it and she bought a study Bible for me. This is when I started reading and marking. I think that was beginning of my change" (Transcript #1, 3).

Feeling dissatisfied with his family background in Chinese religions and practices, an informant talked about receiving a Bible as a gift from his Christian brother. There is an aspect of the Bible, which he found critical toward his transformation. He said, "My older brother, he was converted to Christianity in another church. He gave me a Bible. As I tried to relate to the Bible events, what I know about Jesus, with what I knew in school from my history classes, I found the Jesus described in the Bible was very different from what has been described in history books. I think I read Genesis, Exodus, the four gospels, excerpts of Romans, so from reading the Bible I knew that Jesus was no ordinary person" (Transcript #4, 2).

A third informant talked about reading Josh McDowell's *More Than a Carpenter*, as a helpful resource in deciding to become a Christian. Describing himself as a "logical, rational kind of thinker," he recalled "the book help me a lot." He continued, "I became a lot more receptive, because of the factual and logical kind of reasoning. So I started to read the Bible, from the book of Genesis, and I started to realize that I could connect with what it was saying. So I went and joined the Alpha class and met facilitators and everyone was very approachable and the whole environment was very open, which I never thought of Christians. These things all lined up along the way, so then I accepted Christ toward the end of Alpha class" (Transcript #8, 2).

Another informant recalled receiving a Bible to read during a period when he was searching for meaning and reading self-help books. There was something "so amazing" about the Bible, he recalled. "To be honest," he said, "I initially convinced myself that only the OT was true because it validates my three religions—Islam, Judaism, and Christianity" (Transcript #14, 2–3). However, after reading Lee Strobel's *A Case for Christ*, he was convinced that "everyone is a sinner and we need a savior" because "these twelve people who wrote about Christ were willing to die for him," underscoring the historicity of the Bible (Transcript #14, 3).

The idea of the historicity of the Bible is expressed in another interview. Coming from a Buddhist background, his initial impression of Christianity was admittedly "not very good." However, his friends at his mission school kept inviting him to their church. So he reluctantly accepted "because I wanted to see my friends in the church" (Transcript #16, 2). What was ultimately impressive to him regarding Christianity was his initial reading of the Bible. He said, "So then when I read the Bible, I realized that many of the things look very reasonable and historical" (Transcript #16, 2). In contrast, he continued, "When I read the Buddhist scriptures, many of the stories look like myth, very unreal and a lot of deities, a lot of gods, beings, things like that I had a lot of questions how the world came into being" (Transcript #16, 3).

When asked to share about what or who influenced him to become a Christian, a university student said, "I became a Christian through one of the meet-up with the facilitators for Bible study" on campus. "I was convinced that this gospel was something that's real, different from the things that my family believes," he said (Transcript #15, 2). When asked to clarify the difference, he asserted, "There's a creator in this world and that's what I really got out of those gospels we try to read and those series of weekly Bible study" (Transcript #15, 2).

Similarly, a student mentioned about Christian "friends" who exhibited "something different about the way they look at life from the way I look at life" as a non-believer (Transcript #17, 3). She continued, "Another factor, which leading up to my conversion, was actually when I was able to meet this person for one-to-one Bible studies. It was about reading the Bible for about four to six months then I made the decision to accept Christ" (Transcript #17, 4).

The most significant observation, however, is that of the thirty-five informants interviewed, twenty-seven people (77.1 percent) were introduced or converted to Christianity in the context of a school environment. Furthermore, out of those twenty-seven informants, ten had attended a mission school at one point or another. Those two statistical facts underscore not only the positive influence mission schools make on their students but the school venue in Singapore as a religiously neutral space in which many conversions take place.

Christianity as the True Religion

The religious conversion experience indeed involves the complex interface of personal, existential, religious, and social factors. However, when asked to clarify why they were convinced that Christianity was the true religion in comparison to Chinese religions, informants offered more nuanced explanations of Christianity as the preferred religion. The informants' responses on their perceptions of the truth of Christianity can be organized into two broad categories, including the personal and experiential dimension of religious faith, and the biblical basis of Christianity.

Personal Relationship with and Experience of God

A major reason why informants favored Christianity is the spiritual dimension of Christianity. Of the thirty-five people interviewed, fourteen referred to Christianity as the true religion because of their personal relationship with or experience of God. In particular, five informants reported that a personal relationship with God was what convinced them about the truth of Christianity over Chinese religions. It is noteworthy that informants talked about their relationship with God in the context of contrasting it with Chinese religions. One informant identified his personal relationship with God as a point of contrast to *Guan Yin*. When asked about why he preferred Christianity, he said: "That's easy—a relationship with God. That is one of the clearest things for me. When I became a Christian, I could tell God, 'I love you.' And God could tell me through scripture, through people, through the Holy Spirit that he loves me as well. There is love because God is love. But I could never, for the life of me, say that to *Guan Yin*" (Transcript #2, 12).

A college student said her relationship with God is "what makes the difference" between Christianity and Buddhism. She explained, "I guess in many ways I couldn't find that in Buddhism or any other religion. There is no such thing. There is no personal relationship" (Transcript #12, 13). "So when you are, let's say, worshipping or praying a prayer to the idols or the statues, what were those like to you? I mean who did they . . . did they represent anything to you or whether any meaning behind that," she asked? (Transcript #12, 13)

Likewise, another informant was critical of Buddhism due to his inability to have a personal relationship with *Guan Yin*. He asked rhetorically, "So would you say that you did not have a personal relationship with the Buddha or with any other idols? I mean, what were those idols to you in contrast to your so-called relationship with God now? I mean were they not personal gods or they were very far away?" (Transcript #16, 14)

A fourth informant pointed out that the prospect of having a relationship with God played a decisive role in her conversion to Christianity. She contrasted that relationship, however, with her obligation to obey her parents' example in Taoism. She explained, "I guess it's a personal relationship that stands out in contrast to what I had to follow in the footstep of my parents. So I find that, you know, is the first and foremost difference. And that attracts me" (Transcript #18, 6). One last informant stated his preference for Christianity because, he said, "I felt that I was in a living relationship with God, and, for example, God answered my prayers very quickly so that God was telling me that he is real; he is affirming" (Transcript #25, 3).

Beyond pointing to a personal relationship with God as the decisive factor for Christianity, informants talked about personal experience as what qualified it as the true religion. When informants spoke about experiencing God, several themes emerged. Several, for example, talked about experiencing God through answered prayers. A woman talked about how "God has been very real" to her. The critical turning point in her spiritual life was when she was in a "desperate" situation to find a misplaced test paper. For fear of what her teacher might do to her, she prayed to God for help. Feeling a "strong prompting that it was inside a trash bag," she looked and found the paper (Transcript #20, 18). Another said, she started to attend church and became a Christian, "because I wanted to fulfill my vow" to "repay back" God for answered prayer (Transcript #21, 9).

A distinctive of Christianity, according to one informant, is that "we only pray then look forward to God's blessings or God's love" in contrast to Taoism, which required adherents to practice rituals (Transcript #31, 8). One other informant gave an example of her "personal encounter with God" in terms of an answer to prayer. She asked God for a "sign" on whether she should quit her job. "And then after I prayed and then at the East Coast Park there was this very big rainbow that appeared," she recalled (Transcript #30, 28). She was transformed by that experience and started to "believed in God more and more" (Transcript #30, 28).

To be sure, answered prayer was not the only indicator of why Christianity is the true religion in comparison to Chinese religions. Several informants described their religious experience in other ways. A couple of informants talked about their religious experience of Christianity in terms of feelings. When asked about why she regarded Christianity as the true religion, a young student responded, "So when I use the word true, a lot of feeling is involved, a lot of conviction of the heart and this heart joined with the mind" (Transcript #11, 15). She then clarified what she meant by experiencing God, particularly in a charismatic church. "It's almost like this feeling of the holy, just like you feel that God is here" (Transcript #11, 15), she recalled. Comparing the difference between going to a Buddhist temple and attending a Christian church, an informant said, "we just feel the difference" (Transcript #29, 9). The fundamental difference, he insisted, was "I think that you can feel" in a church service (Transcript #29, 10).

Experiencing God, the decisive factor of true religion for several informants, can be expressed in the love of God. One informant described the love of God in contrast to fear as the motivating factor for practicing ritualistic religions. She explained, "It is about when I go to God, I know more about God. I am more secure. I no longer feel fearful, and uncertain or inferior about myself." She explained that the knowledge of God was "to know that he loves me" (Transcript #7, 18). Another spoke of the love of God as the key motivating factor for self-transformation. In contrast to the practice of Chinese rituals, which drove her to become a good person by fear, the "feeling of the unconditional love of God just became stronger over the years," as she has learned to accept herself and grow from her mistakes (Transcript #26, 22–23).

Biblical Christianity

The uniqueness of Christianity, according to twenty-one informants, is attributed to the important role of the Bible in Christian faith. In contrast to Chinese religions, which are passed down through oral tradition and characterized as "legends" or "myths," Christianity is preferred because it is codified or text-based and the Bible is regarded as the word of God. Acknowledging the existence of the creator God as revealed by Scripture, one informant said, "When I read his word, many times I feel like he is talking to me; he is speaking real things to me. So I guess that is the first differentiating point is when I think about God as the creator and the rest of the religions I know of are truly made by my own human hands" (Transcript #1, 7).

One other talked about the Bible as revelatory in an intellectual sense. He said, "On a cognitive basis, when I hear the message, when I read further, I started to realize and understand what the faith is all about" (Transcript #3, 5). Another informant, from a charismatic background, explained that "He is a speaking God." In contrast to idols who never speak, "but the God that I know in the Bible speaks and I experience him," she said (Transcript #33, 12).

The Bible as God's special revelation is accepted by informants on various grounds. Some validate the truth of the Bible on its self-authenticating quality. One informant explained the truth of the biblical theme of the unconditional love of God as follows: "Because I could forgive. I can forgive a lot of people. I would cry at moments. When I connect that moment you know it's real. And then you know that the word is true" (Transcript #34, 18). Another person said, "I would say that the Bible, whatever is written in the Bible is just true stories. It's just true fact. And sometimes when we are seeking we get answers from the Bible." The factual basis of the Bible is predicated upon "our faith and trust" (Transcript #35, 8). Describing her initial faith as trusting a text, an informant explained, "I think it is a set of faith like trusting textbooks. To me, it was like you trust what the author says is true. So at the point of time, it is really like I have faith that the word of God is true" (Transcript #10, 9). One other informant offered an even more direct statement: "Christianity is founded on the Bible, which claims to be the word of God. So we have to accept what it claims on face value. We cannot prove it" (Transcript #6, 9).

While the above comments expressed a rather fideistic view of the Bible and appeared inconsistent with Christianity as a rational religion, the following respondents grounded the truth of the Bible on something other than its self-authenticating-quality. A few informants, for example, claimed the truth of the Bible based upon its historicity. Characterizing Christianity as a "logical" faith, an informant observed that "it is very concrete, based upon a great set of texts, with historical evidence." This quality, according to him, is "what other religions kind of lack" (Transcript #8, 6). Another informant talked about his attraction to Christianity due, in part, to the truth of the Bible. "Is there a God that stands behind this word," he asked rhetorically. He answered by explaining the basis of his faith in the "historical Jesus who was brought into history" (Transcript #19, 15).

Another informant talked about Christianity's offer of eternal life. When asked why he believed in the teachings of the Bible, he said, "I think to a certain extent some of the Bible narratives or rather the events that occur in the Bible is backed up by history" (Transcript #23, 9). One other informant nicely summarizes the basis of his faith: "Christianity is the true religion to me mainly because I believe the Bible is a faithful witness to the words and acts of God through history and this is all grounded and written in the historicity and truthfulness of the resurrection of Christ" (Transcript #13, 8).

For the most part, however, most informants grounded the truth of the Bible seemingly on the perception that biblical teachings fit the real world. For example, five informants justified the validity of Scripture because it identifies the reality and problem of human sin. One said, "For me, Christianity is true because it speaks to me of my situation and for all mankind as well, because we are sinners" (Transcript #4, 10). Another said, "What truly convinced me was just Christ himself, the idea that everyone is a sinner and we need a savior" (Transcript #14, 3).

Distancing herself from Buddhism, which she characterized as a religion of "self-discovery," one informant stated the beginning point of Christianity is the "awareness that I'm not a good person, I make mistakes, and I need forgiveness." She continued, "I couldn't really find it in Buddhism" (Transcript #17, 6). Similarly, referring to his conversion as an intellectual journey, which involved "a process of acquiring knowledge and figuring things out," an informant finally acknowledged the limitations of head knowledge. "But it reaches to the point where I realized that like what the Bible said, I was really a sinner," he said candidly (Transcript #28, 12).

The perception that the Bible fits real life is evident in comments made by several other informants. An administrator attributes the validity of the Bible due to changed lives. He said, "I would say that in my experience, you find that Christians are more willing to help one another. When your brother needs help, we are more readily to help each other" (Transcript #5, 7). Frustrated by his parents' inability to answer his question "about why so many gods," an engineer found the Bible offering a more reasonable answer. When asked to elaborate, he said, "Reasonable answer is just like, yeah, there's only one God. You know, you cannot have too many gods" (Transcript #22, 12).

One informant argued that the viability of a religion must correspond to life and reality. He explained, "If you want to test a religion, we need to ask four questions, including the origins of the world, of mankind, morality, and the meaning of life" (Transcript #9, 16). Another informant described his belief in the Bible because of "how well it explains the world for you." He continued, "So if you look at Christianity, you know it walks you through every step of the way, from Genesis about the creation of the world, to why Christ had to come down, why his sacrifice was needed" (Transcript #27, 7).

When asked what convinced her about Christianity, another informant said: "Completeness. I think it's more like the Bible from start to end how it addresses everything" (Transcript #24, 9). Asked to clarify, she responded, "In terms of how life began and how life will end on earth" (Transcript #24, 10). One informant referred to the preservation of the Bible through the ages as evidence for its truthfulness. He explained the need to do some personal research, "Because I wanted to understand how it is true that the Bible is actually passed down from all generations. So I think I was convinced that yes it is God's word. Therefore I believe in Christianity and God" (Transcript #32, 9).

Christianity as a Logical or Rational Religion

The central research question of the study examines the extent to which and the ways in which the perception of Christianity as a rational or logical religion is a contributing factor to conversion among younger Chinese Singaporeans. It is noteworthy to point out that of the thirty-five people interviewed, eighteen informants (51.4 percent) described Christianity in Singapore as a "rational" or "logical" religion, without the interviewer introducing those terms in the questions asked. What did informants mean by "logical" or "rational" religion? The following section summarizes what informants meant in describing Christianity as a "rational" or "logical" religion. The comments were generally offered in the contexts of responding to three questions: (1) What is your view on or attitude toward Chinese religions and rituals? (2) How did you convert to Christianity? (3) What convinces you that Christianity is the one true religion?

The Nature of Christianity as a Rational Religion

When asked to talk about the processes, events, and people who influenced their conversion experience, several informants pointed to the intellectual aspect as a significant contributing factor. One individual, a marketing administrator, recalled receiving Josh McDowell's *More Than a Carpenter* as a gift from a friend to read. As a "logical rational kind of thinker," he said the book was helpful "because of the factual and logical kind of reasoning" marshaled by the author in arguing for the truth of Christianity (Transcript #8, 2). A quality of "logical" faith was exemplified by Jesus' audacious claim that he was God. He was either telling the truth or he was the devil or insane, but one cannot claim that he was merely a good teacher (Transcript #8, 5–6). That sparked his interest in reading the Bible. As he began reading the Book of Genesis, he was amazed that he could "connect with what it's saying," as he "tried to understand God's character through the Bible." He eventually joined an Alpha class, met facilitators, and found them "approachable and open, which was something I never thought of Christians" (Transcript #8, 2). He continued, "These were things that all lined up along the way, so then I accepted Christ towards the end of the Alpha class" (Transcript #8, 2).

Another individual decided to become a Christian because he regarded Christianity as "reasonable" and "historical" (Transcript #16, 2). Coming from a Buddhist background, his initial impression of Christianity was admittedly not favorable. However, he went on to study at Anglo-Chinese School, a prominent Methodist mission school, where Christians befriended him. From there, he attended church and Sunday school, where he conversed with his Sunday school teacher and prayed to become a Christian.

When asked to explain what he meant by "reasonable" and "historical," he said, "When I read the Buddhist scriptures, many of the stories look like myth; very unreal and a lot of deities, a lot of gods, beings, things like that and I had lot of questions how the world came into being" (Transcript #16, 3). He commented that the Buddhist scriptures did not answer his questions, like how life came to exist and where we are going. He said, however, "But the Bible, you know, things that have been recorded, when I checked it up, the thing is very historical so I can trust for what had happened" (Transcript #16, 3).

A third individual noted his conversion experience as an intellectual process, a "rational journey." When asked to clarify the meaning of his use of the term "rational," he said it referred to "how people think" (Transcript #27, 7). A lawyer by training, his initial view of Christianity was one of skepticism. However, his intellectual journey began when he attended a creationist versus evolution talk at a local church. From there, he read *The Seven Habits of Highly Effective People*, and reasoned that "all the principles come from natural laws and all natural laws flow from God" (Transcript #27, 4). While his conversion started as a "rational journey," he noted "that there is a point where rationality stops and then there's a part where faith has to take over to get you to the other side" (Transcript #27, 4). Furthermore, in comparison to Buddhism and Taoism, Christianity is rational "because it explains the world for you. So, you know, if you look at Christianity, we know that it walks you through every step of the way, from Genesis, talks about the creation of the world, how the world came about, all the way until, you know, why Christ had to come down, why his sacrifice was needed" (Transcript #27, 7).

In response to the question about the nature of Chinese religions and rituals, informants viewed Christianity as rational and logical in contrast to Buddhism and Taoism. When asked to respond to the teachings of Buddhism and Taoism, one particular person said, "Of course I don't believe in what they teach. I don't believe all these teachings. They don't make sense to me, and some people think it is very logical, but to me no, I don't think so. I cannot accept it" (Transcript #6, 8).

For this teacher, Chinese religions "were founded by humans, and the teachings were written by men, who don't claim to be God" (Transcript #6, 8). She explained why Christianity was attractive because it "gives me a sense of the world as a child of God." Her difficulty with Taoism is that it "teaches you about various gods." She continued, "It is difficult to imagine God as being in so many forms, in form of a kitchen god, in the form of something else. To me, it doesn't make sense. It is not logical either. It is not logical for the god to be so divided in his identity" (Transcript #6, 14).

Another informant was even more pointed in his comparison of Christian and Chinese religions. In comparison to Chinese religions, which "held a strong grip on me in the sense of fear of spirits, fear of the unknown," he insisted that "in Christianity it's more of a rational God, because I appreciate the creation around you" (Transcript #4, 2). Whereas his university training as an engineer in science and technology reinforced his faith in Christianity, it also caused him to view Chinese religions "as a bit backward, irrational, very much superstitious rather than something that is rational, something that can be explained" (Transcript #4, 4). Much of his skepticism of Chinese religions had to do with how people practiced rituals out of fear. They have never read sacred texts on their meaning and that "a lot has to do with trying to appease the unknown" (Transcript #4, 5). Fear is the motivating factor for practicing religious rituals, whereas a personal relationship with God is the hallmark of Christianity (Transcript #4, 8).

Without doubt, one's education seems to have a direct correlation with his or her view on religion. An architecture student from NUS characterized Buddhism and Taoism as "superstitious beliefs" because "they are like myths" (Transcript #12, 3). She went on to explain, "So it's hard for me to believe in something that I believe its folklore." On the other hand, "Christianity to me is like really based on truth like the Bible itself is a piece of documentation that has been passed down for so many years. It is consistent and contains archeological evidences" (Transcript #12, 3–4). When asked whether her education influenced their views, she said, "I think more or less because I actually came from math and science so our teaching is very scientific." In fact, she insisted that her educational background was "really logical" and "so like straightaway, I know the room for mystery is out" (Transcript #12, 9). For her, she saw "consistency" in the Bible because it was written by many people, yet it is one story. She reasoned that the Bible's consistency is evident in "that it's written over long periods of time, and it's more like a book that is based on facts" (Transcript #12, 11).

The correlation between education and religion was posed to an NUS law student. When asked if he felt his educational background impacted his view of Chinese religions, he said, "I guess that would be right, because

I was pretty much doing sciences." With regards to his view on practicing rituals, he said, "I should be more objective, rational, and logical, but you just don't really question because you've been doing it all along, and I'm not really sure what the religion actually does offer" (Transcript #28, 10).

An accountancy student did not think his education impacted his view of Chinese religions. However, as a "practical" and "very logical" person, he consistently considered "whether things make sense or not" (Transcript #32, 7). So when it came to consulting the Chinese zodiac, burning joss sticks, and offering paper houses and other material goods to ancestors, he regarded the rituals as "illogical" (Transcript #32, 7). However, before making a profession of faith in Jesus Christ, he did some reading and researched online, and concluded that the Bible is God's word because "it is written like so many years ago and it was passed down from all generations." When asked to clarify, he said, "So the key thing that I accepted is because this Bible exists and it is God's creation. Therefore I believe in Christianity and God" (Transcript #32, 9).

When asked about what convinced converts that Christianity is the true or right religion in contrast to Chinese religions, many informants described Christianity as "rational." When using this term, it was clear that they did not regard reason as the chief source and test of knowledge concomitant with philosophical ideals of the Enlightenment. While one physics graduate defined his use of the term "rational" as "intellectual," he clarified that he was not referring to a rational worldview (Transcript #19, 22). A law student described Christianity as "objective," but insisted that one has to be convinced subjectively (Transcript #28, 16). Another reported that he initially approached Christianity as a "rational thinker." That is, he regarded Christianity as characterized by a "great set of text with historical evidence, which other religions they kind of lack" (Transcript #8, 6).

For the most part, though, what many informants meant by "rational" referred to the active intellectual engagement of religious ideas, as opposed to passive acceptance of Chinese religious ideas and ritualistic practices. In particular, it seemed clear that the perception of Christianity as a rational religion referred to the process of examining and understanding biblical ideas. For example, an informant stated, "I make sense of the Bible through rationality, yeah, and how I arrived on a conclusion that the Bible is the truth is also through rationality" (Transcript #14, 14).

Similarly, another informant, an undergraduate computer science student, regarded Christianity as a rational religion. She explained, "Yes, I mean, also given that my own journey began intellectually, began with a rational kind of approach, I do believe it makes sense. It is rational but it is not what I would say the entire religion to be simply rational. It is a feature of the faith that is rational but it is not what it is all about. The main point is that it's spiritual; it's Jesus Christ" (Transcript #17, 8). She clarified her definition of a rational religion as an exploration of intellectual matters, such as historical evidences of Christianity, archeology of the biblical world, and the person of Jesus Christ. Christianity is a rational religion because "it makes sense" (Transcript #17, 6). When she worshiped *Guan Yin*, who is supposed to watch over and bless people, she never understood the basis for such beliefs. In Christianity, though, people come to the awareness that they are not good people. She insisted that "They make mistakes and need forgiveness." For her, that has to be the starting point, but she could not find it in Buddhism (Transcript #17, 6).

It is obvious, then, "rational" Christianity is viewed interchangeably with "making sense" or "logical." An NUS sociology student carefully qualified his remark as follows: "Christianity is rational. It is definitely not irrational and yet Christianity is also beyond rationality" (Transcript #13, 8). When asked to clarify his definition of rational, he said, "I would not think of rationality like many people use the term in the sense of a closed system, a universe that excludes supernatural and miraculous activities—that is—what is rational is limited to what can be proven by science." He continued, "However, the way I use rational is just interchangeable with logical" (Transcript #13, 9). When pressed to explain further, he said, "The Christian faith is fully logical in the sense that I have not come across so far any internal self-contradiction in Scripture, not in the doctrines of the Christian faith" (Transcript #13, 9). However, for him, it was not the case with Islam, Buddhism, and Taoism, where inconsistencies abound (Transcript #13, 9–10).

One informant pointed to the so-called "inconsistencies" of Taoism as the primary reason for converting to Christianity. Whereas Christianity "answered all my questions," which is the pull-factor, *Tian Gong* (heavenly grandfather) is amorphous and "we just worship the sky," which is the push factor (Transcript #9, 11). For him, it just "did not make sense" to spend S$20,000 for a Chinese funeral only to come back later to pay another S$10,000 to burn offerings because the deceased is suffering below and in need of a bigger house (Transcript #9, 8–9). Christianity is "true" because of its historical quality and "real" because, when watching National Geographic, he witnessed the amazement of God's creation (Transcript #9, 12). Likewise, a physics student, recalling his initial exposure to reading the Bible, said "I realized that many of the things look very reasonable and historical" (Transcript #16, 2). He was "convinced" of Christianity because of the historical quality of the OT and NT records. According to him, the Buddha was historical, but Buddhist sacred texts "don't look historical when I checked all those were composed hundred years after his death" (Transcript

#16, 11). In the case of Christianity, "All these things did happen and especially both the resurrection and the cross. The records are historical and reliable" (Transcript 16, 11).

A medical doctor recalled her negative view of Taoism because those gods were always remote and angry. Beyond that, she found ancestral worship irrelevant because she never had a relationship with her ancestors. For her, "It's more logical and rational when I look at Christianity" (Transcript #18, 7). When asked to clarify what she meant by "rational," she answered, "That I would be thinking through rather than following in obedience." Of course, what she meant by "following in obedience" was accepting a religion in deference to her parents' wishes. In contrast to Taoism and Buddhism, which is "more of following," she viewed Christianity as "trying to make sense of what I'm doing." She was "uncomfortable" with her negative perceptions of Taoism and Buddhism (Transcript #18, 7). Moreover, she saw herself as a "rational being," primarily because of her education. What is interesting is that she connected her relationship with Jesus Christ and Christianity as a rational religion by examining Jesus' teaching and whether it addressed her needs. She explained, "Like I would be looking at what Jesus said and did. And then it is not something distant but is also addressing me if I would follow him. So after that, it's like a dialogue and so that will be something that makes me want to have this belief rather than something I just have to follow" (Transcript #18, 7).

Another informant agreed that "rational means thinking through the teachings of the Bible" (Transcript #23, 12). Although he admitted to an "intellectual" aspect of religious faith, he insisted that Christian conversion, or the lack thereof, was a supernatural work. He said concerning the rational aspect of Christianity: "I think it's not just Singapore context. I think it's worldwide. The key question is why are the people, especially the grassroots people, not responding to Christianity. I think it's the spiritual aspect of the case" (Transcript #23, 12).

Beyond pointing to rationality as the process of intellectual engagement of religious ideas, several informants said Christianity was rational because it to spoke to life and reality. An engineer described his exposure to the gospel at a youth club as "a very rational and good message." When asked to explain, he said, "The gospel is very clear and specific. Basically, when I hear this message, it is good for my life. The whole thing, the meaning of my life, it became purposeful. I have Christ as my superhero rather than the monkey god" (Transcript #3, 6). It can be surmised that the gospel framed the way in which he viewed himself, his life, and the world. Before he became a Christian, his life was without meaning, purpose, or hope. He continued, "When I became a Christian, even my education changed. My objective, why I wanted to do this, changed. I did well at school. All that changed. For the first few years in secondary school, I was quite a model student. No more trouble" (Transcript #3, 6).

Another engineer, when asked what convinced him that Christianity is the true religion, said, "Chinese religion held a very strong grip on me in the sense of fears of the spirits, fears of the unknown. The Christian, I think, it's more of a rational God. I appreciate the creation around us. Then you can appreciate the human dilemma, human depravity, the need for a savior" (Transcript #4, 2). He continued, "For me, Christianity is true because it speaks to me of my situation. Because we are sinner, we have offended our creator God, and that relationship has to be restored" (Transcript #4, 10).

A law student at NUS expressed his conversion experience as a "rational journey." When asked to explain, he said, "I think you have to look at it in a sense how well it explains the world for you. So, you know, if you look at Christianity, it walks you through every step of the way, from Genesis, talks about the creation of the world, how the world came about, and all the way to why Christ had to come down, and why his sacrifice was needed." He continued, "Christianity explains why there's suffering in the world. Of course, Buddhism would make the same thing. So you have to compare. I think the classic way of looking at Buddhism is that it doesn't really explain where the world came from or that if there is such an explanation, I don't know of a very convincing one" (Transcript #27, 8). Having attended creationist versus evolutionist seminars, he explored the evidential aspect of Christianity as part of his initial intellectual journey in Christian faith.

Perception of Christianity in Singapore

Indeed, the question of whether Christianity in Singapore is perceived as a Western religion needs to be addressed. Of the thirty-five people interviewed, twenty-eight informants (80 percent) said Christianity in Singapore is perceived as a Western religion by those around them, such as parents or relatives, particularly older individuals from Chinese-speaking backgrounds. Of the thirty-five informants, seven people (20 percent) did not offer opinions or made no comments. However, for the informants themselves, twenty-nine out of thirty-five informants (82.8 percent) said they did not perceive Christianity in Singapore as a Western religion at the point of their conversion, nor do they see it as such now. The remaining six individuals offered no opinions or made no comments.

For the most part, informants pointed to their non-Christian parents as those who perceived Christianity in Singapore as a Western religion and discouraged their children from conversion. The reasons contributing to their negative perception were varied but a few common themes can be highlighted. One informant recalled her mother's opinion of Christianity as a Western religion primarily due to the ways Western missionaries carried about. "They speak English in a certain way," or "they don't really speak Chinese and are of upper middle class," she said. This was a stigma, because "like my mother's side of the family would be poorer and go to the temple" (Transcript #11, 21).

Another informant said, "Very foreign! And they can't speak our language. So when we were young growing up, we were like, this is a Western religion. And our parents do inculcate in us and say, 'This is a Western people's religion. Chinese is temple, you know, Westerners is church.' And so it doesn't really help if sometimes we go to church. When we went to church, the final person who has authority to stand up and speak is an Ang Mo [紅毛 or 'red-haired'] Caucasian missionary" (Transcript #1, 10). The perception of Christianity as a Western religion correlated with a negative view of foreigners was resonated in another interview. A young lawyer explained his parents' concerns: "I think that is certainly one worry and they compare Buddhism which has Chinese roots, and then Christianity, which they perceive as having Western roots. I think there's always been this, I mean, I'm not sure how to put this nicely, but there's always a sort of mistrust of foreigners and Westerners from the Chinese" (Transcript #27, 15).

Another young lawyer said his parents correlated Western with book learning. He said, "But I honestly think in Singapore and still in my family, the association of Christianity with Western culture and tradition is still very strong." When asked why, he said, "I think it's still very strong because of the fact that the religion is based on a book" (Transcript #28, 24). A female teacher said, regarding this negative perception, "I still remember my father would see it as like purely Western and therefore do not allow me to join. I still remember what he said then when he would even joke at the Catholics doing the sign of the cross and seeing all the churches were built in very Western styles" (Transcript #10, 11).

One informant explained his father's resistance as follows: "But I think my dad, coming from traditional Chinese background, might be resistant, just because it seems Western to him and he probably cannot connect with it. I remember he spoke very specifically about a savior. He said, 'There is no such thing as someone or something that can save you. Ultimately, it comes down to how you conduct your individual life'" (Transcript #8, 8). The apparent stark contrast between Buddhism and Christianity in Singapore was expressed by another informant. He said, "This question would mean a lot to my father-in-law, who is a Buddhist. He always sees Christianity as something Western, because its beliefs are so different than where we came from. It's seems so jarring to him" (Transcript #2, 15). Extending on the issue of misunderstanding or misinterpreting Christianity, one informant said, "Yes, my mother thinks it's a Western religion. She says it's Western because she is Hokkien and she says, *sia kao*, which means 'eat god.' The Hokkien people say the church people eat a part of god when you do holy communion, right?" (Transcript #34, 27).

Family relationship was another point of contention related to the perception of Christianity as a Western religion. When asked if his parents perceived Christianity as a Western religion, a male informant said, "Maybe. I'm not sure of whether they consider it as a Western religion. But I think subconsciously they may feel that they're losing a son because they ask questions like, 'why you become a traitor' or 'who is going to carry the urn?'" (Transcript #23, 16). The subject of family and identity was extended in another discussion. A female informant said, "Even my grandmother before she passed away complained about believers not partaking of food offered to the idols. So to her, it's more like segregating yourself from your family. It's like Western religion is causing you to break off ties from your ancestors" (Transcript #33, 24).

In general, informants explained that the negative perception of Christianity in Singapore as a Western religion has often been shaped by the media. These include depictions of Jesus as a Caucasian, Western church architecture in Singapore, Western missionaries in Singapore, English language, British colonial history, mistrust of foreigners, class distinction, and the correlation of Chinese ethnicity and religions.

Christian converts, however, did not view Christianity as a Western religion at the point of their conversion. The most common justification for their perspective was that Christianity began in the Middle East, expanded into the West and then embraced by many Westerners. As such, informants did not perceive Christianity in Singapore as a Western religion because many of their Asian friends are Christians (Transcript #17, 3).

For a few informants, they acknowledged their perceptions have been colored, to a large extent, by their Western education. Concerning the difference between Western and Asian Christianity, one informant said, "For me, because I have been brought up with in Western educational system, I don't see the difference much. Even though you may communicate in English and worship in a Western environment, Western hymns and in Western traditions, people continue to maintain their Chinese traditions and practices together with their Christian faith. I don't think they end up thinking that it is a Western religion, because it is still very communal; it feels like part of the family" (Transcripts #4, 11).

One informant attributed the perception of Christianity in Singapore as a Western religion to its colonial history and that many of the mission schools were founded by Western missionaries. However, she reiterated this observation in a positive light. She said, "So I think the schools, my parents will tell me that they are very good because they like you to go learn English, become more educated, get better jobs, and get better connections. One of the advantages is because they see there is a lot of money coming from the West" (Transcript #10, 13).

In discussing her negative perception of Buddhism and Taoism, one informant described her experience as "it's more of following." In comparison, Christianity is "trying to make sense of what I'm doing," he said. She then concluded: "I guess whether it's my education or that we are rational beings" (Transcript 18, 7). One last informant said regarding the association of Christianity with Western education, "Definitely, I think people who perceived Christianity as a Western religion, maybe in their mind it's equated with English education" (Transcript #28, 25).

The thirty-five informants offered various characterizations of Christianity in Singapore. One informant observed that Christianity in Singapore is influenced by the West. He added, "But culturally I think we are just Chinese Singaporean. So there is still hope for us not moving into that direction of Western Christianity" (Transcript #5, 8). For him, Christianity in Singapore is a "combination of West and East" (Transcript #5, 8). When asked if he regarded Christianity in Singapore as a Western religion, one informant said he used to think that way only because it was perceived as a "very trendy and cool thing, especially during his days in school" (Transcript #9, 17). He then qualified his remark about his attraction toward Christianity by insisting: "It would have been different if Christianity had been brought by Indians" (Transcript #9, 17). One university student argued that Christianity in Singapore is not a Western religion because "it originated in the Middle East" (Transcript #12, 16). Furthermore, she said, "It's actually a religion for everybody because I mean Christ said so himself." As such, her family and friends are quite open because "they'll always be globalized" (Transcript #12, 17). One other student offered his opinion when asked if he thought Christianity in Singapore was a Western religion, to which he replied, "Christianity is not tied to anybody or a particular culture, but it did come to us in Singapore through Western missionaries." He added, "I want to shift the emphasis away from culture to spirituality and to what Christianity means to us as human beings" (Transcript #13, 13). Another student was quite insistent when asked the same question. He said, "Christianity is not a religion; it's truth and it's meant for all. So it's meant to reach those who are willing to open their hearts" (Transcript #14, 17). One student insisted that

Christianity was not a Western religion, although it "felt Western to me" at the time when he was in a mission school (Transcript #16, 16). He explained what he meant by Western: "In a Methodist school, I was forced to attend chapel. It's not like in a very strange architecture and the priest was doing something I didn't understand" (Transcript #16, 16). So when I was in ACS (Anglo-Chinese School), Christianity to me is "modern." That is, "Modern is something attractive to me. Something trendy" (Transcript #16, 16). In contrast to Buddhism, which is "a bit old-fashioned," Christianity is "contemporary and socially acceptable at least to our peers" (Transcript #16, 18).

An informant referred to her Western education when asked about whether Christianity in Singapore is perceived as a Western religion. She clarified that it was not a matter of one or the other. "In my education, we are pursuing Western thought. So it's a split of East and West. What is important is truth. So even in Eastern ways, not everything is right. And, of course, in the Western way, some things we cannot subscribe to. But it's really what is true to you and what is relevant to you. How is Christianity relevant to you," she said (Transcript #18, 8). Admitting that Christianity is perceived as a Western religion in Singapore, an informant attributed the observation to false depictions of Jesus as a Caucasian in popular artworks. She pointed out, however, that he was "Middle Eastern," and felt slighted whenever that reference is directed to herself as an Asian (Transcript #20, 28). One other informant insisted that he does not associate Christianity with cultural values or identities. He said, "I don't differentiate myself from any Asian values or Western values because I still maintain this—I only have faith in God and that is what I believe. No values. Whether I'm Asian or whether I'm a Westerner because we are all still praying to the same one God" (Transcript #31, 12). Lastly, an informant acknowledged that he grew up with the perception of Christianity as a Western religion, partly because of its association with English language. But now, "I don't think it is. I wouldn't say it's a Western religion. I just think it doesn't belong to any like East or West. It's just international," he said (Transcript #32, 19).

Formation of Christian Identity

Researchers typically argue that religious conversion involves a process of adjustment in self-identification through at least some nominal acceptance of religious beliefs and practices that are considered true, appropriate, and useful. As such, the process of religious conversion is not only a gradual examination and acceptance of beliefs but the formation of a new identity as well. The locus of the new and emerging self-identity is, in fact, grounded in those religious beliefs. For Christians in Singapore, the Bible's teaching, as was passed through tradition and interfaced with culture, is a primary basis of belief and practice. The findings on the formation of Christian identity from the thirty-five interviews with Singaporean Christians can be arranged in four major themes, namely, beliefs, practices, relationships, and ethnicity. Particular attention is also given to probing whether Singaporean Christians perceive Christianity as a Western religion.

Religious Beliefs

With regards to grounding identity on religious beliefs, one informant seemed to speak for everyone in her statement: "My identity is basically formed by all these (biblical) stories. It's like otherwise we have no reason for doing anything" (Transcript #11, 13). An important conviction voiced by several informants regarding their Christian identity is that they are a "child of God." Whereas Buddhism teaches about reincarnation, one informant viewed herself as a "child of God" because of "having a share of salvation" (Transcript #6, 14). A student referred to herself as a "child of God," because "she has been bought with a price," and that gave her a healthier self-esteem (Transcript #30, 44). For another informant, being a child of God meant security, because "whatever happens in life, God is still my father, and I am still his child" (Transcript #4, 13). The subject of trust was expressed in another interview. When asked to clarify what he meant by child of God, he said, "You have to understand that what the father does is for your own good and you have to trust in what the father does. It's for your own good because he knows better and he is God" (Transcript #25, 7). One last informant admitted that he was a "child of God," but underscored the fact that he was also "Asian" by virtue of cultural heritage and geographical location. "My geography and my history and my culture affect the way I view my identity," he said (Transcript #19, 25).

For a couple informants, however, being a Christian was understood in relational terms as having a relationship with God. When asked about how he viewed himself as a Christian, an accountant said, "So to me is each day I will spend time at least talking to God, and it can be throughout the day. Because many got blessing and stuff, and also I spend time to read his word. For this, I follow the *Daily Bread*, which is very good" (Transcript #29, 18–19). A similar, yet slightly more theological, description of his Christian identity is offered by the use of the phrase, "in Christ." An informant clarified, "I recognize that my Christian identity is not something merely theoretical but it is in fact mystical. It is supernatural and it's something that

I would not be able to fully describe or explain beyond saying that in a very real sense, I am in Christ. I am a part of his body and all the benefits and promises and blessings that the Bible speaks of cannot be extracted from Christ" (Transcript #13, 10).

A couple of informants used the biblical term "disciple" to speak of Christian identity. Given the various shades of meaning and connotations, it was not surprising to hear their attempts to unpack this term. For one, he simply viewed it in terms of Christ's Great Commission (Matt 28:19)—"to go forth and make disciples of all nations across the world," he said (Transcript #27, 17). That meant, in particular, to share the gospel message with those around him and to find his place in the church. He explained, "I've been trying to find my role, maybe my gift that I can use in the church and, you know, see myself as a small part of a big thing, just as every part of my body has to work properly for the body to be healthy" (Transcript #27, 17). Another just said: "I see myself as a disciple trying to follow Christ, to become like him. In a way, he has given me the potential to already become the person I was meant to be. But it's more realizing what he has done and shaking all the habits of the past, I suppose" (Transcript #28, 17).

Identity Formation as a Process

While, on the one hand, most informants spoke of their identity as a present reality, a few, on the other hand, viewed their identity formation as an on-going process. One informant, who recently became a Christian, offered a rather realistic estimation of the stage of his journey. He said, "So my identity is still that of a learning Christian, because I think of sanctification as something that requires a lifetime and there is no one state wherein you are truly perfect" (Transcript #14, 18). A young accountant, likewise, admitted that he has much to learn and room for growth. "I guess I see myself as a very young Christian, who still doesn't fully understand the Bible and sometimes I have own doubts as well. So I will ask around for help for them to answer my questions, and I will still sometimes commit like certain sins," he said (Transcript #32, 18). Aware of his personal struggles as a relatively new Christian, one student was brutally honest about himself: "I see that as a Christian I was still a work in progress. As I'm going through in this life, there are still a lot of things that I love and needing to work on" (Transcript #15, 18).

The characterization of Christian conversion or identity formation as a "journey" emerged in a few interviews. Acknowledging her personal struggles as a person, one informant spoke of her Christian experience as follows: "It gives me a discovery on the journey to know about, you know, religion, God, and myself. As I come asking who I am, so it's like guiding me to know what God has made me to become" (Transcript #18, 8). That discovery, she continued, was "to know without tinted glasses of my strength and weaknesses and how those are relevant to myself and to others around" (Transcript #18, 9). Having been a Christian for a few years, one informant talked about the need to discern where he is at this point in his journey. "This is the journey of being a Christian. The juncture that I am in now is asking God to help me to understand him in Christianity to be even more relevant, making it more relevant in my adult life," he said (Transcript #23, 17). Having gone through the initial euphoria of her newfound faith in Christ, one informant discussed about coming down from the so-called "high" point of her experience to what she regarded as present reality. She explained, "But after a while I realized that it was really about perseverance to the end, like how knowing God should change the way I live my life genuinely" (Transcript #17, 8).

Religious Practices

Beyond the topic of religious beliefs, informants also talked about their outward manifestations. Given their newfound faith, how would Chinese Christians deal with their practice of Chinese religious rituals? The need for a Christian to be consistent in belief and practice was quite evident in a few interviews. For one informant, being a Christian simply meant "submit and obey" (Transcript #22, 27). "But we have to accept his way. It's not my way," he said (Transcript #22, 26). When asked to talk about her identity, one informant said, "My identity as a Christian now is very strong. I would like to think that when people look at me, they see me as somebody who lives the talk" (Transcript #20, 25).

In particular, the transformation of interpersonal relationship was cited as an important manifestation of religious belief for a couple of people. Coming out of a Buddhist and Taoist background, a young student talked about the impact of Christianity on how she viewed herself. "I think in terms of how I relate to others," she said (Transcript #24, 13). She explained that, in the past, she related to people conditionally on how they treated her. But her conditional treatment of people has since changed after she became a Christian. When asked to describe her Christian identity, an executive said: "I guess a more caring person. You know, after the incident, my relationship with my son has been even closer than before and even my son's character seems to have changed for the better as well" (Transcript #21, 19). Recalling how she has changed since becoming a Christian, a teacher talked about her relationship with her mother. "I remember my temper was very bad toward my mum. So it was only after reading the Bible about 'in your anger do not sin' that I didn't want to be a Christian hypocrite. So I followed what the Bible said that I saw transformation" (Transcript #10, 18). In describing her Christian identity, one last informant, without hesitation, said, "Okay, I will show my love. I try to love as much as I can, and I try to humble myself" (Transcript #35, 11).

In response to the question of whether becoming Christian meant the total eclipse or rejection of former religious practices and identities, informants offered a variety of answers. One informant reasoned that many, if not all, Chinese traditional customs and practices have their basis in Chinese religions. Consequently, it is nearly impossible to tease out the cultural aspects from the religious tenets. He said, "Like we give *ang bao* (red envelopes or gifts), celebrate Chinese New Year, these mean luck. You know it is kind of religious belief behind them. You know the two Mandarin oranges that we give to others refer to luck. Oranges means gold. So a lot of belief is actually behind Chinese customs and practices" (Transcript #1, 11).

While informants typically shunned Chinese religious rituals as unacceptable for themselves as Christians, many viewed participation in Chinese festivals as cultural, not religious matters. For those who were unclear about the distinction between cultural and religious elements, they would simply consult others on how to discern the differences. An informant discussed the difficulty of discerning cultural and religious matters on the occasion of his wedding. Tension was created because he wanted a Christian wedding but his in-laws wanted some Chinese traditions, which involved religious elements. He explained, "When we went to the shop in Chinatown and we were served by a Christian. And he was a referee in it. I remember him telling me, 'okay, this is the religious part, this is the Chinese part.' For anything that was cultural, I'm game for it. I take pride in being ethnic Chinese. But I don't bother with those things that border on superstition like releasing chicken underneath your bed and see which side of the bed it comes out from" (Transcript #2, 16).

One informant reasoned that although he no longer performed religious rituals, such as burning joss sticks and paper for the dead, that does not mean he will stop doing everything that he used to do in the past. Listening to him, he seemed to convey a certain degree of intuitive knowledge when it comes to discerning what to continue and what not to continue. He said, "Technically, I guess the homecoming, the reunion dinner, those are very Chinese stuff. No, those are blessings. I am bringing you well-wishes. I mean I don't see the struggle. There are good things I can use, where the things that I mean directly conflict with God, obviously not. I guess I can roughly know where to draw the line" (Transcript #3, 9).

Another informant clearly expressed that he has become somewhat of a "hybrid" after converting to Christianity. When it comes to negotiating his religious past and present practices, there are "overlaps in Christian values with other religions" (Transcript #4, 12). For him, there are certain matters which define Chinese identity. Those are all acceptable even for a Chinese who converted to Christianity. "I think maybe food, the practice of certain Chinese customs like the family dinner, the wedding dinner, some of the Chinese festivals, including Moon-Cake festival, the Dumpling festival, and reunion dinner," he explained (Transcript #4, 12).

The religious and cultural dimensions seem to be quite flexible in another interview. The informant was adamant that one can tell the difference between religious and cultural aspects. She said, "The Chinese New Year to many people is non-religious but a big part of the Chinese culture" (Transcript #6, 12). But she seemed to rationalize her actions when it comes to eating food that has been offered to idols. "But I did eat. I think to me it is still okay. What causes eating the food itself is not wrong, if you don't bow down to the idols," she said (Transcript #6, 13).

One discussion seemed to illustrate that informants tend to reinterpret religious occasions or practices in somewhat arbitrary ways. On where to draw the line concerning the use of joss sticks and papers, he said the line was quite flexible. He said, "But my personal stand is no. I don't want to but if it's at the expense of offending some people, then I will reconsider that then" (Transcript #8, 12). While he was clear about participating in Chinese festivals, he was ambivalent about continuing in ancestor worship. He said, "I can be there to kind of remember this person and respect him for what he's done. I don't see anything wrong with that *per se*. But if you ask me to hold a joss stick, then I will question like 'what difference it's going to make?' If it is gonna be religious, then of course, I would not" (Transcript #8, 13).

Another informant said that she continued to eat food offered to idols and held joss sticks after becoming a Christian. She has since continued those practices even though the church taught her to stop those practices. When asked how she dealt with this tension, she said, "I think I take the cue from my parents" in determining what is respectful or dishonoring to them. She said she has "no scruples" in participating in rituals if her non-participation disrespected her unbelieving parents (Transcript #10, 16). It is clear from the above interviews that the demarcation between the religious and cultural aspects of Chinese religious practices seemed subjectively defined and varied from person to person.

Chinese and Christian Identities

When a Chinese Singaporean becomes a Christian, how does the conversion process impact his or her ethnic identity? Does the new Christian identity eclipse or replace the Chinese identity? Are those identities mutually exclusive in the narratives concerning the beliefs and practices of Chinese Singaporean Christians? More importantly, do the Chinese converts perceive Christianity in Singapore as a Western religion?

All thirty-five informants (100 percent) indicated that becoming Christian did not mean the eclipse or denial of their Singaporean or Chinese identities. The informants were quite clear about what they regarded as markers of Chinese identity and their desire to negotiate Chinese and Christian identities. For informants, Chinese identity markers included ability to speak Mandarin or dialects, skin color, food choice, participation in Chinese festivals, and filial piety.

One informant insisted that, for Singaporeans, "Chinese identity is that you must speak Chinese, or in dialect" (Transcript #2, 16). He went on to explain the "core identity element of Chinese culture" was "filial piety" (Transcript #2, 18). The definition of filial piety, according to one informant was "respect to the elderly," and that it was "very important" to him (Transcript #5, 9). Identifying himself as Chinese, an informant was adamant about "skin color" and "language" as crucial markers (Transcript #9, 19). When asked what constituted Chinese identity in Singapore, one informant said: "I think maybe food is one thing because I still prefer rice. I think the practice of certain Chinese customs, like Chinese New Year, Moon-Cake festival, and Dumpling festival is a big part as well" (Transcript #4, 12). He still considered speaking in Chinese or dialect important, though he acknowledged that young people prefer to speak to their parents in English (Transcript #4, 13).

Concerning the potential tension of adhering to multiple identities, one informant insisted that there was no conflict between his Singaporean Chinese and Christian identities. He said, "For me, I don't really feel conflicted. I feel my (Chinese) values have always been very strongly grounded. And as I become a Christian, my values are even more rooted towards the faith" (Transcript #8, 9). When asked to explained what he meant by Singaporean Chinese values, he clarified: "Yes, few values that I would associate myself with, being family-oriented, filial piety, being hard-working, maybe a bit pragmatic. But with things like being materialistic, being very achievement-driven, these are things that I don't ally myself with" (Transcript #8, 9). Concerning his understanding of filial piety, he explained: "Filial piety means no matter what happens, what situation, we cannot forsake our parents. I mean in the most tricky scenario it is always maybe between your spouse or your parents. If I have a spouse that doesn't align with that—we are not gonna to leave our parents—then to me that is a no goal" (Transcript #8, 10).

Indeed the concept of "filial piety" was considered as a key marker of Chinese identity in the narratives of Singaporean Christians. Moreover, it was also clear that informants viewed filial piety as a cultural trait rather than a tenet of Chinese religious belief. A young mother said, "Being a Chinese Singaporean, as a Christian, I never think I need to abandon my culture. Someone was asking 'is it that you cannot celebrate Chinese New Year anymore?' I say, no, because to me that is only a culture. I can celebrate but the whole thing is, if the whole thing involved into religious practice, then I will not involve" (Transcript #7, 20). She insisted that the "core of Chinese culture" is still filial piety (Transcript #7, 21). Concerning filial piety, she said, "I don't see there is a clash because it is not an issue to me. Maybe in my mind I understand what is the core importance. Anything that is against God I will not put it in" (Transcript #7, 22). Likewise, a teacher gave her opinion regarding filial piety: "I think that is something different from religion. Every child should be filial to their parent, whether you are Christian or non-Christian. It is not a religious thing" (Transcript #6, 13). When asked to clarify why she considered filial piety non-religious, she replied, "It is universal. I think it is a universal value. Every culture, every society values this" (Transcript #6, 13).

Recognizing the potential conflict between his Chinese and Christian identities, an informant clarified his priority: "So when I think of myself as a Christian now, my identity is a Christian first" (Transcript #1, 11). Then he went on to explain his approach to dealing with his Chinese identity, particularly as it related to practicing religious rituals. He said, "So there are times I think the practices there are some conflicts. But I guess some of these practices have lost their religious significance. It is handed down and now becomes a tradition with no religious thinking behind. So it is just for the significance of tradition. Some I would not do. Some of them I think it doesn't matter" (Transcript #1, 11).

Another admitted to feeling ambivalent about not burning offerings to the ancestors when he became a Christian. Because he is the oldest in the family, his parents were afraid that "no one would send them things" when they died (Transcript #3, 8). According to the informant, many Chinese, particularly Chinese-speaking Singaporeans, would not convert to Christianity because they fear the consequences of abandoning their ancestors (Transcript #3, 9). As a Christian, he clarified that he still participates in two Chinese festivals, including the homecoming and reunion dinner, but he would no longer hold joss sticks, participate in funeral rites, and burn paper money to the dead (Transcript #3, 9).

Admittedly, not all informants were able to provide clear-cut demarcations between Chinese and Christian identities. A few conceded to having some form of hybrid identities between Chinese and Western influences. When asked about her traditional Chinese identity, an informant retorted, "I think that's a tough question, because sometimes I view myself in-between" (Transcript #26, 32). She clarified herself: "Yeah, I'm educated in a Western manner, but Christianity needs to be or should be contextualized. There are no Singaporean songs or Chinese songs written locally that, you know, express our way of worshipping God" (Transcript #26, 33).

Recognizing her Singaporean Chinese identity, one woman clarified that she is still Chinese, except she no longer practices Chinese religious rituals. Moreover, she admitted that she is "more Western" in the sense that Singaporeans are "more open to new ideas" (Transcript #33, 26). She identified herself as Christian, albeit a "modern Christian," because she no longer holds to certain Chinese customs or cultural things that her mother embraced (Transcript #32, 27). Concerning not feeling the need to have an elaborate Chinese wedding when she got married, she said, "Yeah, it's actually pointless" (Transcript #32, 28).

Having attended a Roman Catholic school in his adolescence, a period of time when he felt Christianity was very westernized, a recent convert identified himself as "Mainly a Christian or world Christian, then Singaporean, then Chinese" (Transcript #16, 19). However, he did not regard Christianity in Singapore to be a Western religion for a couple of reasons. One, he said, "I knew that Buddhism was also not Chinese, yet it's here in Singapore." Moreover, he reasoned, "Although many Westerners embraced Christianity, so have many in Asia" (Transcript #16, 19). For him, Christianity is a "universal religion; it's a world religion" (Transcript #16, 19).

7

Analysis of Research Findings

RELIGIOUS CONVERSION IS A major area of interest for those in theological or religious circles, but it is also an important subject of inquiry in the social sciences, particularly, anthropology, psychology, and sociology.[1] In sociology, religious conversion indicates the shift in personal belief and identity.[2] As such, the phenomenon of conversion involves much more than the mere reorientation of religious belief. Conversion is a process of evaluating—intellectually and affectively—new religious ideas and biographical information to reconstruct new identities as a way to help solve life problems.[3] Evangelical missiologists, who examine Christian conversion as a way to facilitate effective mission, deal with issues related to the interface of biblical truth and the changing realities of the world in which we live.

This chapter seeks to analyze new empirical findings on Christian conversion experience in Singapore, and how the gospel relates to those changing realities. The chapter aims then to explain the meaning and the importance of the data in the light of the three literature reviews, and to provide evidence for each point. Whereas the previous chapter is descriptive and discusses *what* is happening, with regard to Christian conversion in Singapore, this chapter is analytical and explains *why* it is happening by exploring emerging themes and patterns. Any attempt to analyze and examine the shifting religious landscape in Singapore will have to take into account both the micro-level factors of individual crises and choices as well as the

---

1. Rambo, "Theories of Conversion," 259.

2. Beckford, "Accounting for Conversion," 253–58; Balch, "Looking behind the Scenes," 137.

3. Snow and Machalek, "Sociology of Conversion," 167–90; Hefner, "World Building," 17; Woods, "Geographies of Religious Conversion," 440.

macro-level factors of situating Singapore in broader contexts of modernization and globalization.

The chapter argues from the research findings that the perception of Christianity as a rational religion is a significant factor in the conversion among younger Chinese Singaporeans to Christianity. In fact, data gathered from interviews appear to corroborate with Tong's thesis that religions in Singapore, including Christianity, are intellectualized and rationalized due to the processes of modernization. Related to the perception of Christianity as a rational religion is the question of whether Singaporeans view it as a Western religion. One researcher has even acknowledged the anomaly that Chinese Singaporeans are attracted to Christianity precisely "because of its Western features."[4] Our findings indicate that an overwhelming majority of the thirty-five respondents who converted to Christianity did not perceive Christianity as a Western religion at the time of their conversion. Christian conversion in Singapore does not involve a total repudiation of a former identity, but can be characterized as a hybridization of religious beliefs, practices, and identities.

Summary of Research Findings

Before we analyze the empirical data on Christian conversion in Singapore, it would be appropriate to summarize some key findings from the thirty-five interviews. One, informants converted from Chinese religions primarily because of four reasons. Informants reported that their lack of understanding of Chinese religious beliefs and practices was a major point of dissatisfaction. Coming from educated backgrounds, particularly the hard sciences, informants could no longer accept religious belief on a passive basis but required explanation or justification for them. Because they perceived Chinese religions as passed down through oral tradition, sometimes lacking historical reference, they rejected them largely as superstitions and illogical. Interestingly, while many informants reported about Christian accounts of miracles, they accepted them due primarily to their perception of supernatural elements portrayed as historical events in the Bible. Not only did informants not sense intellectual struggles with Christian faith, but they did not report problems over issues such as evolutionism, problem of evil, and the reliability of Scripture. It seems clear that converts' formation of a biblical worldview trumped the scientific worldview.

Yet in spite of their lack of understanding of Chinese religions, informants reported participation in religious rites and practices out of deference

4. Hwa, "The Gospel," 93.

to their parents. Religious belief or practice was viewed primarily as a gesture of respect for parents and Chinese culture, not as transcendent truth. Some regarded religious rituals as distasteful because they were often practiced as a commercial transaction to gain blessings or positive results. In a world in which self-help and success could be approached in a variety of ways, informants found it difficult to differentiate Chinese religions and practices from the rampant and empty commercialism of modern Singapore society. Beyond this, informants also voiced their disdain for Chinese religious practices, because they viewed them as motivated by unfounded fear.

A second key finding from the thirty-five interviews is that informants reported a keen desire to search for meaning and purpose in life, as they encountered personal challenges and crises. This was significant, as informants complained about not finding purpose and meaning in religious rituals on transcendent matters, other than to seek protection from harm and favor from the gods on temporal matters. Moreover, as many informants were exposed to Christianity in mission school environments or had contact with Christians, they reported experiencing answered prayers and signs from God as part of the conversion process. The encounters or experiences of God not only served to validate the veracity of new religious ideas but provided, in many cases, feelings of calm and peace. It was noted in the previous chapter that the vast majority of converts experienced extensive interactions with Christians prior to conversion or during the process of discovering or learning about Christianity through church attendance or campus Bible studies. In fact, twenty-seven out of thirty-five conversions took place within or involved a school context to a certain extent. The geography of Christian conversion in Singapore is no doubt significant, as religious practices are clearly demarcated in public places.

A third important finding from the interviews concerns the informants' perception of Christianity as the true religion in a context where ethnic and religious diversity flourish. Informants reported about their relationship with God as the grounds for their belief. A relationship with the Christian God was, in fact, a key distinguishing feature from Chinese gods, deities, idols, statues, and ancestors because of their inability to relate with them. The Christian faith, with a codified text in the Bible, was also preferred to Chinese religions. The latter was viewed as inferior because they were passed down from oral tradition and practiced out of duty or obligation to parents and Chinese culture. In light of their contrasting perceptions of Chinese religions and Christianity, it is interesting to note that eighteen of the thirty-five informants characterized Christianity as "logical" or "rational," as these terms were often used interchangeably. When informants used the term "rational" with reference to Christianity, they meant Christian faith "is logical," "makes sense," "corroborates with reality or learning," "is objective or intellectual because it can be examined," and "answers the questions of the origin of the world and life." While admitting to a factual component or the textual basis of Christian faith as the beginning in their spiritual quest, informants spoke of their faith in Christ as confirmed by religious experience.

Lastly, on whether informants perceived Christianity as a Western religion in Singapore, it is striking that twenty-eight out of thirty-five informants said "yes" for their non-Christians friends and relatives. However, twenty-nine out of thirty-five informants insisted that they did not regard Christianity as a Western religion at the point of or subsequent to their conversion experience. The remaining six informants either had no opinion or did not comment. There is thus a stark contrast in the perception of Christianity as a Western religion between ordinary non-believing Singaporeans and those who converted to Christian faith. A few informants acknowledged that their Western education, particularly in the sciences, colored the way they view Christianity in Singapore as transcending cultural and ethnic boundaries. What is interesting is that all informants interviewed did not believe becoming Christian meant the denial or eclipse of their Singaporean and Chinese identities. What is not clear from the findings is the degree to which the perception of Christianity as a Western religion hinders non-believing Singaporeans from converting. Although this question is beyond the scope of this study, it would be an important issue to explore in future research.

Christian Conversion in Singapore

From the aforementioned summary, various stages and levels of Christian conversion are highlighted. On a personal or micro-level, informants talked about conversion in terms of a process or stages. That is, they discussed about their religious background and crises as contributing factors to searching for meaning and purpose in life. In the search process, they encountered Christianity as an alternative and reported about significant interactions with individual and or communities of faith. At some point or another, the informants expressed a commitment to the newfound faith, which led them to decisions that demanded personal change or transformation. Those stages of conversion are highlighted in Rambo's, *Understanding Religious Conversion*, which presents a psychological analysis of religious conversion. In general, religious conversion refers to "turning from and to new religious groups, ways of life, systems of belief, and modes of relating to a deity or the nature of reality."[5] Specifically, conversion refers to a change "in the person."[6] In contrast to classical conversion literature, which depicts the conversion as a sudden event, Rambo argues that the religious conversion experience is a contextual process and involves a number of factors with distinct "stages" of progression.[7] The seven stages include context, crisis, quest, encounter, interaction, commitment, and consequences.[8]

In general, the notion of "context" refers to the biographical background of individuals, including ethnicity, upbringing, education, life experiences, and religious affiliation and practices. The context of one's life explains, in part, a person's identity formation as he or she is today. "Crisis" plays a significant role in the process of conversion when challenges tend to destabilize one's identity, assumptions, and religious beliefs. Situations stemming from doubts about religious faith, identity confusion, health problems, and family struggles are leading causes for distress. Moreover, difficulties in life often lead to breaking points, resulting in conflict and emotional responses. Those episodes lead people to reexamine their position in life and seek out alternative paths. This is the phase that Rambo calls the "quest." In searching for meaning and purpose in life, people turn to religious options and come into "encounter" with Christians or communities of faith. The aspect of "interaction" refers to one's participation in religious activities and getting to know the religious beliefs and practices. In other words, people do not experience religious transformation in isolation but are aided by resources made available to them. Aside from resources and interactions, people express "commitment" as part of the conversion process. The commitment to the newfound faith is often expressed when the convert formally and ritually joins a religious community. After one has made a commitment to follow a new religion, certain "consequences" or outcomes are manifested that suggest transformation in behaviors, relationships, attitudes, and plans of action.

Beyond the micro-level of conversion, there is the contextual or meso-level of the Christian conversion process, which involves examining conversion within the overall context of Singapore society. Specific issues unique to Singapore need to be addressed. Who are converted to Christianity? Why and how are people converted? What impact do those considerations have on Christian identity formation? This present study focuses on younger Chinese Singaporeans who converted from Chinese religions to Christianity.

5. Rambo, *Understanding Religious Conversion*, 3
6. Paloutzian et al., "Religious Conversion," 1053.
7. Rambo, *Understanding Religious Conversion*, 5.
8. Ibid., 16–17.

There is a simple reason for limiting this study to the Chinese. According to the 2010 census of population, most conversions to Christianity occurred primarily among the ethnic Chinese (20.1 percent), while the percentage of Indians and Malays remain very small.[9] Researchers observe that the heterogeneous nature of traditional Chinese religions is less of a marker of cultural identity.[10] Thus, Chinese Singaporeans are more susceptible to conversion than Indians and Malays, whose cultural identity is intricately bound to Hinduism and Islam respectively.

Of the thirty-five people interviewed, with the exception of four who have diplomas, all are university degree holders or are working toward a degree. The informants are either university students or graduates, working in some kind of professional vocation. The findings seem to support the notion that Christian conversion in Singapore is socially structured in terms of relationships and institutions. This is especially evident in the sense that most conversions occurred in school contexts or at least involved some kind of school context. Many converts, in fact, attended Christian mission schools and experienced significant interactions with Christians as part of their conversion process.

From the aforementioned findings, it seems clear that Christian conversion takes place within a specific socioeconomic sector (SES) of the Singapore population, at least in terms of ethnicity, age, education, and occupation.[11] Since most of the interviewed were younger people, who converted to Christianity at a rather early age, this pattern does seem to give credence to Tong's observation that an optimal window of conversion exists for those between the ages of ten and nineteen (40 percent) and twenty and twenty-nine (32 percent). One can surmise that people between the ages of fifteen and twenty-nine are in a period when they are in secondary, undergraduate or post-graduate educational programs, and are still relatively open to changing their views and convictions.[12] Moreover, as Tong claims, religious conversion in Singapore is related to social mobility, as those who are better-educated with higher economic status are more inclined to convert to Christianity from traditional Chinese religions. Thus, there seems to be a growing social class gap between Christians who hold higher social status and those who remain in Chinese religions, though this negative trend is rarely acknowledged.[13]

9. Wong, "Census of Population 2010," 11.
10. Tong, *Rationalizing Religion*, 65.
11. Ibid., 82.
12. Ibid., 84–85.
13. Ibid., 82–83.

Active Engagement Over Passive Acceptance of Religion

Christian conversion experience must be examined not only on the individual or micro-level, the contextual or meso-level, but also the structural or macro-level of religious change. What is abundantly clear from the thirty-five interviews is that all voiced their dissatisfaction with Chinese religious beliefs and practices as a key factor for their switch to Christianity because it offered a more active and personal way of expressing religiosity than Chinese religious practices. Informants reported about their dissatisfaction with Chinese religions and practices primarily for four reasons: (1) a lack of understanding of Chinese religious beliefs and practices, (2) performing rituals merely out of deference to their parents, (3) performing rituals as commercial transactions, and (4) practicing of rituals as motivated by unfounded fear.

A strong consensus emerged from the interviews that informants, before they were converted, practiced religious rituals out of passive acceptance. Informants insisted that not only did they not understand Chinese religions and practices, but they were discouraged by their parents from investigating them. In other words, they were taught to accept them without question. Since many informants were trained in the hard sciences, where they were taught to explain and justify their understanding, Chinese religions were unconvincing to them. Additionally, because Chinese religions were passed down primarily through oral tradition, informants simply viewed them as folklores, legends, myths, and lacking in historical reference. Chinese religions were perceived by many, in the end, as superstitions and illogical. A few informants even discussed sarcastically learning about Chinese religions from watching popular television programs and movies. It was also quite evident that informants rejected Chinese religions as superstitious, yet many did not struggle with Christian accounts of miracles and supernatural elements, because they regarded the former as legends or myths and the latter as historical elements taught in the Bible. Several talked disapprovingly about being offered to deities as god-sons or god-daughters at an early age when they lacked understanding.

Yet in spite of their lack of understanding, informants reported participation in religious rites and practices out of deference to their parents. Religious belief or practice was viewed primarily as a gesture of respect for parents and Chinese culture. Informants regarded Chinese religions and rituals as forms of filial piety, not personal expressions of inner conviction. Several informants regarded religious rituals as distasteful, because they were compelled by selfish motives and practiced as commercial transactions to gain blessings or positive results. At the same time, some informants viewed religious rituals as a self-help resource, and found it difficult to differentiate them from the rampant and empty commercialism of modern Singapore society. Above all, many informants voiced their disapproval of Chinese religious practices, because they viewed them as backward, irrational, and motivated by unfounded fear of the unknown.

These findings corroborate explanations offered by sociologists, such as Tong, regarding the "push" factors of conversion from Chinese religions to Christianity as reflecting a shift in the perception of religion in the context of modernization. According to Tong, a major so-called push factor is the younger Chinese's dissatisfaction with traditional Chinese religion. The whole idea of religious rituals, such as burning paper material belongings to the dead, is generally viewed as "illogical," "unrealistic," and "superstitious" for educated individuals who are trained to think critically.[14]

Informants expressed their disapproval of Chinese religions and practices, because they viewed them as essentially oral traditions past from one generation to another, highly syncretistic, amorphous in belief, devoid of codified canonical systems, and mainly expressed in terms of obligatory ritualistic practices. Here, the findings are consistent with Tong's statement: "Chinese religion emphasizes the ritual performance itself, rather than an internalization of the ideas and meanings of the religious practices."[15] The findings also indicated that those who followed Chinese religions and their rituals did so primarily out of obligation and duty in upholding such Chinese values as *xiao* (孝) or "piety," *li* (禮) or "propriety," and *zhong* (忠) or "loyalty," not out of personal conviction.[16]

In the context of modern Singapore society, which promotes voluntarism, such a view of religion is unacceptable because it suppresses individual choice.[17] This shift can be explained by the processes of modernization. As a process of modernization, pluralization engenders "the contestation of ideas, and the contestation of religions, opening up the possibility of multiple constructions of what constitutes the social order."[18] Thus, a key feature of modern life involves the increasing availability of options and choices.[19] In modern, pluralistic societies like Singapore, people have the ability to

14. Ibid., 113.
15. Ibid.
16. Ibid., 115.
17. Ibid.
18. Ibid., 115–16.
19. Berger et al., *Homeless Mind*, 23–82.

make religious choices that were not available to them in premodern times. The breakdown in traditional religions is due to the "individualization of the religious process."[20]

The modern preference for active involvement in religious beliefs, as opposed to passive acceptance of religious traditions, must be examined at the macro-level of modernization. The structural approach considers the process of modernization and its impact on social structures as a key driver of religious conversion.[21] According to Weber, the modern world in which we live is undergoing a continuous and increasing process of rationalization, and "One of the most important aspects of the process of rationalization of action is the substitution for the unthinking acceptance of ancient custom for deliberate adaptation to situations in terms of self-interests."[22] Whereas action is determined largely by habitual and affective elements in traditional societies, they are controlled by conscious ideas in modern societies. That is, rational action is motivated by perceptions of irrational action. Three key premises underscore religious conversion as a result of modernization. (1) Social and religious change occurs as people constantly reorient themselves in accordance with increasing rational thought and action. (2) World religions, such as Judaism, Buddhism, Islam, and Christianity, represent superior forms of religious rationalization when compared with traditional counterparts, such as animism and ancestor worship. (3) Religious rationalization occurs not only within world religions but also instigates conversion between religions.[23] Through the processes of modernization, traditional religions, regarded as superstitious and irrelevant, are slowly replaced by rationalized world religions that effectively address the emotional, ethical, and intellectual issues of modern life.[24]

Sociologist Tong observes that traditional Chinese religious practices in Singapore are slowly replaced by world religions, such as Christianity. Religious shifts take place as rationalization involves searching for answers to the intellectual, emotional, ethical challenges of modern life. Christianity, in part, meets this need because it proclaims a transcendent reality that is superior to that of temporal reality.[25] Tong's observation of Christian conversion in Singapore is one such example of rationalization of religion. He argues that Singapore's science-oriented and Western-styled educa-

20. Tong, *Rationalizing Religion*, 116.
21. Woods, "Geographies of Religious Conversion," 442.
22. Molloy, "Max Weber,"
23. Woods, "Geographies of Religious Conversion," 442.
24. Hefner, "World Building," 8.
25. Ibid.

tion system and the concomitant "intellectualization" of the population facilitates a growing number of conversions from Buddhism and Taoism to Christianity. The preference for more active and "rational" Bible teachings over religious practices reflects a shift "from an unthinking and passive acceptance of religion" to a religion that is believed to be "more systematic, logical, and relevant."[26] Tong describes the preference for Christianity as one "where conscious ideas emerge in the orientation of action and becomes more rational."[27]

According to Tong, it is this perception of Christianity as a rational religion, which has attracted so many younger Chinese Singaporeans.[28] To younger Chinese Singaporeans, who live in a modernized and globalized society and are educated in Western-styled, scientific and analytical environments, Chinese religion, as expressed in unquestionable rituals and practices, is simply unacceptable. This is especially true for those living in modern societies, which emphasize voluntarism, personal choice, and freedom to express their opinions.[29] Dissatisfaction with Chinese religion in general and disdain for rituals and practices in particular is a major factor for Singaporean's preference for Christianity as a rational religion. Perhaps unbeknownst to Christian converts, changes in the social structure of Singapore society actually play a significant role in one's religious choice.

Once converted, informants talked about renouncing their participation in religious rituals, albeit to varying degrees. Most said they would no longer use joss sticks and papers or participate in funeral rituals. Although their decision to opt out was often met with disapproval from family members, more converts are now experiencing greater degree of tolerance from non-believing family members. The main concern on the part of Chinese parents, in the event of their children converting to Christianity, is not having someone perform funeral rituals for them when they die.[30] This observation was largely confirmed by interviews with informants. While insisting that they would no longer participate in funeral rituals, including offering sacrifices, burning paper goods, setting up altars, and taking part in processions, most, if not all, informants indicated that they would attend religious funerals to show honor and respect to their family members.

However, informants also reported that not all elements from their religious background need to be discarded as a result of their conversion.

26. Tong, *Rationalizing Religion*, 4.
27. Ibid., 114.
28. Ibid.
29. Ibid., 115.
30. Ibid., 116.

Over ten informants indicated that there was no clear demarcation between religion and culture aspects. For example, some would continue to eat food offered to idols while others would not. A few said that they continue to hold joss sticks even after their initial conversion to Christianity, though they later abandoned the practice. Most, if not all, participated in religious festivals because they considered them as cultural, not religious matters. Some informants expressed that they would continue to accompany their family members to temples and graveyards on religious occasions to show respect and honor to their family members. At least three informants argued that the way to distinguish cultural and religious matters was to simply ask others for their opinions. These findings seem to support Goh's contention that Christians in Singapore hold to somewhat "relaxed" attitudes regarding ancestor ritualistic practices. Goh concludes that of the seventeen rituals examined in his qualitative research, eleven were reported as acceptable for Christian participation.[31] The five rites considered unacceptable include burning incense and paper goods, preparing ritualistic items and setting the altar at funerals, and offering sacrifices and burning incense at the grave or columbarium.[32]

The above observations confirm, to a large extent, Tong's theory that many Christian converts in Singapore continue to observe certain Chinese customs and festivals because they "rationalize" that they are cultural rather than religious events.[33] At the very least, a few informants reinterpreted participation in Chinese customs and festivals with Christian teaching, such as arguing for filial piety as a biblical mandate. The virtue of filial piety—particularly expressed in terms of respecting and honoring parents—is viewed as consistent with biblical teaching. It can be surmised that filial piety has become a "catch-all" virtue responsible for the rather fluid and sometimes subjectively determined demarcation between cultural and religious boundaries in Singapore society.

The fact that a few informants indicated the way to determine between religious and cultural aspects was by "asking others" seems to be rather arbitrary and subjective. It is no wonder that many Christian converts from Chinese religions have no scruples in attending religious funerals, and participating in customs and festivals, particularly if they view those events in association with filial piety. Conversely, informants also indicated that not all Christian rites, such as baptism, need to be adopted for fear of parental

---

31. Goh, "Practice of Ancestor Rites," 221.
32. Ibid., 167.
33. Tong, *Rationalizing Religion*, 118.

opposition.[34] Most converts accepted baptism but several delayed participation of this rite out of respect for and in fear of alienating their non-Christian Chinese parents. The hybridization of religious beliefs and practices in Christian conversion underscores the challenge of coming to grips with the complex relationship and distinction between culture and religion.

It appears that Singaporeans often fail to understand the complex relationship between culture and religion, particularly when proponents of Buddhism and Taoism seek to make clear demarcations between them. For example, while acknowledging the growing apathy among younger Chinese Singaporeans toward Chinese customs and rituals, representatives of the Singapore Federation of Chinese Clan Associations insist that "the customs and rituals related to Chun Jie (Chinese New Year) can be practised whether one is a Christian, Buddhist, Taoist, atheist or agnostic."[35] This is so because traditional Chinese practices are distinct from Buddhist and Taoist religious practices, and the practice of "Chinese customs and rites cut across religious boundaries."[36]

The tendency to conflate cultural and religious elements (the latter of which is often rejected by younger Chinese Singaporeans) explains why Chinese customs and practices are rejected in total when younger people associate them with Chinese religions. The assumption of a clear distinction between culture and religion results, for example, in an understanding of filial piety as a catch-all virtue for preserving Chinese culture, and as a moral value "that holds a nation together and help ensure a stable and peaceful society."[37] In contrast, Western culture, religion, and the English language are viewed as underlying reasons for the erosion of Chinese culture, customs, and rituals in Singapore.[38]

Perception of Christianity as a Rational Religion

The findings from the thirty-five interviews revealed a variety of reasons why informants found Christianity to be an attractive alternative to Chinese religions and practices. While informants talked about their dissatisfaction with Chinese religions as a key "push factor," they also highlighted the spiritual benefits of Christianity as the "pull factors" for conversion. For example, experiencing a personal relationship with God was favored over

34. Ibid., 117.
35. Wee, "Forward," 9.
36. Ibid., 5.
37. Ibid., 9.
38. Ibid., 11.

worshiping idols and ancestors, which were viewed as remote and impersonal. Informants also talked about receiving answered prayers and signs from God as additional spiritual benefits. All these are consistent with what Tong discussed as the spiritual reasons for conversion.[39]

Social benefits of Christianity were also mentioned as pull factors for conversion. On this point, informants received significant influences from relatives and friends, including extensive exposures to Christian communities as part of their conversion experience. This, too, is consistent with Tong's contention that peer influence plays a significant role in one's conversion process. Moreover, the venue of Christian conversion also plays an important role in conversion, because Singapore maintains clear demarcations between public and private religious spaces. In fact, many informants attended mission schools at one point or another in their lives.

Beyond the aforementioned factors, one particular element stands out as a significant factor for Christian conversion. When asked what convinced them that Christianity is the true religion in comparison to Chinese religions, eighteen out of thirty-five informants reported their view of Christianity as a logical or rational religion as a basis for their conversion. Although it is difficult to determine the extent to which their view contributed to their decision to switch, it played an important role, nonetheless. Here, the process of rationalization is an important contributing factor for conversion as evidenced by the strong correlation between education and religion. According to Tong, Singapore's science-oriented education system and the resultant "intellectualization" of the population is the underlying factor for the growing number of conversions to Christianity. The appeal of Christianity is that Christians perceive it as a "rational" religion in contrast to Buddhism and Taoism, which are perceived as "irrational" and "illogical."[40]

In times of personal crises, for example, informants spoke of the need to find meaning and purpose in life. According to Tong, religion serves its purpose best when it "provides man with the cognitive, affective, and moral capacity to deal with the world he lives in."[41] It was obvious that Chinese religions failed to provide those who converted to Christianity with intellectual, spiritual, social and relational benefits needed for one to navigate life in the modern world.

Informants found Christianity helpful because it met particular existential and spiritual needs. Some experienced relief from fears, answered prayers, and miraculous signs from God. They consistently pointed to their

---

39. Tong, *Rationalizing Religion*, 110–12.
40. Ibid., 82.
41. Ibid., 119.

personal relationship with God and the textual basis of Christianity in the Bible as the distinguishing features of Christianity from Chinese religions. Moreover, the findings also revealed that since most Chinese Singaporeans experienced significant interactions with Christians either prior to or during the course of their conversion experience, the social and relational benefits of Christian faith are rightly considered as pull factors.

What seems striking from the findings is that informants talked extensively about the intellectual dimension of Christianity. This dimension or the doctrinal aspect of Christianity is an important characteristic of Christianity as a rational religion. Converts characterized Christianity as a rational religion because it "makes sense," or "it corroborates with reality," or "it answered the questions about the origins of the world." Informants, particularly university students, accepted Christianity because they perceived it as a "logical" or "rational" religion.[42] In fact, many used the terms "logical" and "rational" interchangeably in describing Christianity. Their perceptions did not mean, however, they were able to resolve all intellectual questions regarding Christianity. Although converts did not mention specific intellectual issues, eighteen out of thirty-five informants discussed about the rational nature of Christian faith, with its basis in the Bible and historical narratives, allowed for active investigation and intellectual inquiries. In the final analysis, a few described Christianity as a spiritual journey.

The findings seem to be consistent with Tong's argument that the "intellectualization" of religion in Singapore, with its roots in the science-oriented education system, is responsible for a growing number of conversions to Christianity.[43] Tong maintains, "It is this perception of Christianity as a modern, English-based, ethnically neutral religion that partly explains for its attractiveness to the younger generation in Singapore, who are themselves socialized into an English-stream western-oriented educational system."[44] Christian converts' preference for a more rational religion, with its textual basis in the Bible over Chinese ritualistic practices, reflects a shift from an unthinking and passive acceptance of religion to one that people perceive as more "rational, systematic, and intellectual."[45]

By using the term "rational" to describe their religion of choice, what Singaporeans really meant was that they preferred a religion whose validity they can evaluate for themselves. In the gradual course of conversion, this evaluation process involved both intellectual and affective aspects of

---

42. Ibid., 104.
43. Ibid.
44. Ibid., 91.
45. Ibid., 114–15.

Christianity.[46] Moreover, Christianity's emphasis on Bible study, whereby informants explored for themselves the validity of its truth claims, indicated a modern preference for "active" investigation rather than "passive" acceptance of faith.[47] The findings seem consistent with the view of religion in modernity when one shifts from passive acceptance to active search for meaning when he or she is confronted with religious options. Notably, the decision to convert involves not only a view of religion as a "problem solving mechanism," but an attempt to align religion with self-identity and worldview or as an avenue to facilitate identity transformation.[48]

Compared with Taoism, for example, Christianity is a rational religion because it involves cognitive and affective evaluation of religion. Far from an instantaneous event, the conversion process is a "sequential trying out of new beliefs and identities in an effort to resolve felt difficulties."[49] Traditional views on conversion often characterize the phenomenon as a radical turning point, whereby one puts off an old self and puts on a new self. However, it is probably more accurate to view Christian conversion within the larger socio-cultural context of Singapore and to acknowledge that "religious affiliation is socially structured" in terms of relationships and institutions.[50]

In recent discussions with Tong via email, he expressed little surprise about our research findings. A few important points emerged from those conversations. Firstly, he insisted that he has not changed his views since the publication of his book in 2007. Secondly, perhaps with the exception of Daniel Goh's 1999 study, "Rethinking Resurgent Christianity in Singapore," he noted that "he has not read anything that contradicts" his work. In response to Goh's critique of his thesis, Tong writes, "Goh suggests that people convert to Christianity because of a need for transcendence. I find that a weak argument and with little empirical proof. Why should people need transcendence? And if they do, why convert to Christianity?" Thirdly, Tong confirmed that "it is the older Singaporeans who view Christianity as a Western religion, but this is not the case for younger Singaporeans." Lastly, he stated that the "real question to be answered is: why do converts view Christianity as a rational religion compared with Chinese religions, and what are the independent associations or causalities?" In probing informants' perception of rationality, it was apparent that some referred to

46. Ibid., 105.
47. Ibid.
48. Ibid.
49. Ibid.
50. Ibid., 106.

historical and empirical evidences, as neutral or universal criteria in adjudicating competing religious truth claims. Thus, the perception of Christianity as an "intellectual" and "objective" religion gave rise to the opinion that Chinese religions, which deemed to have little or no basis in reality, were "myths," "legends," and "superstitions." The subject of "independent associations or causalities" in adjudicating competing religious truth claims would be another viable topic for further research.

Perception of Christianity as a Western Religion

Related to the perception of Christianity as a rational religion is the question of whether Chinese Singaporeans view it as a Western religion. Of the thirty-five informants, twenty-eight said that Christianity was a Western religion among their non-Christian friends and family members. This was particularly true for older individuals from Chinese-speaking backgrounds, but twenty-nine of those interviewed insisted that they did not view Christianity as a Western religion at the point of their conversion. Informants discussed extensively, in the chapter on research findings, about experiencing resistance from their non-Christian parents precisely because they regarded Christianity as a Western religion. For the non-believing parents of a few informants, seeing their children convert to Christianity was tantamount to losing them to a foreign god or the abandoning of their Chinese family, identity, and culture.

How does one account for the stark contrast in the perception of Christianity as a Western religion among older non-Christian Singaporeans and younger converts who viewed it as a global, international, or ethnically neutral religion? Why did informants associate their Western-styled education with their view of Christianity as an ethnically neutral religion? What is the interrelationship between Christianity and education in Singapore that shape Christian identity? First, the interview findings essentially corroborate Tong's contention that it is the older Singaporeans who view Christianity as a Western religion, but this is not the case for younger Chinese converts.

The hybridized nature of Christian beliefs, behaviors, and identities is helpful to explain this reality. In his chapter on "Singapore" in *Christianity in Southeast Asia*, Robbie B. H. Goh talks about the "social influence" of Christianity in Singapore as mediated primarily through the establishment of various well-respected "mission schools."[51] Goh observes that Christian educational ministries became a very effective tool for churches to bridge

---

51. Goh, *Christianity in Southeast Asia*, 35.

the initial gap between British colonizers and immigrant people.[52] Those schools not only provided reputable and affordable "Anglophone" education but opened the door to employment opportunities for locals under the colonial government .[53] Local Singaporeans naturally perceived Christianity as associated with higher education, better income, and middle-class identity.[54]

According to Goh, statistics bear out his claims, whereby Christians in Singapore are represented by the highest percentage of college graduates, people with better income and housing.[55] More importantly, though, Christians account for a higher percentage of people who spoke English at home, reinforcing the perception of the English language as the *lingua franca* in Singapore and English-speakers with "cosmopolitan" social identities.[56] Goh observes: "Christianity is often perceived as the religion of English-speaking, middle-class cosmopolitans who studied at a good school (if not specifically a mission school), had the opportunity to study in a university (possibly an overseas one), and who are now in a professional or managerial position with a comfortable middle-class lifestyle."[57] Given its strategic location, prosperity, and openness, Goh predicts that Singapore will continue to serve as a "hub" for Christian organizations and ministries in Southeast Asia. [58]

The argument for the hybridization of Christian faith, practices, and identities is nuanced and reflected in the observation that Christians in Singapore actually hold in tension both the "cosmopolitan" and "heartland" identities.[59] Goh argues that Christianity exists in Singapore within the tension of national impulses and globalized networks. On the one hand, Christianity, like all religions in Singapore, is regulated by and conforms to state policies under the "Maintenance of Religious Harmony Act" in terms of religious space, practices, and multiculturalism. Under Singapore's multicultural policy, race and religion are conflated with government definition and control of those boundaries.[60]

---

52. Ibid., 38.
53. Ibid., 39.
54. Ibid., 35.
55. Ibid., 41.
56. Ibid., 42.
57. Ibid.
58. Ibid., 45.
59. Goh, "Christian Identities in Singapore," 1.
60. Ibid.

On the other hand, Christianity, unlike religions that are ethnically correlated (i.e., Islam, Hinduism, Buddhism, and Taoism), is perceived by many in Singapore as a Western religion, one which is obliged to expand itself at the expense of ethnic or race-based religions. With its roots in colonialism, Christianity, along with concomitant association of Western values and ways, is resisted due to fear of cultural "deracination."[61] The perception of Christianity as a Western religion associated with "elite" social status and English-education is thus perpetuated by non-English-speaking Singaporeans.[62] A class divide is thus created when "Anglophone Christians" in Singapore are perceived as linked with university-education, English-speaking, social class elitism, and "cosmopolitan" in identity.[63]

This awkward positioning, according to Goh, compels Christianity in Singapore to constantly rationalize and adapt its processes on two fronts. On the one hand, Christianity in Singapore identifies itself as a rooted aspect of the national community, which preserves the uniqueness of Chinese identity and the "hegemony of the state."[64] On the other hand, it associates with Western languages and cultures, capitalizes on its global networks and its affinities to capitalist modernity, and segregates from traditional religious practices.[65] As such, Singaporean Christians adopt a "flexible identity" by preserving the social bonds with the Singapore "heartland" and channeling the bulk of their evangelical energies outside of Singapore's shores, thus avoiding inter-faith tensions at home, which might be construed as a violation of the Maintenance of Racial Harmony Act. In this way, Christianity creates a "modernity without deracination," holding in tension the "cosmopolitan" and "heartland" identities.[66]

Christian Identity in Singapore

How do the aforementioned considerations influence Christian identity formation in Singapore? To what extent does becoming a Christian impact ethnic or national identities? It is noteworthy that all informants interviewed did not believe becoming Christian meant the denial or eclipse of their Singaporean or Chinese identities. This observation certainly reflects a high degree of hybridization of beliefs and behaviors in Singapore. No

61. Ibid., 9.
62. Ibid.
63. Ibid., 10–11.
64. Ibid., 13.
65. Ibid., 20.
66. Ibid., 14.

religion is completely neutral or free of cultural influences. As noted in chapter three, Tong maintains that Christian conversion in Singapore does involve a process of intellectualization, rationalization, demystification, differentiation, and hybridization of religion. He writes,

> Conversion to another religion does not necessitate a total shift in religious orientation and identity, the negation of an old self and its transplantation by a new self. Rather, given the linkage between religious behavior and the cultural attributes of the population in Singapore, religious conversion often results in a hybridization of beliefs and ritual behavior, not a total repudiation of the previous belief system.[67]

Tong's "hybridization" thesis has important implications on the formation of Christian identity in Singapore. Take, for example, the observation that converts renounced their Chinese beliefs and practices, but did so in ways that either arbitrarily rationalized religious and cultural boundaries or reinterpreted certain Chinese rituals with Christian teachings. This is consistent with Tong's argument that Christian converts, who persist in particular Chinese religious rituals, "rationalize that these practices are not religious but cultural behaviours."[68] In doing so, Christian converts fuse together elements of their religious past with Christian faith and practice. Tong thus concludes, "In Singapore, conversion does not mean the total denial of a past identity and the acquisition of a completely new one. Rather, there is an accommodation between the new religious identity and the cultural forms from which the individual is socialized from young."[69]

The fact that Christian conversion in Singapore occurs within a specific socioeconomic sector of the population reflects a marked shift in attitudes among converts from their view of traditional Chinese religious practices as "illogical" and "irrational" to what they perceive as a more "rational" and "modern" religion in Christianity. Christian conversion in Singapore involves both the "push factor" of Chinese religions and "certain pull factors, such as the nature of Christianity, the linkage between religion and the educational system, and the nature of a modern society."[70] According to Tong, it is this perception of Christianity as a "rational" and "modern" religion, which partly explains why younger, Western-educated, Chinese Singaporeans are more predisposed to convert to Christianity over

---

67. Tong, *Rationalizing Religion*, 78.
68. Ibid., 118.
69. Ibid., 117.
70. Ibid., 82.

the years.[71] Social mobility in Singapore, particularly in terms of education and occupation status, is an underlying factor explaining why individuals representing a particular socioeconomic sector are switching from traditional Chinese religious practices to Christianity.[72]

It must be admitted then that the personal or micro-level and contextual or meso-level aspects of Christian conversion cannot fully account for the changing realities in Singapore. One must situate those perspectives within the larger or macro-level contexts of modernization and globalization on Singapore. The perception of religion in Singapore has changed over the years. Certainly, the processes of modernization and globalization have played a significant role in that transformation. The effects of globalization on Singapore are most evident in terms of the country's British colonial experience, use of the English language, Western education system, and connection to global markets. As one sociologist rightly points out, "Changes in the structure of society, perhaps unknown to converts themselves, therefore play a key role in determining religious choice."[73] The crucial point in understanding Christian conversion experience in Singapore—whether on the micro, meso, or macro-level—is that it reflects the hybridization of beliefs, behaviors, and identities.

Rationality, Rationalization, and Rationalism

At this point, it is important to distinguish rationalization from associated concepts, such as rationality and rationalism. Those terms hold different meanings, whether used in Asian critiques of rationalistic, Western theology in Asia, Tong's thesis of the perception of Christianity as a rational religion, or in our qualitative interviews. In Weber's sociology of religion, the terms "rationality," "rationalization," and "rationalism" are notoriously difficult to define. For example, rationalism refers to ordering of means-end calculation into patterns for the purpose of evaluation, while rationalization refers to the systematization of idea. Rationality indicates the control of action by those ideas.[74] In distinguishing such overlapping concepts, Weber argues that religious systems tend to move beyond magic and rituals to become more systematic and rationalized. One must make a distinction between rationality as the process of the modernization of society and rationalization of religion. The latter, as used by Tong, refers to the process of disenchant-

---

71. Ibid.
72. Ibid.
73. Woods, "Geographies of Religious Conversion," 443.
74. Swidler, "Concept of Rationality," 35–42.

ment, making explicit of the implicit practices, providing an organizational framework, and codifying religious teaching in written form. In discussing rationalization of religion with reference to Singapore, Tong makes two important observations: (1) there is a rationalizing of Christianity among believers, particularly younger Chinese students, and (2) a conversion process where rationalization plays an important role in religious switching.

To be sure, Weber also uses the term rationalism. While the term is often defined in terms of Enlightenment philosophy as a reliance on reason to guide belief and action, Weber uses it in different ways. The term is used to indicate the ordering of action into patterns or worldviews based upon some "value postulate" for the purpose of evaluation. Since the ordering of patterns are done from particular points of view and are situated within particular historical contexts, they are ultimately perspectival in nature. Thus, the term is often used as an intellectual imposition of a coherent and ordered set of ideas upon the world. In Weber's thought, rationalism can take on a variety of forms, including ascetic, Confucian, scientific, technological, and economic rationalism. As a historical concept, rationalism is far from an internally consistent concept. The important point is that human rationality—a methodology to control action by ideas—does not necessarily mean a belief in the predominance of rational motives or a commitment to rationalism in the form of Enlightenment epistemology.

In other words, the reality of the rationalization of Christianity in Singapore should not be construed as tantamount to the intrusion of "rationalistic" or Western theology in Asia, as aligned with eighteenth-century Enlightenment philosophy. Furthermore, one's inclination toward the rational or intellectual dimensions of life, as indicated by interview respondents, does not necessarily require commitment to rationalism as a philosophical tenet. This is so because practical and substantive rationality are distinct ideas in Weberian thought. The prior refers to human capacity for "means-end rational action," while the latter refers to the direct ordering of actions into patterns for evaluation, as reflected in the Enlightenment's faith in reason.[75]

Not only are they distinct ideas, but practical, theoretical, and formal rationalization processes actually dominate substantive rationalization processes in modern Western societies. For example, there was a time when the Judeo-Christian worldview provided the point of reference for major groupings of substantive rationalities in the West. Since the eighteenth century, however, Western societies have witnessed the erosion, if not the complete eclipse of the Judeo-Christian worldview by the scientific worldview.

---

75. Kalberg, "Max Weber's Types," 1168.

Science, as a mode of knowledge, is presumably and analytically distinct from values. And values could no longer define the theoretical rationalization processes in modern times. In the modern era, science is falsely assumed as objective knowledge and distinct from values. However, people rarely recognize this false assumption. The irony is that "This holds true even though the scientific worldview as a whole is itself a substantive rationality" in Weber's sociology of religion.[76]

Explaining Conflicting Viewpoints

This study has argued, thus far, that the perception of Christianity as a rational religion is an important factor for Christian conversion in Singapore. The research findings are in basic agreement with Tong's thesis. In stating this case, it is quite apparent that both Tong and this present study counter the common Asian missiological criticism of the Western, and, hence, alien nature of Christianity in Asia, and that rationalistic theology is inappropriate for effective mission in that part of the world. Asian missiologists and Singaporean sociologist Tong, along with this study, disagree on at least three points.

First, those viewpoints conflict on the role and value of the rational element in Christianity. Asian missiologists attribute the alien nature of Christianity in Asia to the intrusion of rationalistic and Western theology through Western missionaries, whose theological methodology is often aligned with Enlightenment rationalism. Rationalistic theology contributes to rational and Western expressions of Christianity, which are detrimental to effective mission in Asia. Tong's sociological research, on the other hand, indicates that the perception of Christianity as a rational religion is a significant factor for those converting from Buddhist and/or Taoist backgrounds, particularly among younger Chinese Singaporeans who are "socialized into an English stream, scientifically oriented educational system."[77] The research findings corroborate, to a large extent, Tong's thesis in that eighteen out of thirty-five informants indicated their perception of Christianity as a rational religion played an important role in conversion. In other words, the correlation between education and religion is quite evident as Singapore continues on the path of modernization and globalization.

How does one account for this disconnect in scholarly literature? The study has argues that religion, in the Singapore context, is rationalized as the processes of modernization and globalization impact religious change.

76. Ibid., 1173–74.
77. Tong, *Rationalizing Religion*, 4.

Religions, including Christianity, are changing both in substance and in their social significance in Singapore. The rationalization of religion, in terms of Weberian sociology of religion, refers to the intellectualization and systematization of religious ideas. It denotes, in particular, a process whereby one shifts from an unthinking and passive acceptance of religion to one that actively searches for meaning and truth regarded as logical or relevant. It is Tong's contention that the receding of Chinese religions, which are largely perceived as superstitious and illogical, is best explained by this shift from traditional religions directed by habits and emotions to rationalized religions directed by conscious and active ideas.

This study also demonstrates that when informants used the term "rational" with reference to Christianity in Singapore, they meant Christian faith "is logical," "makes sense," "corroborates with reality or learning," "is objective or intellectual because it can be examined," and "answers the questions of the origin of the world and life." What they did not intend to convey, when pointing to the rational quality of Christianity, is a conscious commitment to or agreement with Enlightenment philosophy that views reason as the chief source and test of knowledge. On the this point, the shortcoming of the missiological critique of rational and Western Christianity in Asia reflects the failure on the part of some Asian missiologists to take into account that religions are rationalized in the processes of modernization and globalization. In accounting for religious change, one must not only consider the structural or macro-level factors of conversion but also avoid confusing and conflating terms such as "rational," "rationalistic," and "rationalism."

There is a second apparent disconnect between the views of Asian missiologists and Professor Tong. In identifying rationalistic theology as the root source for the Western and alien expressions of Christianity in Asia, what Asian missiologists assume is that rational correlates with Western. In other words, rational theology is equivalent to Western Christianity. However, this assumption seems quite false in the light of interview data that clearly differentiate rational and Western.

Again, the research findings seem to corroborate Tong's thesis. On the one hand, over half of the informants reported their perception of rational Christianity as an important factor for conversion. On the other hand, while twenty-eight out of thirty-five informants reported that the perception of Western Christianity was a hindrance of conversion for their non-Christians parents and relatives, twenty-nine out of the same thirty-five informants insisted that they did not regard Christianity as a Western religion at the point of or subsequent to their conversion experience. The remaining six informants either offered no opinion or did not comment. Consistent with Tong, who differentiates the perceptions of older and younger Singaporeans, the research findings indicate a stark contrast between the perspectives of older non-believing Singaporeans and those who converted to Christian faith. The former perceived Christianity as a Western religion, while the latter did not perceive Christianity as a Western religion.

Concerning this distinction, the rationalization of religion in Singapore is reflected in terms of the social significance of Christianity within culture, as it is often associated with higher education, social upward mobility, class status, and a cosmopolitan identity. A few informants acknowledged that their Western education, particularly in the sciences, colored the way they view Christianity as a global religion that transcends cultural and ethnic boundaries. Moreover, what is interesting is that all informants interviewed did not believe becoming Christian meant the denial or eclipse of their Singaporean and Chinese identities.

This study points to a third apparent disconnect between Asian critiques of rationalistic and Western theology in Asia and Tong's thesis that Christianity in Singapore is appealing because it is, in part, regarded as a rational religion. How does one explain for these conflicting perspectives? It seems quite evident from literature reviews that not only do Asian missiologists fail to make the important distinction between theology and Christianity, but their critiques of rationalistic theology as being too Western often lapse into general critiques of Christianity as being too Western. The result is the invalid conclusion of the overall inappropriateness of Western Christianity in Asia. Moreover, although informants did not discuss theology as such, their comments about their perception of Christianity as a rational religion suggest that they might not be opposed to a rational element within theology.

8

Conclusions and Missiological Implications

THIS STUDY BEGAN BY posing an important research question: To what extent and in what ways is the perception of Christianity as a rational and/or Western religion a factor in Christian conversion among younger Chinese people in Singapore? The research question emerged when several disconnects were identified in scholarly literature. Asian missiological writers and Singaporean sociologist, Chee Kiong Tong, seem to disagree on several key issues, including the role or value of the rational element in Christianity, the relationship between what is meant by rational and Western, and whether the particular critique of Western theology is the same as the general critique of Western Christianity.

The study approached the central research question by examining it in the light of three distinct yet interrelated domains of literature: (1) the Asian missiological critique of rationalistic, Western theology in Asia, (2) the impact of modernization and globalization on religions, and (3) Christian conversion and identity in Singapore.

In answering the central research question, the study confirms, to a large extent, Tong's thesis that the perception of Christianity as a rational religion is an important factor in Christian conversion among younger Chinese people in Singapore. Of the thirty-five people interviewed, eighteen reported that their perception of Christianity as a logical or rational religion was a compelling factor for conversion. The rational element of Christianity was attractive in contrast to converts' negative perception of Chinese religions as incomprehensible, amorphous, illogical, or irrational. Christian converts favored Christianity because it "is logical," "makes sense," "corroborates with reality," "is objective or intellectual because it can be examined," and "answers the questions of the origin of the world and life." Those claims seem to counter Asian missiologists' assertions that rationalistic theology is not only Western but detrimental to effective Christian mission in Asia. What accounts for those differences in perspective?

This study argues that Christianity in Singapore is rationalized and religious beliefs, practices, and identities are hybridized with local elements. Religions, including Christianity, are changing in Singapore. The changes are evident, both in terms of the substance of Christianity and its social significance in Singapore society. Changes in the perception of Christianity are particularly evident among younger Chinese Singaporean converts who switched from Chinese religions.

The rationalization of religion in Singapore is apparent on several levels of human existence. On a personal, individual, or micro-level, Christian conversion is expressed in one's active search for truth, meaning, and purpose in life, as opposed to the passive acceptance of religious faith and practice typical of traditional society. Christian conversion, viewed primarily as a process rather than a sudden change, underscores the contention that it involves a reconstruction of personal identity in the light of biblical narratives. In the thirty-five interviews, informants discussed, to a large extent, various stages of the conversion process outlined by researchers such as Rambo.

Beyond personal factors, the social structure of Singapore also plays a significant role in determining one's religious choice. On a societal or meso-level, the rationalization of religion in Singapore is manifested in the correlation of religion with ethnicity. With few exceptions, Christian conversion occurs primarily among those from the ethnic Chinese community. Conversion among those from Hindu and Malay communities is indeed very rare. Not only is religion correlated with ethnicity, but research also indicates that conversion occurs primarily within a particular socioeconomic sector of the population represented by people who are younger, English-speaking, university educated, and more "cosmopolitan" in identity. In fact, many informants revealed that their exposures to Christianity and interactions with Christians took place, to some extent, within venues of mission schools or institutions of higher education.

Beyond understanding the phenomenon of Christian conversion in Singapore on micro and meso-levels, this study argues that structural or macro-level factors must also be considered in order to achieve a more balanced understanding of Christian conversion. Following the sociological analyses of religion by Max Weber and Chee Kiong Tong, the study argues that the processes of modernization and globalization are largely responsible for transforming religions in Singapore. As Singapore society becomes increasingly industrialized, modernized, and globalized with the promotion of an English-speaking and science-oriented educational system with vital connections to global markets, Christianity is favored because of the perception of Bible teachings as more rational and intellectual than Chinese religions viewed by converts as myths or legends.

Concerning the question of whether the perception of Christianity as a rational religion necessarily means it is also Western, the research findings clearly indicate that converts did not perceive Christianity in Singapore as a Western religion. This finding has important implications for Asian missiological writings. On the one hand, Asian missiologists insist that rationalistic theology contributes to Western Christianity in Asia. On the other hand, research findings corroborate Tong's observation that those who resist conversion are primarily the older, Chinese-speaking Singaporeans due to their perception of Christianity as a Western religion. However, the same is not true for the younger, English-speaking Chinese Singaporeans, who are educated in English-stream and Western educational systems. This observation is largely supported by informants who reported that Christianity is viewed as a Western religion by their non-believing parents and relatives. However, twenty-nine out of thirty-five informants insisted that they did not regard Christianity as a Western religion at the time of their conversion.

The religious landscape in Singapore is indeed changing. The change in the perception of Christianity as a Western or alien religion to one that is considered ethnically neutral, international, or global reflects the fact that religions are transformed as they respond and adapt to socio-cultural, political, and economic changes in Singapore. Related to the broader topic of religious conversion in Singapore is the more focused subject of Christian identity formation. Not only is Christianity as a religion transformed, but its social significance in Singapore society is changing as well.

What is striking about the thesis of the hybridization of religion with local culture is how converts viewed their newfound Christian identity. Of the thirty-five people interviewed, every informant insisted that becoming a follower of Jesus Christ did not deny or eclipse their Chinese or Singaporean identities. This assertion is largely substantiated by empirical data that describe Christian converts actually blend elements of their religious past with Christian faith and practice. What is important is not only the fact of the hybridization of faith and practice, but the somewhat arbitrary ways in which converts demarcate religious and cultural boundaries in the conversion process. As sociologists contend, Christian conversion and identity formation is not a complete repudiation of one's cultural and religious past, but a realignment of Christian, Singaporean, and Chinese identities. The fact that Christian conversion involves the correlation of education with religion and occurs primarily within a particular socioeconomic sector of society indicates that it serves as a power mechanism for the formation of a "cosmopolitan" social identity in Singapore.

As this study comes to close, it is appropriate to draw out some missiological implications. Three in particular can be enumerated. The first implication concerns the value or role of the intellectual or rational element in Christian faith. The study confirms, to a large extent, that the intellectual appeal of Christianity plays an important role in conversion, particularly for those who are educated in English stream and Western educational systems. However, in acknowledging the intellectual appeal of Christianity in conversion, several qualifications need to be mentioned. Although converts perceived Christianity as a rational religion, this does not mean that Christianity alone is a rational religion or that other religions are not rational in nature. Buddhism, in Singapore, is increasingly rationalized or "Christianized." An important question to ask would be the extent to which young Singaporeans are attracted to Buddhism because of rationality. The limited scope of this study, however, does not allow room to explore the reason and the degree to which some people might be attracted to Buddhism because they too perceive it as a rational religion. Such an inquiry would have to be reserved for another study.

Moreover, this study does not address why some people might reject Christianity because they find it too rational. The role of rationality in Christian faith could certainly be challenged, particularly by those who are more inclined toward a "postmodern" or experiential religious epistemology. This subject, too, is beyond the scope of this study and deserves further research. What this study does demonstrate is the necessity to nuance what one means by "rational." If the term is used as a "catch-all" definition for Enlightenment rationalism that reason is the final arbiter of truth, then it may not be applicable to the Singapore context. However, if rational means the active intellectual examination of religious truth claims or that Christianity is "logical" or it "makes sense," as many informants insist, then it would fit the Singapore context. Certainly, the Weberian concept of the rationalization of religion needs to be seriously considered in accounting for religious change. The main problem with the Asian missiological critique of rationalistic theology and Western Christianity in Asia is its neglect to take into account that religions are rationalized in the processes of modernization and globalization. Hopefully, this study has clarified the need to properly define and nuance terms and concepts, particularly from the competing perspectives of philosophers, theologians, and sociologists.

Secondly, this study demonstrates that the boundaries between religion and culture are highly fluid in the contexts of modernization and globalization. In particular, the categories "Western" and "Asian," used by Asian missiologists with reference to Christianity, are actually not fixed boundaries. This study has argued that Asian missiologists, who criticize the Western and alien nature of Christianity in Asia, do so with the false assumption that rational necessarily means Western. In other words, they tend to correlate those terms and use them interchangeably. While Tong's study does not explicitly demonstrate whether people who converted to Christianity due to their perception of it as a rational religion also regarded Christianity as a Western religion, this study clearly demonstrates that rational and Western are differentiated. Many informants who converted to Christianity perceived it as a rational religion. However, all interviewees did not consider Christianity as a Western religion at the point of their conversion. Christianity, as a global religion, when it interacts with social, economic, and political realities in different historical and cultural contexts, undergoes change in terms of its internal constitution as well as its social significance in society. The relationship between religion and culture overlaps various dimensions of human existence. As a result, the boundaries between them are permeable and become highly fluid. What may be true in the 1980s, with regard to rationalistic theology in Asia, may not be applicable in 2016 in Singapore.

In the contexts of modernization and globalization, it is simply not helpful for missiologists to examine religion as a fixed or static category. In particular, the use of the terms "Western" and "Asian" in a "catch-all" fashion to characterize Christianity in Asia betrays the complexity of the interplay between culture and religion. Many followers of Buddhism in Singapore also regard it as a rational religion, but this does not mean it is Western in nature. Religion, in the contexts of modernization and globalization, is a highly complicated phenomenon and one must not generalize or create cultural stereotypes when it comes to understanding its relation to culture.

As such, when addressing the critique of rationalistic and Western theology in Asia, one must not view those terms as all-encompassing concepts to cover all parts of Asia. While the criticism of Western Christianity may be valid when applied to some parts of Asia, such as a remote fishing village in Japan, it does not seem to be the case in contemporary Singapore. For one thing, what Asian evangelical missiologists have in mind, when using the term "rationalistic" in criticizing Western theology in Asia, is theological methodology—a particular way of doing theology in Asia as associated with Enlightenment philosophy or epistemology. This is certainly not what Christian converts in Singapore had in mind when they reported about their perception of Christianity as a rational religion. It is one thing to criticize Christianity in Asia as Westernized, derived from rationalistic theology, but quite another to report about one's perception of Christianity as a rational religion. As such, this study argues that it may be simplistic to depict "Western" and "Asian," as if they are static in nature, and that rationalistic necessarily means Western.

The third implication concerns what it means to facilitate effective Christian mission in the light of the distinction between the missiologists' critique of Western theology as too rationalistic and Tong's thesis that Christianity in Singapore is appealing because it is perceived as a rational religion. Clearly, there are overlaps between the categories of theology and Christianity, but they are not synonymous. Christian theology, properly understood, is a heuristic tool or an abstract framework in an attempt to translate the meaning of the biblical text to determine its significance and application in various contemporary contexts. In that sense, theology is an invaluable intellectual exercise to formulating the substance of belief and to cultivate virtues for life and practice.

However, it is also true that some theologies are highly abstract and are not at all oriented toward engaging the gospel with lived realities. To be sure, the overly abstract characteristic of so-called Western theology is at the root of Asian missiological complaints against it. Asian missiologists maintain that Western theology is inappropriate because it fails to engage human lived realities. Although this may be true for some forms of Western theology at certain times in the history of Christian mission, it would be a gross over-generalization to characterize all theology from the West in such a fixed category. The crux of the issue concerning theology is not about an "Asian or Western" debate. The real concern with theology is whether it effectively engages human lived realities in facilitating effective mission.

On the other hand, Christianity is a much broader category, covering dimensions that include the full orb of Christian faith and practice and its current state in various parts of the world. Given these distinctions, even if one accepts the thesis that the perception of Christianity as a rational religion plays a significant role in conversion, it does not necessarily invalidate the Asian critique of Western theology as too rational. What is important in seeking to contextualize Christianity appropriately is that one attends to the self-understanding of people and their life situations as they encounter the gospel. This would be true whether one seeks to contextualize Christianity in Asian or Western contexts. Christian missiologists, in order to facilitate effective mission, need to give proper attention to the processes of modernization and globalization and the ways in which they impact lived realities. As Christianity engages a particular religious tradition, what becomes critical is the encounter between the gospel of Jesus Christ and the self-understanding of those who follow that tradition. The apparent problem with some Asian missiologists is that, in their critiques of rationalistic theology as too Western, they often lapse into general critiques of Christianity in Asia as also too Western.

Moreover, while the perception of Christianity as a rational religion may be appealing to younger Chinese Singaporeans, particularly those trained in English-stream and Western educational systems, this does not mean that it would not hinder some other groups in Singapore from conversion. Tong's observation that conversion occurs within a specific socioeconomic sector of the population is quite alarming. Sociologists have wondered aloud if some Western expressions of Christianity in Singapore, including those that emphasize the intellectual aspect and identity with middle class social status, are not inappropriate for Chinese-speaking Singaporeans, particularly the older ones from less affluent backgrounds. The issue, again, is not about depicting Christianity in Asian or Western categories, but whether Christianity is appropriately contextualized, so that the gospel truly engages with the changing lived realities of human cultures across the globe.

The predisposition on the part of some younger Chinese Singaporeans toward the intellectual side of Christian faith raises one last issue. If one admits the goal of Christian mission as a holistic endeavor, including spiritual, social, and physical realities, would an over-emphasis on the intellectual aspect of Christianity not be a cause for concern? Might some Chinese Singaporeans who converted to Christianity be missing something in emphasizing the intellectual aspect of faith, perhaps to the neglect of the experiential, social, physical, and spiritual dimensions of Christian faith? On this point, the church in Singapore must somehow recover the holistic nature of Christian conversion and discipleship in order to facilitate effective mission.

Many observers anticipate that Christianity in Singapore will continue to grow within a limited sector of the population. This negative trend will persist unless the church makes a concerted effort to contextualize Christian faith and practice. The future success of the church in Singapore will depend, to a large extent, on her ability to contextualize Christian faith to reach the heart-landers, the Chinese-speaking population, the religious and ethnic others, and the next generation of Singaporeans with the gospel of Jesus Christ.

Appendix 1

Informant Profiles

Informant	Gender	Age	Degree	Vocation	Church	Conversion
#1	M	32	BS	Teacher	Presby	1998
#2	M	30	BA	Army	AOG	1997
#3	M	28	MA	Engineer	Bible	1996
#4	M	31	BS	Engineer	Method	1980
#5	M	34	MBA	Marketing	Presby	1987
#6	F	33	MA	Teacher	Method	Sec 3
#7	F	31	Diploma	Home	Charis	1993
#8	M	25	BA	e-Marketing	Method	2012
#9	M	33	Diploma	Engineer	Baptist	2009
#10	F	29	BS	Teacher	Baptist	1993
#11	F	32	BA	Editor	Charis	P6
#12	F	22	BS	Architect	Presby	2012
#13	M	28	BA	Student	Anglican	2005
#14	M	24	Soph	Student	Presby	2011
#15	M	25	Junior	Student	Presby	2002
#16	M	32	BS	Teacher	Indep	JC
#17	F	22	Junior	Student	Presby	2011
#18	F	35	MBBS	Doctor	Presby	1995
#19	M	31	MA	Civil servant	Baptist	2007
#20	F	33	BA	Editor	Charis	P2
#21	F	29	MBA	Executive	Method	2013
#22	M	35	MA	IT	Evangel	2009
#23	M	34	Diploma	Engineer	Method	Sec 1
#24	F	21	Junior	Student	Method	Sec 3

APPENDIX 1: INFORMANT PROFILES

Informant	Gender	Age	Degree	Vocation	Church	Conversion
#25	M	29	LLM	Lawyer	Presby	2009
#26	F	27	BA	Soc worker	Anglican	2005
#27	M	27	BA	Law stud	Presby	2012
#28	M	29	LLM	Lawyer	Presby	2009
#29	M	36	MA	CPA	Charis	2009
#30	F	26	BA	Soc worker	Charis	1999
#31	M	?	Diploma	Executive	Method	1995
#32	M	27	BA	Auditor	Presby	2013
#33	F	33	BS	Teacher	Charis	2000
#34	F	36	BA	Banker	Presby	1995
#35	F	33	BA	Admin	Method	2009

Appendix 2
Interview Protocol

1. Please introduce yourself—i.e., age, educational background, occupation, date of conversion, and church or denominational affiliation.

2. How did you become a Christian? What were some key experiences/events that led you to faith in Christ? Who influenced or helped you in this process?

3. Talk about your family and religious backgrounds. What are your parents' occupations? Describe your family's participation in religious festivals, customs, and rituals both at home and in public? How did you feel as a child about those rituals? Why?

4. Talk about your educational experience. Was there any time during your studies when you felt that what you were learning challenged the religious beliefs or practices you accepted as a child?

5. Taoist and Buddhist traditions have their sacred texts and stories about miracles and healings. As a Christian, what is it about the Bible that is different from those texts, or do you think they are all basically the same?

6. As a Christian, when you reflect on those earlier religious beliefs and practices, how do you feel about them now?

7. As a Christian, how do you approach or deal with religious birth, marriage, and death rituals?

8. In comparison to traditional beliefs, rituals, and practices, what is it about the Christian faith that you find most helpful or relevant to you?

9. What convinces you that Christianity is the one true faith?

10. Some criticize Christianity in Singapore as a Western religion. Do you agree or disagree? Why? What to you constitutes Western Christianity?

11. Describe your encounter, if any, with Western culture or Western Christians that may have contributed to your conversion experience.

12. How would you describe your Christian identity at this point in your spiritual journey? How have you changed since becoming a Christian? In what ways are you different from some of your non-believing friends or family members?

13. Since becoming a Christian, how or in what ways are you still loyal to your family, cultural, or ethnic background?

14. What are some hindrances or obstacles that keep you from full commitment to following Jesus Christ?

15. What is your view on Christian baptism? Have you been baptized? If not, why not?

Bibliography

Anane-Asane, Andrew, et al. "Paul G. Hiebert's 'The Flaw of the Excluded Middle.'" *Trinity Journal* 30 (2009) 189–97.
Athyal, Saphir. "Toward an Asian Christian Theology." In *Asian Christian Theology: Emerging Themes*, edited by Douglas Elwood, 67–80. Philadelphia: Westminster, 1980.
Balch, Robert W. "Looking behind the Scenes in a Religious Cult: Implications for the Study of Conversion." *Sociological Analysis* 41, no. 2 (1980) 137–43.
Beckford, James A. "Accounting for Conversion." *British Journal of Sociology* 29, no. 2 (1978) 249–62.
Bellah, Robert N. 1958. "Religious Aspects of Modernization in Turkey and Japan." *American Journal of Sociology* 64, no.1 (1958) 1–5.
Bendix, Reinhard. *Max Weber: An Intellectual Portrait*. New York: Doubleday, 1960.
Benson, B. E. "Postmodernity." In *Evangelical Dictionary of Theology*, edited by Walter Elwell, 939–45. Grand Rapids: Baker, 2001.
Berger, Peter. "The Desecularization of the World: A Global Overview. In *The Desecularization of the World: Resurgent Religion and World Politics*, edited by Peter Berger, 1–18. Grand Rapids: Eerdmans, 1999.
———. *A Far Glory: The Quest for Faith in an Age of Credulity*. New York: Anchor, 1992.
———. "Four Faces of Global Culture." *National Interest* 49 (1997) 23–29.
Berger, Peter, Brigitte Berger, and Hansfried Kellner. *The Homeless Mind: Modernization and Consciousness*. New York: Vintage, 1973.
Beyer, Peter. "De-Centering Religious Singularity: The Globalization of Christianity as a Case in Point." *Numen* 50, no. 4 (2003) 357–86.
———. "What Is Secularism for?" In *Secularism and Its Critics*, edited by Rajeev Bhargava, 486–542. Delhi: Oxford University Press, 1998.
Bhargava, Rajeev. "Introduction." In *Secularism and Its Critics*, edited by Rajeev Bhargava, 1–28. Delhi: Oxford University Press, 1998.
Caldwell, Larry W. "How Asian is Asian Theological Education?" In *Tending the Seedbeds*, edited by Allan Harkness, 23–45. Quezon City, Philippines: ATA, 2010.
Calhoun, Craig, Mark Juergensmeyer, and Jonathan VanAntwerpen. "Introduction." In *Rethinking Secularism*, edited by Craig Calhoun, Mark Juergensmeyer, and Jonathan VanAntwerpen, 3–30. New York: Oxford University Press, 2011.

Campbell, Jonathan. "Releasing the Gospel from Western Bondage." *International Journal of Frontier Missions* 16, no. 4 (1999) 167–71.
Carr, Leslie, and William Hauser. "Anomie and Religiosity: An Empirical Re-Examination." *Journal for the Scientific Study of Religion* 15, no. 1 (1976) 69–74.
Chan, Edmund. "Defining Postmodernism." *Compass* 9, no. 3 (2005) 8–9.
Chan, Simon. "Evangelical Theology in Asian Contexts." In *Cambridge Companion to Evangelical Theology*, edited by Timothy Larsen and Daniel Treier, 225–40. Cambridge: Cambridge University Press, 2007.
———. "Problem and Possibility of an Asian Theological Hermeneutic." *Trinity Theological Journal* 9 (2000) 47–59.
———. "The Problem of Transcendence and Immanence in Asian Contextual Theology." *Trinity Theological Journal* 8 (1999) 5–18.
Chang, David. "Nation-Building in Singapore." *Asian Survey* 8, no. 9 (1968) 761–73.
Chang, T. C., and S. Y. Lim. "Geographical Imaginations of 'New Asia-Singapore.'" *Geografiska Annnaler* 86, no. 3 (2004) 165–85.
Chew, Melanie. "Human Rights in Singapore: Perceptions and Problems." *Asian Survey* 34, no. 11 (1994) 933–48.
Chew, Phyllis Ghim-Lian. "Religious Switching and Knowledge among Adolescents in Singapore." In *Religious Diversity in Singapore*, edited by Lai Ah Eng, 381–410. Singapore: Institute of Southeast Asian Studies, 2008.
Chia, Philip. "Biblical Studies in the Rising Asia: An Asian Perspective on the Future of the Biblical Past." *Sino-Christian Studies* 12 (2011) 33–65.
Chin, Karen. "Seeing Religion with News Eyes at the Asian Civilisation Museum." *Material Religion* 6, no. 2 (2010) 192–217.
Chong, Terence. "Filling the Moral Void: The Christian Right in Singapore." *Journal of Contemporary Asia* 41, no. 4 (2011) 566–83.
Chong, Terence, and Hui Yew-Foong. *Different under God: A Survey of Church-Going Protestants in Singapore*. Singapore: Institute of Southeast Asian Studies, 2013.
Clammer, John. "Culture, Values, and Modernization in Singapore: An Overview." In *Understanding Singapore Society*, edited by Ong Jin Hui, Tong Chee Kiong, and Tan Ern Ser, 502–12. Singapore: Times Academic, 1997.
———. *Race and State in Independent Singapore, 1965–1990: The Cultural Politics of Pluralism in a Multiethnic Society*. Brookfield, VT: Ashgate, 1998.
———. "Religious Pluralism and Chinese beliefs in Singapore." In *Chinese Beliefs and Practices in Southwest Asia*, edited by Cheu Hock Tong, 199–221. Malaysia: Pelanduk, 1993.
———. *Singapore: Ideology, Society, Culture*. Singapore: Chopmen, 1985.
———. "Singapore: Urbanism, Culture, and the Church." *Urban Mission* 7, no. 4 (1990): 6–20.
———. *The Sociology of Singapore Religion: Studies in Christianity and Chinese Culture*. Singapore: Chopmen, 1991.
Clark, David K. *To Know and Love God*. Wheaton, IL: Crossway, 2003.
Cole, Graham. "Thinking Theologically." *The Reformed Theological Review* 48, no. 2 (1989) 51–62.
Comber, Leon. *Chinese Ancestor Worship in Malaya*. Singapore: Moore, 1954.
Conn, Harvie. "Conversion and Culture: A Theological Perspective." In *Down to Earth: Studies in Christianity and Culture*, edited by John Stott and Robert Coote, 147–72. Grand Rapids: Eerdmans, 1980.

———. *Eternal Word and Changing Worlds: Theology, Anthropology, and Missions in Trialogue*. Grand Rapids: Zondervan, 1984.

Cox, Harvey. "Thinking Globally about Christianity." In *The Oxford Handbook of Global Religions*, edited by Mark Juergensmeyer, 245–53. New York: Oxford University Press, 2006.

Dawson, Lorne. "Self Affirmation, Freedom, and Rationality: Theoretically Elaborating 'Active' Conversions." *Journal for the Scientific Study of Religion* 29, no. 2 (1990) 141–63.

Dearman, J. Andrew. "Observations on 'Conversion' and the Old Testament." *Ex Auditu* 25 (2009) 22–36.

DeBernardi, Jean. "Global Christian Culture and the Antioch of Asia." In *Religious Diversity in Singapore*, edited by Lai Ah Eng, 116–41. Singapore: Institute of Southeast Asian Studies, 2008.

Dyrness, William. *Learning about Theology from the Third World*. Grand Rapids: Zondervan, 1990.

———. *How Does America Hear the Gospel?* Grand Rapids: Eerdmans, 1989.

Eisen, Arnold. "The Meanings and Confusions of Weberian 'Rationality.'" *The British Journal of Sociology* 29, no. 1 (1978) 57–70.

Elwood, Douglas. "Asian Christian Theology in the Making: An Introduction." In *Asian Christian Theology: Emerging Themes*, edited by Douglas Elwood, 23–39. Philadelphia: Westminster, 1980.

England, John. *Asian Christian Theologies: A Research Guide to Authors, Movements, Sources*. Vol. 2. Delhi: ISPCK, 2003.

Erickson, Millard. *Christian Theology*. 3rd ed. Grand Rapids: Baker, 2013.

Eriksen, Thomas Hylland. *Globalization: The Key Concepts*. Oxford: Berg, 2007.

Feng, Robin Chee Ming, and James Chen. "Shopping for God: Media and Religion in Singapore." In *Mediating Piety: Technology and Religion in Contemporary Asia*, edited by Francis Khek Gee, 161–81. Leiden: Brill, 2009.

Fleming, John R. "Singapore, Malaysia and Brunei: The Church in a Racial Melting Pot." In *Christ and Crisis in Southeast Asia*, edited by Gerald Anderson, 81–106. New York: Friendship, 1968.

Fraser, D. A. "Globalization." In *Global Dictionary of Theology*, edited by William Dyrness and Veli-Matti Kärkkäinen, 336–43. Downer Grove, IL: InterVarsity, 2008.

Freedman, Maurice. *The Study of Chinese Society*. Stanford: Stanford University Press, 1979.

Freedman, Maurice, and Marjorie Topley. "Religion and Social Realignment among the Chinese in Singapore." *Journal of Asian Studies* 21, no. 1 (1961) 3–23.

Friedman, Thomas. *The Lexus and the Olive Tree: Understanding Globalization*. New York: Anchor, 1999.

———. *The World Is Flat: A Brief History of the Twenty-First Century*. New York: Farrar, Straus and Giroux, 2005.

Gay, Craig. "An Ironic Cage: The Rationalization of Modern Economic Life." In *Faith and Modernity*, edited by Philip Sampson and Vinay Samuel, 252–72. Oxford: Regnum, 1994.

Geisler, Norman, and Paul Feinberg. *Introduction to Philosophy*. Grand Rapids: Baker, 1980.

Gener, Timoteo. "Contextualization." In *Global Dictionary of Theology*, edited by William Dyrness and Veli-Matti Kärkkäinen, 192–96. Downers Grove, IL: InterVarsity, 2008.

Geertz, Clifford. *The Interpretation of Cultures*. New York: Basic, 1973.

Giddens, Anthony. *The Consequences of Modernity*. Stanford, CA: Stanford University Press, 1990.

Gilbert, Pierre. "Further Reflections on Paul Hiebert's 'The Flaw of the Excluded Middle.'" *Direction* 36, no. 2 (2007) 206–18.

Gille, Zsuzsa, and Sean O Riain. "Global Ethnography." *Annual Review of Sociology* 28 (2002) 271–95.

Gilliland, Dean. "Contextualization." In *Evangelical Dictionary of World Missions*, edited by A. Scott Moreau, 225–27. Grand Rapids: Baker, 2000.

Gispert-Sauch. "Asian Theology." In *The Modern Theologians*, edited by David F. Ford, 455–73. 2nd ed. Oxford: Blackwell, 1997.

Gnanakan, Ken. "Asian Theologies." In *Evangelical Dictionary of World Missions*, edited by A. Scott Moreau, 88–90. Grand Rapids: Baker, 2000.

Goh, Daniel P. S. "Christianity in Post-Colonial Singapore." *Sojourn: Journal of Social Issues in Southeast Asia*. 25, no. 1 (2010) 54–89.

———. "Rethinking Resurgent Christianity in Singapore." *Southeast Asian Journal of Social Science* 27, no. 1 (1999) 89–112.

Goh, Robbie B. H. "Christian Identities in Singapore: Religion, Race, and Culture Between State Controls and Transnational Flows." *Journal of Cultural Geography* 26, no. 1 (2009) 1–23.

———. *Christianity in Southeast Asia*. Singapore: Institute of Southeast Asian Studies, 2005.

———. "Mission Schools in Singapore: Religious Harmony, Social Identities, and the Negotiation of Evangelical Cultures." In *Religious Diversity in Singapore*, edited by Lai Ah Eng, 362–80. Singapore: Institute of Southeast Asian Studies, 2008.

Goh, Wah Seng Jeremiah. "A Study in the Practice of Ancestor Rites Among the Diaspora Chinese Protestant Christians in Singapore." PhD diss., Asbury Theological Seminary, 2011.

Grice, Kevin, and David Drakakis-Smith. "The Role of the State in Shaping Development: Two Decades of Growth in Singapore." *Transactions of the Institute of British Geographers* 10, no. 3 (1985) 347–59.

Guillen, Mauro. "Is Globalization Civilizing, Destructive or Feeble? A Critique of Five Key Debates in the Social Sciences Literature." *Annual Review of Sociology* 27 (2001) 235–60.

Han, Chul Ha. "A Critical Evaluation of Western Theology." *Evangelical Review of Theology* 7, no. 1 (1983) 3–47.

———. "A Critical Evaluation of Western Theology: Towards a Reappraisal of the Biblical Faith." In *The Bible and Theology in Asian contexts*, edited by Bong Rin Ro and Ruth Eshenaur, 31–47. Seoul: ATA, 1984.

Harkness, Allan. "De-schooling the Theological Seminary: An Appropriate Paradigm for Effective Pastoral Formation." In *Tending the Seedbeds*, edited by Allan Harkness, 103–28. Quezon City, Philippines: ATA, 2010.

Hefner, Robert. "Multiple Modernities: Christianity, Islam, and Hinduism in a Globalizing Age." *Annual Review of Anthropology* 27 (1998) 83–104.

———. "World Building and the Rationality of Conversion." In *Conversion to Christianity: Historical and Anthropological Perspectives on a Great Transformation*, edited by Robert Hefner, 3–45. Berkeley: University of California Press, 1993.

Heinze, Ruth-Inge. "The Nine Imperial Gods in Singapore." *Asian Folklore Studies* 40, no. 2 (1981) 151–71.

Hesselgrave, David. "Brian McLaren's Contextualization of the Gospel." *Evangelical Missions Quarterly* 43, no. 1 (2007) 92–100.

Hiebert, Paul G. *Anthropological Insights for Missionaries*. Grand Rapids: Baker, 1985.

———. *Anthropological Reflections on Missiological Issues*. Grand Rapids: Baker, 1994.

———. "Beyond Anti-Colonialism to Globalism." *Missiology* 19, no. 3 (1991) 263–81.

———. "The Category 'Christian' in the Mission Task." *International Review of Mission* (1983) 421–27.

———. "Conversion and Worldview Transformation." *International Journal of Frontier Missions* 14, no. 2 (1997) 83–86.

———. "Conversion, Culture, and Cognitive Categories." *Gospel in Context* 1, no. 4 (1978) 24–28.

———. "Critical Contextualization." *Missiology* 12, no. 3 (1984) 287–96.

———. "Critical Contextualization." *International Bulletin of Missionary Research* 11 (1987) 104–11.

———. *Cultural Anthropology*. Grand Rapids: Baker, 1976.

———. "Cultural Relativism and Theological Absolutes." *Direction* (1973) 2–6.

———. "The Flaw of the Excluded Middle." *Missiology* 10, no. 1 (1982) 35–47.

———. "Form and Meaning in Contextualization of the Gospel." In *The Word among Us*, edited by Dean Gilliland, 101–20. Eugene, OR: Wipf and Stock, 1989.

———. "Metatheology: The Step beyond Contextualization." In *Reflection and Projection: Missiology at the Threshold of 2001*, edited by Hans Kasdorf and Klaus Muller, 383–95. Bad Liebenzel, West Germany: Liebenzeller Mission, 1988.

———. *Missiological Implications of Epistemological Shifts: Affirming Truth in a Modern/Postmodern World*. Harrisburg, PA: Trinity, 1999.

———. "Sets and Structures: A Study of Church Patterns: A Study of Church Patterns." In *New Horizons in World Missions*, edited by David Hesselgrave, 217–27. Grand Rapids: Baker, 1979.

———. *Transforming Worldviews: An Anthropological Understanding of How People Change*. Grand Rapids: Baker, 2008.

Hiebert, Paul, R. Daniel Shaw, and Tite Tiénou. "Responding to Split-Level Christianity and Folk Religion." *International Journal of Frontier Missions* 16, no. 4 (1999) 173–81.

Hill, Michael. *Conversion and Subversion: Religion and the Management of Moral Panics in Singapore*. Victoria, New Zealand: Asian Studies Institute, 2000.

———. "The Making of a Moral Panic: Religion and State in Singapore." In *Challenging Religion*, edited by James Beckford and James Richardson, 114–25. London: Routledge, 2003.

Hinton, Keith. *Growing Churches Singapore Style: Ministry in an Urban Context*. Singapore: OMF, 1985.

Horrell, J. Scott. "Doing Theology: An International Task." *Evangelical Missions Quarterly* 41, no. 4 (2005) 474–78.

Huntington. Samuel P. *The Clash of Civilizations and the Remaking of World Order*. New York: Touchstone, 1996.

Hwa, Yung. "The Gospel in Twenty-First Century Asia." *Trinity Theological Journal* 13 (2005) 87–102.

———. A Fresh Call for United States Missionaries. *Christianity Today* 55, no. 11 (2011) 42–46.

———. *Mangoes or Bananas? The Quest for an Authentic Asia Christian Theology*. Oxford: Regnum, 1997.

———. "Mission and Evangelism: Evangelical and Pentecostal Theologies in Asia." In *Christian Theology in Asia*, edited by Sebastian Kim, 250–70. Cambridge: Cambridge University Press, 2008.

———. "A 21st Century Reformation: Recover the Supernatural." *Christianity Today* (2010) 3–4.

Inglehart, Ronald. *Modernization and Postmodernization: Cultural, Economic, and Political Change in 43 Societies*. Princeton, NJ: Princeton University Press, 1997.

Jenkins, Philip. *The Next Christendom: The Coming of Global Christianity*. New York: Oxford University Press, 2002.

———. "Reading the Bible in the Global South." *International Bulletin of Missionary Research* 30, no. 2 (2006) 67–73.

Jones, Lindsay, ed. *Encyclopedia of Religion*. 2nd ed. Farmington, MI: Gale, 2005.

Jordan, David K. "The Glyphomancy Factor: Observations on Chinese Conversion." In *Conversion to Christianity: Historical and Anthropological Perspectives on a Great Transformation*, edited by Robert Hefner, 285–303. Berkeley: University of California Press, 1993.

Juergensmeyer, Mark, ed. *Global Religions: An Introduction*. New York: Oxford University Press, 2003.

———. "Thinking Globally about Religion." In *The Oxford Handbook of Global Religions*, edited by Mark Juergensmeyer, 3–14. New York: Oxford University Press, 2006.

Kalberg, Stephen. "Max Weber's Types of Rationality: Cornerstones for the Analysis of Rationalization Processes in History." *American Journal of Sociology* 85, no. 5 (1980) 1145–79.

———. "The Rationalization of Action in Max Weber's Sociology of Religion." *Sociological Theory* 8, no. 1 (1990) 58–84.

Kau, Ah Keng, and Charles Yang, ed. *Values and Lifestyles of Singaporeans: A Marketing Perspective*. Singapore: Singapore University Press, 1991.

Kitamori, Kozoh. *Theology of the Pain of God*. Richmond, VA: Knox, 1965.

Kluver, Randolph, and Pauline Cheong. "Technology Modernization, the Internet, and Religion in Singapore." *Journal of Computer Mediated Communication* 12, no. 3 (2007) 1–29.

Koch, Andrew. "Rationality, Romanticism and the Individual: Max Weber's 'Modernism' and the Confrontation with 'Modernity.'" *Canadian Journal of Political Science* 26, no. 1 (1993) 123–44.

Kong, Lily. "Negotiating Conceptions of 'Sacred Space': A Case Study of Religious Buildings in Singapore." *Transactions of the Institute of British Geographers* 18, no. 3 (1993) 342–58.

Koyama, Kosuke. *Water Buffalo Theology*. Maryknoll, NY: Orbis, 1974.

———. *Water Buffalo Theology*. Rev. ed. Maryknoll, NY: Orbis, 1999.

Kuo, Eddie C. Y., and Riaz Hassan. "Some Social Concomitants of Interethnic Marriage in Singapore." *Journal of Marriage and Family* 38, no. 3 (1975) 549–59.

Kuo, Eddie C. Y., Jon S. T., and Tong Chee Kiong. *Religion and Religious Revivalism in Singapore*. Singapore: Report Prepared for Ministry of Community Development, October 1988.

Lechner, Frank, and John Boli. "General Introduction." In *The Globalization Reader*, edited by Frank Lechner and John Boli, 1–4. Oxford: Blackwell, 2004.

Lechner, Frank, and John Boli, eds. *The Globalization Reader*. 2nd ed. Oxford: Blackwell, 2004.

Lee, Kuan Yew. *From Third World to First: The Singapore Story 1965–2005*. New York: HarperCollins, 2000.

Lee, Moon Jang. "Asian Theology." In *Global Dictionary of Theology*, edited by William Dyrness and Veli-Matti Kärkkäinen, 74–77. Downers Grove, IL: InterVarsity, 2008.

———. "Reading the Bible in the Non-Western Church: An Asian Dimension." In *Mission in the 21st Century: Exploring the Five Marks of Global Mission*, edited by Andrew Walls and Cathy Ross, 148–56. Maryknoll, NY: Orbis, 2008.

———. "Reconfiguring Western Theology in Asia." *Trinity Theological Journal* 10 (2002) 31–40.

Lee, Sharon Meng Chee. "Intermarriage and Ethnic Relations in Singapore." *Journal of Marriage and Family* 50, no. 1 (1988) 255–65.

———. "Religious Conversion Among Chinese Singaporeans: An Examination of the Over-Tolerance Concept." *Asian Journal of Religion* 2, no. 4 (2008) 4–10.

Leong, Heng Keng. *Chinese Customs and Festivals in Singapore*. Singapore: Singapore Federation of Chinese Clan Associations, 1989.

Lim, Francis, ed. *Mediating Piety: Technology and Religion in Contemporary Asia*. Leiden: Brill, 2009.

Lowe, Chuck. "Christianity and Social Context: Foundational Principles. In *Ministry in Modern Singapore: The Effects of Modernity on the Church*, edited by Wong Chan Kok and Chuck Lowe, 1–30. Singapore: Singapore Bible College, 1997.

MacDougall, John, and Chew Sock Foon. "English Language Competence and Occupational Mobility in Singapore." *Pacific Affairs* 49, no. 2 (1976) 294–312.

Madsen, Richard. "Secularism, Religious Change, and Social Conflict in Asia." In *Rethinking Secularism*, edited by Craig Calhoun, Mark Juergensmeyer, and Jonathan VanAntwerpen, 248–69. New York: Oxford University Press, 2001.

Mathews, Mathew. "Accommodating Relationships: The Church and State in Singapore." In *Christianity and the State in Asia: Complicity and Conflict*, edited by Julius Bautista and Francis Khek Gee Lim, 184–200. New York: Routledge, 2009.

———. "Christianity in Singapore: The Voice of Moral Conscience to the State." *Journal of Contemporary Religion* 24, no. 1 (2009) 53–65.

———. "Negotiating Christianity with Other Religions: The View of Christian Clergymen in Singapore." In *Religious Diversity in Singapore*, edited by Lai Ah Eng, 571–604. Singapore: Institute of Southeast Asian Studies, 2008.

Matthes, Joachim. "Religious Change and the Modernization Process: The Case of Singapore." *Southeast Asian Journal of Social Science* 10, no. 2 (1982) 23–28.

McKnight, Scot. *Turning to Jesus: The Sociology of Conversion in the Gospels*. Louisville: Westminster John Knox, 2002.

McKnight, Scot, and Hauna Ondrey. *Finding Faith, Losing Faith*. Waco, TX: Baylor University Press, 2008.

Mehden, Fred R., von der. *Religion and Modernization in Southeast Asia*. Syracuse, NY: Syracuse University Press, 1986.

Molloy, Stephen. "Max Weber and the Religions of China: Any Way Out of the Maze?" *British Journal of Sociology* 31, no. 3 (1980) 377–400.

Mullins, Mark. *Christianity Made in Japan: A Study of Indigenous Movements*. Honolulu: University of Hawaii Press, 1998.

Mutalib, Hussin. "Singapore Muslims: The Quest for Identity in a Modern City-State." *Journal of Muslim Minority Affairs* 25, no. 1 (2005) 53–72.

———. "The Socio-Economic Dimensions in Singapore's Quest for Security and Stability." *Pacific Affairs* 75, no. 1 (2002) 39–56.

Netland, Harold A. "Apologetics, Worldviews, and the Problem of Neutral Criteria." *Trinity Journal* 12 (1991) 39–58.

———. *Dissonant Voices: Religious Pluralism and the Question of Truth*. Grand Rapids: Eerdmans, 1991.

———. *Encountering Religious Pluralism*. Downers Grove, IL: InterVarsity, 2001.

———. "Evangelical Missiology and Theology of Religions: An Agenda for the Future." *International Journal of Frontier Missiology* 29, no. 1 (2012) 5–12.

———. "Introduction: Globalization and Theology Today." In *Globalizing Theology*, edited by Craig Ott and Harold Netland, 14–34. Grand Rapids: Baker, 2006.

———. "Is Christianity the Only True Religion?" In *Pluralism: Paul Knitter and Harold Netland in Dialogue*, edited by Robert Stewart, 1–19. Minneapolis: Fortress, 2011.

———. "Religious Pluralism and the Question of Truth." In *Biblical Faith and Other Religions: An Evangelical Assessment*, edited by David W. Barker, 21–42. Grand Rapids: Kregel, 2004.

———. "Religious Pluralism and Truth." *Trinity Journal* 6 (1985) 74–87.

———. "Theology of Religions, Missiology, and Evangelicals." *Missiology* 23, no. 2 (2005) 141–58.

———. "Thinking Theologically About Religious Diversity in the West." *Cultural Encounters* 2, no. 1 (2005) 19–35.

———. "Toward Contextualized Apologetics." *Missiology* 16, no. 3 (1988) 289–303.

———. "Truth, Authority and Modernity: Shopping for Truth in a Supermarket of Worldviews." In *Faith and Reason*, edited by Philip Sampson, Vinay Samuel, and Chris Sugden, 89–115. Oxford: Regnum, 1994.

Newbigin, Lesslie. *Foolishness to the Greeks: The Gospel and Western Culture*. Grand Rapids: Eerdmans, 1986.

———. *The Gospel in a Pluralistic Society*. Grand Rapids: Eerdmans, 1989.

Ng, Kwai Hang. "Seeking the Chinese Tutelage: Agency and Culture in Chinese Immigrants' Conversion to Christianity." *Sociology of Religion* 63, no. 2 (2002) 195–214.

Nyce, Ray. "Gospel and Chinese Religions Today." *South East Asia Journal of Theology* 14, no. 2 (1973) 46–55.

Ott, Craig. "Conclusion: Globalizing Theology." In *Globalizing Theology*, edited by Craig Ott and Harold Netland, 309–36. Grand Rapids: Baker, 2006.

Pagolu, Augustine. "Reading the Bible in an Asian Context." *Journal of Asian Evangelical Theology* 17, no. 1 (2013) 5–21.

Paloutzian, Raymond, James Richardson, and Lewis Rambo. "Religious Conversion and Personality Change." *Journal of Personality* 67, no. 6 (1999) 1047–79.

Parratt, John. *An Introduction to Third World Theologies.* Cambridge: Cambridge University Press, 2004.
Peace, Richard. *Conversion in the New Testament.* Grand Rapids: Eerdmans, 1999.
Pereira, Alexius A. "Religiosity and Economic Development in Singapore." *Journal of Contemporary Religion* 20, no. 2 (2005) 161-77.
Photiadis, John, and Arthur Johnson. "Orthodoxy, Church Participation, and Authoritarianism." *American Journal of Sociology* 69 (1963) 224-48.
Pieterse, Nederveen. *Globalization and Culture: Global Mélange.* 2nd ed. New York: Rowman & Littlefield, 2009.
Polluck, Donald. "Conversion and Community in Amazonia." In *Conversion to Christianity*, edited by Robert Hefner, 165-98. Berkeley: University of California Press, 1993.
Poon, Michael. "Documentation, Social Tradition, and the Emergence of Asian Pacific Christianity." In *Mission, Memory and Communion: Documenting World Christianity in the Twenty-First Century*, edited by Michael Poon, 70-86. Singapore: Trinity Theological College, 2013.
Popp-Baier, Ulrike. "Conversion as Social Construction: A Narrative Approach to Conversion Research." In *Social Constructionism and Theology*, edited by C. A. M. Hermans et al., 41-61. Leiden: Brill, 2002.
Priest, Robert. "'I Discovered My Sin!': Aguaruna Evangelical Conversion Narratives." In *The Anthropology of Religious Conversion*, edited by Andrew Buckser and Stephen D. Glazer, 95-108. Lanham, MD: Rowman & Littlefield, 2003.
Ramachandra, Vinoth. *The Recovery of Mission: Beyond the Pluralist Paradigm.* Grand Rapids: Eerdmans, 1996.
Rambo, Lewis R. "Anthropology and the Study of Conversion." In *The Anthropology of Religious Conversion*, edited by Andrew Buckser and Stephen D. Glazer, 211-22. Lanham, MD: Rowman & Littlefield, 2003.
———. "Current Research on Religious Conversion." *Religious Studies Review* 8 (1982) 146-55.
———. "Theories of Conversion: Understanding and Interpreting Religious Change." *Social Compass* 46, no. 3 (1999) 259-71.
———. *Understanding Religious Conversion.* New Haven: Yale University Press, 1993.
Reader, Ian. "Buddhism in Crisis? Institutional Decline in Modern Japan." *Buddhist Studies Review* 28, no. 2 (2011) 233-63.
———. "Secularisation, R.I.P.? Nonsense! The Rush Hour Away From the Gods and the Decline of Religion in Contemporary Japan." *Journal of Religion in Japan* 1 (2012) 7-36.
Richards, Lyn. *Handling Qualitative Data: A Practical Guide.* 2nd ed. London: Sage, 2009.
Ritzer, George. *The McDonaldization of Society.* Thousand Oaks, CA: Sage, 1993.
———. *The McDonaldization of Society.* Thousand Oaks, CA: Pine Forge, 2000.
———. "Professionalization, Bureaucratization and Rationalization: The Views of Max Weber." *Social Forces* 53, no. 4 (1975) 627-34.
Ro, Bong Rin. "Asia." In *Evangelical Dictionary of World Missions*, edited by A. Scott Moreau, 80-84. Grand Rapids: Baker, 2000.
———. "Asian Theology." In *Evangelical Dictionary of Theology*, edited by Walter Elwell, 106-8. Grand Rapids: Baker, 2001.

———. "Contextualization: Asia Theology." In *The Bible and Theology in Asian Contexts*, edited by Bong Rin Ro and Ruth Eshenaur, 63–77. Seoul: ATA, 1984.

Robbins, Joel. "The Globalization of Pentecostal and Charismatic Christianity." *Annual Review of Anthropology* 33 (2004) 117–43.

Robertson, Roland. "Globalization and Societal Modernization: A Note on Japan and Japanese Religion." *Sociological Analysis* 47 (1987) 35–42.

———. "Globalization and the Future of 'Traditional Religion.'" In *God and Globalization*, edited by Max Stackhouse, 1:53–68. Harrisburg, PA: Trinity, 2000.

———. *Globalization: Social Theory and Global Culture*. Newbury Park, CA: Sage, 1992.

———. "Glocalization: Time-Space and Homogeneity-Heterogeneity." In *Global Modernities*, edited by Mike Featherstone, Scott Lash, and Roland Robertson, 25–44. Thousand Oaks, CA: Sage, 1995.

Roxborgh, John. "Singapore." In *Evangelical Dictionary of World Missions*, edited by A. Scott Moreau, 879. Grand Rapids: Baker, 2000.

Rubin, Herbert, and Irene Rubin. *Qualitative Interviewing: The Art of Hearing Data*. 3rd ed. Thousand Oaks, CA: Sage, 2012.

Russell, Sue A. *Conversion, Identity, and Power: The Impact of Christianity on Power Relationships and Social Exchanges*. New York: University Press of America, 1999.

Said, Edward. *Orientalism*. New York: Vintage, 1978.

Salaff, Janet. *State and Family in Singapore: Restructuring a Developing Society*. Ithaca, NY: Cornell University Press, 1988.

Sanneh, Lamin. *Whose Religion is Christianity? The Gospel beyond the West*. Grand Rapids: Eerdmans, 2003.

Schmidt, Roger, et al. *Patterns of Religion*. 2nd ed. Belmont, CA: Wadsworth, 2004.

Schneiders, Sandra. "Biblical Interpretation: The Soul of Theology." *Australian Biblical Review* 58 (2010) 72–82.

Shenk, Wilbert. "Forward." In *Globalizing Theology*, edited by Craig Ott and Harold Netland, 9–11. Grand Rapids: Baker, 2006.

———. "Modernity." In *Evangelical Dictionary of World Missions*, edited by A. Scott Moreau, 650–51. Grand Rapids: Baker, 2000.

Siew, Yau Man. "Theological Education in Asia: An Indigenous Agenda for Renewal." In *With an Eye on the Future: Development and Mission in the 21st Century*, edited by Duane Elmer and Lois McKinney, 58–68. Monrovia, CA: MARC, 1996.

Sinha, Vineeta. "Constituting and Reconstituting the Religious Domain in the Modern Nation-State of Singapore." In *Our Place in Time: Exploring Heritage and Memory in Singapore*, edited by Kian-Woon Kwok et al., 76–95. Singapore: Singapore Heritage Society, 1999.

———. "Theorising 'Talk' About 'Religious Pluralism' and 'Religious Harmony' in Singapore." *Journal of Contemporary Religion* 20, no. 1 (2005) 25–40.

Smart, Ninian. *The Phenomenon of Religion*. New York: Herder and Herder, 1973.

———. *Religions of Asia*. Englewood, NJ: Prentice-Hall, 1993.

———. *The World's Religions*. 2nd ed. New York: Cambridge University Press, 1998.

———. *Worldviews: Crosscultural Explorations of Human Beliefs*. 2nd ed. Englewood Cliffs, NJ: Prentice-Hall, 1995.

Sng, Bobby E. K. "Church, Ethnicity and Culture." In *Church and Culture: Singapore Context*, edited by Bobby E. K. Sng and Choong Chee Pang, 126–30. Singapore: Graduates' Christian Fellowship, 1991b.

———. "Gospel and Culture." In *Church and Culture: Singapore Context*, edited by Bobby E. K. Sng and Choong Chee Pang, 1–15. Singapore: Graduates' Christian Fellowship, 1991a.

———. *In His Good Time: The Story of the Church in Singapore 1819–1978*. Singapore: Bible Society of Singapore, 1980.

———. *In His Good Time: The Story of the Church in Singapore 1819–2002*. 3rd ed. Singapore: Bible Society of Singapore, 2003.

Sng, Bobby E. K., ed. *Church and Society: Singapore Context*. Singapore: Graduates' Christian Fellowship, 1989.

Sng, Bobby E. K., and Poh Seng You. *Religious Trends in Singapore with Special Reference to Christianity*. Singapore: Graduates' Christian Fellowship, 1982.

Snow, David A., and Richard Machalek. "The Sociology of Conversion." *Annual Review of Sociology* 10 (1984) 167–90.

Song, Choan-Seng. *Third-Eye Theology: Theology in Formation in Asian Settings*. Maryknoll, NY: Orbis, 1979.

Stark, Rodney, and William Bainbridge. *A Theory of Religion*. Toronto: Lang, 1987.

Stiver, Dan R. Theological Method. In *The Cambridge Companion to Postmodern Theology*, edited by Kevin J. Vanhoozer, 170–85. Cambridge: Cambridge University Press, 2003.

Stott, John R. W. "Theology: A Multidimensional Discipline. In *Doing Theology for the People of God*, edited by Donald Lewis and Alister McGrath, 3–19. Downers Grove, IL: InterVarsity, 1996.

Stromberg, Peter G. *Language and Self-Transformation: A Study of the Christian Conversion Narrative*. New York: Cambridge University Press, 1993.

Stults, Donald Le Roy. *Grasping Truth and Reality: Lesslie Newbigin's Theology of Mission to the Western World*. Eugene, OR: Wipf and Stock, 2008.

Sugirtharajah, R. S. 1995. *Voices from the Margin: Interpreting the Bible in the Third World*. Maryknoll, NY: Orbis.

Swidler, Ann. "The Concept of Rationality in the Work of Max Weber." *Sociological Inquiry* 43, no. 1 (1973) 35–42.

Tamney, Joseph B. "An Analysis of the Decline of Allegiance of Chinese Religions: A Comparison of University Students and Their Parents." In *Analysis of an Asian Society*, edited by R. Hassan and J. B. Tamney, unpublished chapter, 2005.

———. "Conservative Government and Support for the Religious Institution in Singapore: An Uneasy Alliance." *Sociological Analysis* 53, no. 2 (1992) 201–17.

———. "Religion in Capitalist East Asia." In *A Future for Religion? New Paradigms for Social Analysis*, edited by William Swatos, 55–72. London: Sage, 1993.

———. *The Struggle Over Singapore's Soul: Western Modernization and Asian Culture*. Berlin: de Gruyter, 1996.

Tamney, Joseph, and Riaz Hassan. *Religious Switching in Singapore: A Study of Religious Mobility*. Singapore: Select, 1987.

Tamney, Joseph, and Linda Hsueh-Ling Chiang. *Modernization, Globalization and Confucianism in Chinese Societies*. Westport, CT: Praeger, 2002.

Tan, Charlene. "Creating 'Good Citizens' and Maintaining Religious Harmony in Singapore." *British Journal of Religious Education* 30, no. 2 (2008) 133–42.

Tan, Eugene K. B. "Re-Engaging Chineseness: Political, Economic and Cultural Imperatives of Nation-Building in Singapore." *China Quarterly* 175 (2003) 751–74.

Tan, Kevin. "Accounting for Conversion: Becoming a Christian in Singapore." Unpublished paper, Department of Sociology, National University of Singapore, 1997.

Tano, Rodrigo D. *Theology in the Philippine Setting: A Case Study in the Contextualization of Theology*. Quezon City, Philippines: New Day, 1981.

Taylor, Charles. "Modes of Secularism." In *Secularism and Its Critics*, edited by Rajeev Bhargava, 31–53. Delhi: Oxford University Press, 1998.

———. *A Secular Age*. Cambridge, MA: Harvard University Press, 2007.

Tenbruck, Friedrich H. "The Problem of Thematic Unity in the Works of Max Weber." *British Journal of Sociology* 31, no. 3 (1980) 316–51.

Teiser, Stephen. "Popular Religion." *Journal of Asian Studies* 54, no. 2 (1995) 378–95.

Tennent, Timothy C. *Theology in the Context of World Christianity*. Grand Rapids: Zondervan, 2007.

Thompson, Mark. "The Survival of 'Asian Values' as 'Zivilisationskritik.'" *Theory and Society* 29, no. 5 (2000) 651–86.

Tiénou, Tite, and Paul Hiebert. "From Systematic to Biblical to Missional Theology." In *Appropriate Christianity*, edited by Charles Kraft, 117–33. Pasadena, CA: William Carey Library, 2005.

Tiénou, Tite. "Christian Theology in an Era of World Christianity." In *Globalizing Theology*, edited by Craig Ott and Harold Netland, 37–51. Grand Rapids: Baker, 2006.

Tiryakian, Edward. "From Modernization to Globalization." *Journal for the Scientific Study of Religion* 31, no. 3 (1992) 296–323.

Tong, Chee Kiong. *Chinese Death Rituals in Singapore*. London: Routledge, 2004.

———. "The Rationalization of Religion in Singapore." In *Understanding Singapore Society*, edited by Ong Jin Hui, Tong Chee Kiong, and Tan Ern Ser, 189–212. Singapore: Times Academic, 1997.

———. *Rationalizing Religion: Religious Conversion, Revivalism and Competition in Singapore Society*. Leiden: Brill, 2007.

———. "Religion." In *The Making of Singapore Sociology: Society and State*, edited by Chee Kiong Tong and Kwen Lian Fee, 370–413. Singapore: Times Academic, 2002.

———. *Religious Conversion and Revivalism: A Study of Christianity in Singapore*. Singapore: Report prepared for Ministry of Community Development, August 1989.

———. "Religious Trends and Issues in Singapore." In *Religious Diversity in Singapore*, edited by Lai Ah Eng, 28–54. Singapore: Institute of Southeast Asian Studies, 2008.

———. "Traditional Chinese Customs in Modern Singapore." In *Asian Traditions and Modernization*, edited by Yong Mun Cheong, 67–88. Singapore: Eastern University Press, 2004.

———. *Trends in Traditional Chinese Religion in Singapore*. Singapore: Report prepared for Ministry of Community Development, 1988.

Tong, Chee Kiong, and Chan Kwok Bun. "One Face, Many Masks: The Singularity and Plurality of Chinese Identity." *Diaspora* 10, no. 3 (2001) 361–89.

Tong, Chee Kiong, and Ho Kong Chong, Lin Ting Kwong. "Traditional Chinese Customs in Modern Singapore." In *Asian Traditions and Modernization: Perspectives from Singapore*, edited by Yong Mun Cheong, 67–88. Singapore: Eastern University Press, 2004.

Topley, Marjorie. "The Emergence and Social Function of Chinese Religious Associations in Singapore." *Studies in Society and History* 3, no. 3 (1961) 289–314.
Turnbull, C. M. *A History of Modern Singapore: 1819–2005.* Singapore: National University of Singapore Press, 2009.
Vanhoozer, Kevin J. "But That's Your Interpretation: Realism, Reading, and Reformation." *Modern Reformation* 8, no. 4 (1999) 21–28.
———. *The Drama of Doctrine: A Canonical and Linguistic Approach to Christian Theology.* Louisville: Westminster John Knox, 2005.
———. *Is There a Meaning in This Text?* Grand Rapids: Zondervan, 1998.
———. "One Rule to Rule Them All? Theological Method in an Era of World Christianity." In *Globalizing Theology*, edited by Craig Ott and Harold Netland, 85–126. Grand Rapids: Baker, 2006.
Wallace, Walter. "Rationality, Human Nature, and Society in Weber's Theory." *Theory and Society* 19, no. 2 (1990) 199–223.
Walls, Andrew. "The Gospel as the Prisoner and Liberator of Culture." In *Landmark Essays in Mission and World Christianity*, edited by Robert Gallagher and Paul Hertig, 133–45. Maryknoll, NY: Orbis, 2009.
———. *The Missionary Movement in Christian History: Studies in the Transmission of Faith.* Maryknoll, NY: Orbis, 1996.
Wan, Enoch. "Christianity in the Eye of Traditional Chinese." *Chinese around the World* 169 (1999) 21–24.
———. "Critiquing the Method of Traditional Western Theology and Calling for Sino-Theology. *Chinese around the World* (1999) 12–17.
———. "Jesus Christ for the Chinese: A Contextual Reflection." *Chinese around the World* (2000) 13–19.
———. "Practical Contextualization: A Case Study of Evangelizing Contemporary Chinese." *Chinese around the World* (2000) 18–24.
———. "Sailing in the Western Wind." *Chinese around the World* 167 (1999) 18–21.
———. "Theological Contributions of Sino-Theology to the Global Christian Community." *Chinese around the World* (2000) 17–21.
Wang, Jiafeng. "Some Reflections on Modernization Theory and Globalization Theory. *Chinese Studies in History* 43, no. 1 (2009) 72–98.
Waters, Malcolm. *Globalization.* 2nd ed. New York: Routledge, 2001.
Weber, Max. *Economy and Society.* Edited by Guenther Roth and Claus Wittich. Translated by Ephraim Fischoff. Berkeley: University of California Press, 1978.
———. *The Protestant Ethic and Spirit of Capitalism.* Translated by Talcott Parsons. New York: Scribner's Sons, 1958.
———. *The Sociology of Religion.* Translated by Ephraim Fischoff. Boston: Beacon, 1963.
Webster, Leonard, and Patricia Mertova. *Using Narrative Inquiry as a Research Method: An Introduction to Using Critical Event Narrative Analysis in Research on Learning and Teaching.* New York: Routledge, 2009.
Wee Cho Yaw. "Forward." In *Chinese Customs and Festivals in Singapore*, edited by Wee Cho Yaw, 4–11. Singapore: Singapore Federation of Chinese Clan Associations, 1989.
Weerstra, Hans M. "De-Westernizing the Gospel: The Recovery of a Biblical Worldview." *International Journal of Frontier Missions* 16, no. 3 (1999) 129–34.

Weerstra, Judy. "Rediscovering the Sacred Myth." *International Journal of Frontier Missions* 16, no. 3 (1999) 135–40.
Wells, David F. "Comparing Modern-Day Alternatives to Biblical Conversion." *International Journal of Frontier Missions* 16, no. 4 (1999) 199–204.
———. "The Nature and Function of Theology." In *The Use of the Bible in Theology: Evangelical Options*, edited by Robert K. Johnston, 175–99. Atlanta: Knox, 1985.
———. *No Place for Truth: Or Whatever Happened To Evangelical Theology?* Grand Rapids: Eerdmans, 1993.
———. *Turning to God: Biblical Conversion in the Modern World*. Grand Rapids: Baker, 1989.
Wilson, Bryan R. "Secularization." In *Encyclopedia of Religion*, edited by Lindsay Jones, 12:8214–20. 2nd ed. Farmington Hills, MI: Gale, 2005.
Wilson, John F. "Modernity." In *Encyclopedia of Religion*, edited by Lindsay Jones, 9:6108–12. 2nd ed. Farmington Hills, MI: Gale, 2005.
Wong, Chan Kok, and Chuck Lowe, eds. *Ministry in Modern Singapore: The Effects of Modernity on the Church*. Singapore: Singapore Bible College, 1997.
Wong, James Y. K. *Singapore: The Church in the Midst of Social Change*. Singapore: Church Growth Study Centre, 1973.
Wong, Wee Kim. "Census of Population 2010: Statistical Release 1 on Demographic Characteristics, Education, Language And Religion." Singapore Department of Statistics, January 12 2011.
Woods, Orlando. "The Geographies of Religious Conversion." *Progress in Human Geography* 36, no. 4 (2012) 440–56.
Yang, Fenggang. *Chinese Christians in America: Conversion, Assimilation, and Adhesive Identities*. University Park: Pennsylvania State University Press, 1999.
———. "Chinese Conversion to Evangelical Christianity: The Importance of Social and Cultural Contexts." *Sociology of Religion* 59, no. 3 (1998) 237–57.
———. "Lost in the Market, Saved at McDonald's: Conversion to Christianity in Urban China." *Journal for the Scientific Study of Religion* 44, no. 4 (2005) 423–41.
Yen, Ching Hwang. *The Chinese in Southeast Asia and Beyond: Socioeconomic and Political Dimensions*. Singapore: World Scientific, 2008.
———. *The Overseas Chinese and the 1911 Revolution, with Special Reference to Singapore and Malaysia*. New York: Oxford University Press, 1976.
Yen, Ching Hwang, ed. *Community and Politics: The Chinese in Colonial Singapore and Malaysia*. Singapore: Times Academic, 1995.
Yeo, Peggy Bee Tin. "Conversion to and Continuation in the Christian Faith among Multi-Generation Chinese Protestant Families in Singapore (1900–1990)." PhD diss., Westminster College, 1992.
Yeow, Choo Lak. "Christ in a Multi-Cultural Context." In *The Asian Church in the New Millennium*, edited by Raul Fernandez-Calienes, 151–93. Delhi: ISPCK, 2000.
———. *Doing Christian Theology in Asian Ways*. Singapore: Association for Theological Education in Southeast Asia, 1993.
Yeung, Arnold M. K. *Theology of Reconciliation and Church Renewal*. Hong Kong: Seed, 1987.
Yieh, John Y. H. "Chinese Biblical Interpretation: History and Issues." In *Ways of Being, Ways of Reading*, edited by Mary Foskett and Jeffrey Kuan, 17–30. St. Louis: Chalice, 2013.

Yoder, Michael, et al. "Understanding Christian Identity in Terms of Bounded and Centered Set Theory in the Writings of Paul G. Hiebert." *Trinity Journal* 30 (2009) 177–88.

Yu, Carver T. *Being and Relation: A Theological Critique of Western Dualism and Individualism*. Edinburgh: Scottish Academic, 1987.

Yuen, Chee Wai John. "A Christian Understanding of and Response to the Social Impact of Meritocracy on Family Life in Singapore." *Asia Journal of Theology* 17, no. 2 (2003) 403–30.

Zhang, Wei Bin. *Singapore's Modernization: Westernization and Modernizing Confucian Manifestations*. Huntington, NY: Nova Science, 2002.